Property Rights and the Environment
Social and Ecological Issues

Edited by
Susan Hanna
and
Mohan Munasinghe

Beijer International Institute of Ecological Economics
and
The World Bank

CONTENTS

FOREWORD

Institutions are the rules of the game in a society or, more formally, are the humanly devised constraints that shape human interaction. In consequence they structure incentives in human exchange, whether political, social, or economic. Institutional change shapes the way societies evolve through time and hence is the key to understanding historical change.

Douglas North, Nobel Prize Laureate 1993
in *Institutions, Institutional Change and Economic Performance*
Cambridge University Press, 1990

When analyzing environmental problems, economists have traditionally searched for ways of extending the rules of social cost–benefit analysis so as to include the environmental side effects associated with investment projects. This they have done by estimating the "economic" value of side effects. Such side effects are often called "externalities" in the economics literature. Economists have also studied the efficacy of various policy instruments—such as the taxation of resource use or the use of tradeable permits for environmental pollution—for directing economic activity in decentralized economic environments. Recently economists have inquired into the environmental side effects of macroeconomic policies.[1] However, a more fundamental question, concerning the nature of the institutions of society that shape the use of environmental resources, has only recently begun to be studied.

One such program of research, conducted at the Beijer International Institute of Ecological Economics, on the ecology and economics of biodiversity loss, explored the notion that a significant cause of much biodiversity loss lies in inadequate institutions, in particular, ill-defined property rights.[2] It was a natural next step for the Institute to launch a more general program of research on property rights and environmental resources. Towards this end, the Institute was fortunate to receive generous economic support from the MacArthur Foundation in Chicago. Subsequently, this support was augmented by the World Bank's Vice Presidency on Environmentally Sustainable Development. This enabled the two institutions to work together in what we believe to be a vital area of concern. We are particularly grateful to Professor Susan Hanna of Oregon State University (also Director of the Property Rights Programme at the Beijer Institute), and to Dr. Mohan Munasinghe of the Environment Department of the World Bank (also Fellow of the Beijer Institute) for the able manner in which they have developed the joint program of activities and produced these two volumes.

Much remains to be done on the design of institutions that would improve upon the current patterns of use of environmental resources. For example, we need to better understand the relationship between various property rights regimes and the speed and direction of technological change because the use of environmental resources is greatly shaped by the technologies in operation. Future programs, both at the Beijer Institute and the World Bank, will hopefully address these issues.

---

1. See M. Munasinghe and W. Cruz, *Economywide Policies and the Environment* (Washington, D.C.: World Bank, 1994).

2. For an overview of this research program, see the special issue of *Ambio* 1993, and E. Barbier, J. Burgess, and C. Folke, *Paradise Lost* (London: Earthscan, 1994).

The subject of property rights covers a wide field, as reflected in these volumes. The relevance of property rights for any study of environmental problems should be self-evident. Nevertheless, the bulk of the efforts that have been made to date for improving the state of the environment in developing countries has been devoted to a support of appropriate investment projects. It is time to place more emphasis on aid that is directed at improving the institutional framework within which resources are used. Indeed, institutional reforms that are aimed at a better management and use of environmental resources should now complement those reforms that are usually called structural adjustment programs. These two volumes should be read with this background in mind.

Ismail Serageldin
Vice President
Environmentally Sustainable
    Development
The World Bank
Washington, D.C.

Partha Dasgupta
Chairman of the Board
Beijer International Institute
    of Ecological Economics
Stockholm

Karl-Göran Mäler
Director
Beijer International Institute
    of Ecological Economics
Stockholm

ABOUT THE CONTRIBUTORS

Fikret Berkes is Professor and Director of the Natural Resources Institute, University of Manitoba. His research interests include common property resources, applied ecology, and ecological economics. He has been fascinated for a long time with the interface between natural systems and social systems, and reports in this volume on a research project that spans over twenty years in the James Bay area of Canada.

Biliana Cicin-Sain is Professor and Co-Director of the Center for the Study of Marine Policy at the University of Delaware, and Co-Editor-in-Chief of the international journal *Ocean and Coastal Management*. She has written extensively on a wide range of marine policy studies, including fisheries management, marine mammal management, offshore oil development, multiple use conflicts, and international marine policy.

Partha Dasgupta is Frank Ramsey Professor of Economics at the University of Cambridge, Fellow of St. John's College, and Chairman of the Board of the Beijer International Institute of Ecological Economics, the Royal Swedish Academy of Sciences. His research has included environmental, development, and welfare economics; and game theory, industrial market structure and technological progress, population, and the economics of malnutrition and destitution. His most recent book is *An Inquiry into Well-Being and Destitution*.

Carl Folke is Deputy Director of the Beijer International Institute of Ecological Economics, the Royal Academy of Sciences, and an Associate Professor in the Department of Systems Ecology at Stockholm University. His research interests are in the transdisciplinary field of Ecological Economics.

Susan Hanna is Associate Professor of Marine Economics in the Department of Agricultural and Resource Economics at Oregon State University, and Director of the research program, Property Rights and the Performance of Natural Resource Systems, at the Beijer International

Institute of Ecological Economics, the Royal Swedish Academy of Sciences. Her research areas are fishery economics, natural resource management, economics of common property resources, and the economic history of marine resource use.

Veijo T. Kaitala is a Senior Research Fellow of the Academy of Finland at the Systems Analysis Laboratory of the Helsinki Institute of Technology. His fields of interest are environmental economics, environmental and ecological systems analysis, and modeling. He has studied dynamic game theory models of international negotiations on resource management and the environment since the early 1980s.

Robert W. Knecht is Professor and Co-Director of the Center for the Study of Marine Policy at the University of Delaware and Co-Editor-in-Chief of the international journal *Ocean and Coastal Management*. Prior to his academic appointments, Professor Knecht served in a number of public policy positions, including director of the U.S. coastal zone management program, U.S. representative to the Law of the Sea negotiations, and mayor of the city of Boulder, Colorado.

Karl-Göran Mäler is Professor of Economics at the Stockholm School of Economics and Director of the Beijer International Institute of Ecological Economics, the Royal Swedish Academy of Sciences. He has published a number of books and articles on environmental economics. His current research interests are national income accounts and environmental resources, valuation of environmental resources, transboundary environmental problems, and problems of development and the environment.

Bonnie J. McCay is Professor of Anthropology in the Department of Human Ecology, Rutgers University. Her research has been in fisheries and coastal communities of the North Atlantic and has focused on how people—as individuals and as members of different social units—respond to and affect marine ecological change. She has served on committees of the

National Research Council and the Mid-Atlantic Fisheries Management Council and is a Fellow of the American Association for the Advancement of Science.

Mohan Munasinghe is Chief, Environmental Economics Division, the World Bank, and Fellow of the Beijer International Institute of Ecological Economics, the Royal Swedish Academy of Sciences. He is also Distinguished Visiting Professor of Environmental Management, University of Colombo, Sri Lanka. During 1982–1986, he served as Senior Advisor to the President of Sri Lanka. He has authored or edited more than fifty books and several hundred technical papers on environmental economics, energy, water resources, and informatics.

Gordon R. Munro is a professor in the Department of Economics, University of British Columbia. Since the mid-1970s, he has specialized in the economics of fisheries management and has given particular emphasis to resource management issues arising under the New International Law of the Sea. He has published extensively in the field.

Elinor Ostrom is Arthur F. Bentley Professor of Political Science and Co-Director of the Workshop in Political Theory and Policy Analysis at Indiana University. She is the author of *Governing the Commons* (1990), *Crafting Institutions for Self-Governing Irrigation Systems* (1992); and co-author with R. Keohane of *Local Commons and Global Interdependence* (1995), R. Gardner and J. Walker of *Rules, Games and*

Common-Pool Resources (1994), and L. Schroeder and S. Wynne of *Institutional Incentives and Sustainable Development* (1993).

Samuel G. Pooley has been Industrial Economist with the National Marine Fisheries Service's Honolulu Laboratory since 1981. He is responsible for their Fishery Management and Performance Investigation, which monitors U.S. domestic fishing in the area around Hawaii. Most of his research has involved cost–earnings analysis of commercial fishing fleets and seafood market analysis with an orientation towards fishery management applications.

Ralph E. Townsend is Professor of Economics at the University of Maine. His research has focused on economic evaluation of alternative fisheries management institutions. Much of his current research is directed at the exploration of new approaches to economic management of fisheries, including ideas such as corporate management, transferable dynamic stock rights, bankable ITQs, and fractional licenses.

Michael D. Young is an ecological economist with the CSIRO Division of Wildlife and Ecology in Canberra, Australia. He has worked on property rights systems for arid land leasing, kangaroo shooting, timber harvesting, trade waste permits and, most recently, fishing. In each of these areas he has focused on the design of systems to the stage that they can be implemented. His last, a fishing share system in New South Wales, breaks new ground in fishery management.

Introduction

1

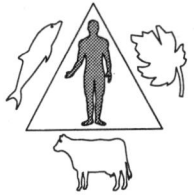

An Introduction to Property Rights and the Environment

Susan Hanna and Mohan Munasinghe

THIS BOOK AND ITS COMPANION VOLUME, *Property Rights in a Social and Ecological Context: Case Studies and Design Applications*, concern the institutional dimensions of environmental sustainability. Humans interact with their environment through systems of property rights that are embedded in social, political, cultural, and economic context. The outcome of that interaction affects both the quantity and quality of environmental resources. It is becoming increasingly clear that although national and international economic policies have often ignored the environment, economic development ultimately depends on institutions that can protect and maintain the environment's carrying capacity and resilience (Arrow and others 1995). The knowledge of how property rights regimes, as particularly important types of institutions, function in relation to humans and their use of the environment is critical to the design and implementation of effective environmental protection.

The papers collected in these books are products of a research program of the Beijer International Institute of Ecological Economics, the Royal Swedish Academy of Sciences, Stockholm, Sweden. The research program "Property Rights and the Performance of Natural Resource Systems" began in 1993 with support from the World Environment and Resources Program of the John D. and Catherine T. MacArthur Foundation and the Environment Department of the World Bank. The program's goal is to further the scientific understanding of ways humans relate to their natural environments through the mechanism of property rights regimes. A major objective of the program is to bring together social scientists and natural scientists to address research questions in their full social and ecological dimensions.

More than fifty international scholars have participated in interdisciplinary research projects. These projects address questions of the design of governance systems for sustainability; the relationships among equity, stewardship, and environmental resilience; the use of traditional knowledge in resource management; the mechanisms that link humans to their environments; and the role played by poverty and population. The chapters in this volume present the theoretical and conceptual background of these five general issues of property rights and the environment. The companion volume, *Property Rights in a Social and Ecological Context: Case Studies and Design Applications*, presents a number of case studies that address questions of design application in the same five areas.

Sustainability, Sustainable Development, and Property Rights

Property rights regimes consist of *property rights*, bundles of entitlements defining rights and duties in the use of natural resources, and *property rules*, the rules under which those rights and duties are exercised (Bromley 1991). Property rights regimes matter to the use of environmental resources, a fact that has long been well established, if not well practiced. In 1911 Jens Warming wrote of the dangers of fisheries overexploitation without ownership, an argument enhanced by Scott Gordon in 1954 (Warming 1911; Gordon 1954). Garrett Hardin's 1968 article, "The Tragedy of the Commons," focused widespread attention on the problem of environmental degradation in the absence of rules governing use (Hardin 1968). For a number of years the general interpretation of Hardin's argument was that collectively owned property was the culprit and that private property was necessary to sustain environmental resources. However, a rapidly expanding body of scientific evidence indicates that sustaining environmental resources is not dependent on a particular structure of property regime, but rather on a well-specified property rights regime and a congruency of that regime with its ecological and social context.

Sustainability is a difficult concept because it has a wide range of meanings based on different disciplines and world views. What is being sustained, how it is to be sustained, and over how long a period of time are all open to interpretation. Regardless of the specific meaning used, it is clear that, to some extent, sustainability is a human construct. Humans use their environment for a range of objectives, including subsistence, commodity production, aesthetic pleasure, and indirect ecosystem services. These objectives have their basis in the desire to sustain human life, enhance standards of living, maintain culture, and protect environmental quality for generations to follow. The different objectives for the use of environmental resources lead to different expectations as to what is to be sustained, and who is to have claims on environmental services.

It is becoming increasingly clear that the question of sustainability is a complicated one whose answer involves more than the generic application of a property rights regime. Property rights regimes, to be effective in modulating the interaction between humans and their environment, must reflect both general principles and specific social and ecological contexts. General principles are the structural and functional attributes of property rights regimes which transcend a particular context. General principles are the necessary conditions of effective property rights regimes because a property rights regime cannot succeed over the long run without them. They include the congruence of ecosystem and governance boundaries; the specification and representation of interests; the matching of governance structure to ecosystem characteristics; the containment of transaction costs; and the establishment of monitoring, enforcement, and adaptation processes at the appropriate scale (Eggertsson 1990; Ostrom 1990; Bromley 1991; Hanna 1992).

General principles are necessary, but not sufficient in themselves for effective property rights regimes. In addition to the general principles, specific attributes of social and ecological context must be represented. Social contexts contain all the dimensions of the human relationship to environmental resources, including social arrangements, cultural practices, economic uses, and political constraints. Ecological contexts contain the structure of ecosystems in which humans live and work, as well as the particular functional properties of those ecosystems. The particular details of the social and ecological context are what give a human–environmental interaction its variety in detail. The match between a property rights regime and the contextual characteristics of the affected humans and ecosystems will determine success or failure in terms of sustainability.

The scientific (biogeophysical) concepts and measures of sustainability have been explored in a recent volume that made a number of recommendations and set out several areas for further study (Munasinghe and Shearer 1995). Meanwhile, those concerned with poverty and development are exploring how to implement some of these approaches to sustainability. The now well-known definition of sustainable development, succinctly paraphrased from the Bruntland Commission report as "meeting the needs of the present generation without jeopardizing the ability of future generations to meet their needs," must be elaborated further, for practical application (World Commission on Environment and Development 1987). The current concept of sustainable development encompasses three key elements—the economic, social, and environmental (Munasinghe 1993).

The *economic* approach to sustainability is based on the Hicks–Lindahl concept of the maximum flow of income that can be generated while at least maintaining the stock of assets (or capital) which yield these benefits. The *social* concept of sustainability is people-oriented, and seeks to maintain the integrity of social and cultural systems, including the reduction of destructive conflicts (Munasinghe and McNeely

1994). Equity is an important aspect of this approach. The *environmental* view of sustainable development focuses on the stability of biological and physical systems. The emphasis is on preserving the resilience and dynamic ability of such systems to adapt to change, rather than conservation of some "ideal" static state. Natural resource degradation, pollution, and loss of biodiversity reduce system resilience. Reconciling these various concepts and implementing them as a means to achieve sustainable development is a formidable task, since all three elements of sustainable development must be given balanced consideration.

The correct economic valuation of environmental and sociocultural assets, and their internalization in the price system is one means of ensuring that market forces lead to more sustainable resource use. The more equitable distribution of resources and assets is a step toward poverty reduction and social sustainability, as is greater participation and empowerment of disadvantaged groups. Clearly, property rights regimes that specify access to the natural resource base and rights of use have a crucial role to play in this context (Dasgupta 1993).

The body of research addressing questions of property rights and environmental resource use is growing, but there remain areas characterized by large gaps in knowledge. Five of these areas form the focus of the Beijer Institute's Property Rights Research Program and are represented by the sections of these books. These areas are the design of governance systems, the development of stewardship and equity in environmental management and its contribution to environmental resilience, the management role of traditional ecological knowledge, the mechanisms by which humans are linked to their environmental resource base, and the relationship between poverty, population, and environmental degradation.

The Volume on *Property Rights and the Environment: Social and Ecological Issues*

In the overview chapter of this book, **Hanna, Folke, and Mäler** summarize the findings on property rights and environmental resources—focusing on why property rights matter, the general problems they address, their structural forms, design principles, mechanisms by which they create linkages between human and ecological systems, and mechanisms by which they coordinate uses at different scales. They argue that policies addressing environmental problems must focus on general principles of property rights regimes and on the context in which such regimes are placed.

Governance

Questions of governance over environmental resources have to do with the ability to predict and oversee both human behavior and ecosystem behavior. Success in prediction and oversight depends on a number of variables. The complexity of the human systems and ecosystems affects the ability to extract consistent objectives, design meaningful control systems, and monitor response. The scale of the ecosystem in comparison with scales of social organization or legal jurisdiction determines the extent of the match between the human and environmental systems. The clarity of lines of authority over environmental decisions and the degree to which authority is coordinated or fragmented is critical to relating actions to outcomes. Finally, the ways in which governance is coordinated between authorities at different levels determine consistency across scales. **Ostrom** addresses both complexity and scale. Since many biological processes occur at small and medium, as well as large scales, governance arrangements that can cope with this level of complexity also need to be organized at multiple scales and linked effectively together. The importance of nested institutional arrangements is emphasized, with quasi-autonomous units operating at very small, up through very large, scales.

Two further chapters address the question of the distribution of authority. **Townsend and Pooley** present the concept of distributed governance—how rights and responsibilities are distributed among the central government, industry, and local communities—analyzing competing models of cooperative management, comanagement, and rights-based management in the context of fisheries. They pay attention to both internal and external governance issues. **Hanna**'s chapter focuses on the effect of distributed authority on governance efficiency and in particular on the role played by user participa-

tion in lowering management costs. The contribution of user participation to governance efficiency is analyzed in terms of the structure and function of user participation and its effect on management costs.

Kaitala and Munro's chapter addresses the question of governance coordination over multiple jurisdictions, as exemplified by transboundary fishery resources categorized as highly migratory fish stocks and straddling fish stocks. The high seas portion of the stocks are exploited both by coastal states and distant water fishing nations. The problem of managing such resources (characterized by ill-defined property rights over the high seas portion of the resources) is now seen as severe, and has become the focus of a major United Nations intergovernmental conference.

Equity, Stewardship, and Environmental Resilience

It is a general finding of the property rights literature that the degree of equity represented by a property rights regime helps create the incentive structure which either promotes or inhibits stewardship of environmental resources. The degree of stewardship practiced, in turn, affects the level of ecosystem resilience, or the ability of an ecosystem to absorb external shocks. Exactly how equity affects stewardship, and how specific stewardship practices affect resilience is still a matter of research. It is becoming clear that definitions of equity, stewardship practices, and environmental resilience reflect a combination of local context, appropriate incentive structures, and adaptation to environmental change.

The goals of equity and stewardship are commonly considered to be inconsistent with efficiency in environmental management. In a departure from the usual approach, **Young and McCay** look at efficiency-driven, market-based property rights systems and evaluate them for their ability to accommodate equity, stewardship, and resilience, offering suggestions about ways these criteria can be built into the design of adaptive and flexible management regimes. They consider a number of different types of property rights systems for a variety of resources.

Traditional Knowledge

Long-standing systems of environmental resource management and their use of traditional ecological knowledge are yielding insights into some current resource management problems. The documentation and use of traditional ecological knowledge is now a part of international environmental policy. **Cicin-Sain and Knecht** review and assess major developments at the international level that have recently emphasized the importance of reconciling systems of traditional knowledge with modern approaches to the management of natural resources. They look at the varying conceptions of the role of traditional knowledge and indigenous peoples in these international agreements, and analyze implementation challenges that both regional and national-level entities will face as they endeavor to enhance the role of indigenous knowledge and participation.

Linking Mechanisms

Linkages between humans and environmental systems operate in different ways according to their structure, the systems they link, and the process by which the linkage is made. Some linkages are constructed by the informal observation of environmental characteristics on the part of users, and the gradual evolution of behavioral response. Others are established as more rapid responses to change. In cases of environmental overuse, linking mechanisms are often weak or absent, cutting off the interaction between environmental condition and human response. The particular structure of a linking mechanism reflects the economic, social, and ecological context in which it is established. The structure determines what information will be monitored, how it will be monitored, and what will be done with the information once acquired. The key question is whether the governance system promotes or even allows behavioral adaptation to environmental change. Linkages affect both ecosystem and human system adaptation and evolution through the type of feedbacks allowed.

Folke and Berkes look at the structure and processes by which ecological systems and human systems are connected. They extract from the common property literature lessons about the interface between ecological and social systems.

A systems view of social and ecological interactions is presented, which stresses the need for active social adaptations to environmental feedbacks and the use of traditional ecological knowledge. Particular attention is paid to the lessons that can be learned to assist in the design of more sustainable resource management systems—improving their adaptiveness and resilience.

Poverty and Population

Population is importantly linked to poverty and the erosion of the environmental resource base. The population policy literature reflects the current conclusion that previous successes in population policy directed at family planning, the supply side of population growth, cannot be sustained without serious attention to the need to reduce both the demand for births and the momentum of population growth (Bongaarts 1994). Proposed policy foci include the education of women to enhance economic standing, incentives to postpone childbearing to later years, and establishment of formalized systems of property rights to resources (Bongaarts 1994; de Soto 1993).

Dasgupta applies economic analysis to rural households in poor countries to examine the forces underlying population growth—finding that it is in varying degrees linked to poverty, to gender inequalities in the exercise of power, to communal sharing of child-rearing, and to an erosion of the local environmental–resource base. These linkages suggest that population policy should contain not only such measures as family planning programs, improved female education, and employment opportunities, but also those measures that are directed at the alleviation of poverty—such as improved credit, insurance, and savings opportunities—and improved availability of basic household needs—such as potable water and fuel.

The Volume on *Property Rights in a Social and Ecological Context: Case Studies and Design Applications*

Governance

The first three illustrative case studies in this book apply various principles of governance to the environmental challenges of air pollution, fishery management, and pesticide use. **Tietenberg** examines the question of governance design and scale through an analysis of the use of market-based mechanisms in his chapter on the transferable permits approach to pollution control problems in the United States. From the various examples described, he extracts lessons for both the implementation process and program design.

Townsend and Pooley consider the question of appropriate levels of authority—through a potential application of the distributed governance concept to the lobster fishery of the Northwestern Hawaiian Islands. In their chapter, they pay particular attention to how rights and responsibilities would be distributed among central government, industry, and local communities.

Gren and Brännlund approach the issue of coordination by examining enforcement of regionally adjusted environmental regulations. Although geographic differences in environmental impacts may call for region-specific environmental regulations, regional differences in enforcement costs will lead to different levels of cost-effective regulation.

Equity, Stewardship, and Environmental Resilience

The next three chapters demonstrate the difficulties of crafting equitable schemes that promote better stewardship and resilience for the conservation of natural resources. **Gadgil and Rao** examine the incentives for managing biodiversity contained in India's folk traditions of nature conservation, in conjunction with a vigorous state-sponsored program of protected areas. They focus on the efficiency and equity gains possible through reestablishing conservation approaches based on positive incentives to local communities. This attractive option is contrasted with current unsuccessful regulatory methods that are too centralized, sectoral, and bureaucratic.

Żylicz looks at the difficulties posed by abrupt changes in property rights regimes for perceptions of equity, incentives for stewardship, and the maintenance of conservation goals. Analyzing an example of the conflict between conservationists and a municipality in Northeastern Poland, he illustrates how changing property

right regimes have influenced the social context of the protection of nature. Parts of national parks are being claimed by previous landowners who feel they were not reimbursed fairly, there are private or communal enclaves left within park boundaries, and neighboring landowners protest against development constraints implied by the park's existence. The fate of the protection of nature crucially depends on the ability of conservationists to demonstrate economic benefits from investing in natural capital, rather than letting it be degraded.

Parks and Bonifaz examine the incompatibility of incentives in the joint use of environmental resources by looking at the inconsistencies of short-term commodity production with long-term environmental sustainability in open-access Ecuadorian mangrove–shrimp systems. They identify incentives to maximize short-term profits through shrimp mariculture, which have led to destruction of larval-shrimp habitats as mangrove ecosystems were converted to shrimp ponds.

Traditional Knowledge

Three further case studies examine the use of traditional and nontechnical knowledge by itself, in combination with modern scientific knowledge, and in the restoration of previously established property rights. **Pálsson** considers the use of practical knowledge obtained by Icelandic fishing skippers in the course of their work, exploring how fishermen's knowledge differs from that of fishery scientists, and to what extent the former could be brought more systematically into the process of resource management for the purpose of ensuring resilience and sustainability. He outlines many of the benefits of engaging fishermen and using their practical knowledge of fishing for the purpose of sustainable resource use and responsible management.

Berkes presents a case study of Cree Indians from the Canadian subarctic, analyzing the evidence regarding the distinctions of the local indigenous knowledge from Euro-Canadian, science-based wildlife and fishery management knowledge. He notes that resource development policies have rarely taken into account local systems of knowledge and resource use. Along with increasing attention to the social impacts of development, there is more interest in traditional indigenous knowledge. Yet, concepts of traditional knowledge and resource management systems have remained elusive, not only for development policymakers, but also for scholars engaged in such research.

Ruddle focuses on the use of traditional knowledge to reestablish claims to former rights. For the New Zealand Maori, traditional property rights have been recognized by customary law. Bodies of local knowledge have been accepted as legal evidence in the process of restoring usurped rights. The codification of existing rights and customary laws within a system of statutory law in various cultural settings is a contemporary process in many nations in the Pacific Basin, which might provide useful precedents for application worldwide.

Linking Mechanisms

The question of linkages is addressed in four chapters that examine their function in nested forest tenure systems, fisheries, and joint farming–forestry systems. Alcorn and Toledo examine Mexican resource tenure systems, which function as "shells" that provide the superstructure within which activities are developed and operate. Such shells are linked in very specific ways to the larger "operating system" in which the shell is embedded. The evidence from Mexico suggests that the best course of action for promoting ecologically sustainable resource management is to support existing structures that have served this function earlier.

Hammer focuses on the links between ecological and social systems in Swedish fisheries, especially in the Baltic Sea. An important aspect of fisheries management is the degree to which property rights systems can be developed that reflect the ecological and socioeconomic context, and that sustain or improve the resilience of the life-supporting ecosystem. Hammer compares traditional small-scale and current large-scale management systems, in terms of how they promote linkages between social and ecological systems, and finds that large-scale systems are more vulnerable because of their failure to process ecosystem feedbacks.

Wilson and Dickie also look at fisheries. They present a view of social and ecological linkages that is based on the broader parametric effects of fishing on the whole biotic and environmental system. Fishing activity leads to a degradation of the biotic or physical environment of desirable species, upsetting their feeding patterns and disrupting normal life cycles. However, the fundamental cause of overfishing lies in the social institutions that either cannot grasp the complexities of biological interactions, or have insufficient means to control the inputs. This institutional difficulty, combined with the uncertainty characterizing marine systems, suggest the appropriateness of a multilevel governance system that captures the social–ecological linkages on different scales.

Pradham and Parks look at Nepal, where deforestation and forest land use change have both socioeconomic and environmental linkages. The interactions between forests and subsistence agricultural systems in Nepal's villages are influenced by the activities of rural farming communities that depend on the forest for various subsistence products. It is because of this reliance on forest resources that such communities often have been blamed for the country's deforestation problem and its associated environmental consequences. Recent government efforts to protect forest resources by excluding local communities have resulted in the opposite effect. Destruction of the social–ecological linkages at the local level has resulted in a new perception by village residents of forests as open-access resources, which has led to further environmental degradation.

Poverty and Population

The links among poverty, population, and the environment are explored in a case study that examines how poverty affects resource use behavior based on desperation. Jodha examines the current unsustainable pattern of resource use in the Himalayas—finding the root cause in the replacement of traditional conservation-oriented resource management systems with more extractive systems. He examines the driving forces that induced or forced the communities to treat natural resources differently under the traditional and current contexts, and discusses ways to restore some of the beneficial properties of the traditional systems.

Lessons Learned and Conclusion

These two volumes provide powerful evidence of the importance of both general principles and specific social and ecological context to the design, implementation, and maintenance of property rights regimes for environmental resources.

Governance: General principles of governance are discussed in relation to the need to match the scale and complexity of ecological systems with their property rights regimes, to ensure that the sets of rules are consistent across different levels of authority, to design a distribution of authority that achieves representation and contains transactions costs, and to coordinate between jurisdictions. Specific properties of governance are presented in the contexts of controlling air pollution, managing a fishery, and enforcing regional environmental regulations.

Equity, Stewardship, and Environmental Resilience: General principles are discussed in terms of the relationship between equity, stewardship, environmental resilience, and efficiency in property rights regimes designed for a range of environmental resources. Specific properties of equity, stewardship, and environmental resilience are presented in the contexts of traditional systems for maintaining biodiversity in India, changing property rights to national parks in Poland, and mangrove–shrimp production systems in coastal Ecuador.

Traditional Knowledge: General principles of traditional knowledge are discussed in terms of the interaction between international environmental policy on the use of traditional knowledge and the implementation of local-level resource management systems that use traditional knowledge. Specific properties of traditional knowledge are presented in the contexts of practical knowledge acquired by fishing skippers in Iceland, fishery and wildlife management in the Canadian subarctic, and the restoration of Maori property rights in New Zealand.

Linking Mechanisms: General principles of mechanisms that link humans to their environment are discussed in terms of their structures and the processes by which they allow humans to observe environmental change, adapt their behavior to reflect environmental change, and create knowledge in the process. Specific properties of linking mechanisms are presented in the contexts of forest tenure systems in Mexico, fisheries management in Sweden and elsewhere, and the interaction between agriculture and forestry in Nepal.

Population and Poverty: General principles of the connection between population and poverty are discussed in terms of the intermediate linkages of gender equality, child-rearing practices, women's education, and general employment opportunities. Specific properties of the population–poverty connection are presented in the context of the relationship of population growth to poverty and unsustainable forest practices in Nepal.

The chapters cover a wide range of general principles and specific contexts. Despite their diversity, the chapters are woven together by a common thread—the interaction of social and ecological systems through property rights to produce environmental outcomes. Each chapter demonstrates in its own way the importance of the social and ecological context. The ecological context shapes human organization and behavior, and the human context in turn shapes ecological organization and response. The structure of governance, values of equity and stewardship, traditional knowledge, linking mechanisms, and conditions of poverty and population all form a part of that context. It is, most important, the interaction of social and ecological contexts that determine the co-evolutionary path that humans and their environment follow. The more we understand about the mechanisms of their interactions and the role of property rights regimes in shaping that interaction, the better able we will be to structure that path.

The editors gratefully acknowledge the invaluable contributions of the chapter authors. Thanks are also due to Adelaida Schwab and Stephanie Gerard, as well as to Rebecca Kary and Jay Dougherty of Alpha-Omega Services, Inc., for assistance in the editing and production stage. Judith Smith of Soleil Associates designed the elegant cover.

Bibliography

Arrow, K., B. Bolin, R. Costanza, P. Dasgupta, C. Folke, C. Holling, B.-O. Jansson, S. Levin, K.-G. Mäler, C. Perrings, and D. Pimentel.

1995. "Economic Growth, Carrying Capacity, and the Environment." *Science* 268:520–21.

Bongaarts, J. 1994. "Population Policy Options in the Developing World." *Science* 263:771–76.

Bromley, D. W. 1989. *Economic Interests and Institutions: The Conceptual Foundations of Public Policy.* Oxford, U.K.: Basil Blackwell.

Bromley, D. W. 1991. *Environment and Economy: Property Rights and Public Policy.* Oxford, U.K.: Basil Blackwell.

Dasgupta, Partha. 1993. *An Enquiry into Well-Being and Destitution.* Oxford, U.K.: Oxford University Press.

de Soto, H. 1993. "The Missing Ingredient." *The Economist* 328(7828):8–12.

Eggertsson, T. 1990. *Economic Behavior and Institutions.* Cambridge, U.K.: Cambridge University Press.

Gordon, Scott. 1954. "The Economic Theory of a Common Property Resource: The Fishery." *Journal of Political Economy* 62(2):122–42.

Hanna, Susan. 1992. "Lessons for Ocean Governance from History, Ecology, and Economics." In B. Cicin-Sain, ed., *Ocean Governance: A New Vision.* Center for the Study of Marine Policy, Graduate College of Marine Studies, University of Delaware, Newark, pp. 23–25.

Hardin, Garrett. 1968. "The Tragedy of the Commons." *Science* 162:1243–48.

Munasinghe, Mohan. 1993. *Environmental Economics and Sustainable Development.* Washington, D.C.: World Bank.

Munasinghe, Mohan, and J. McNeely, eds. 1994. *Protected Area Economics and Policy.* Geneva and Washington, D.C.: World Conservation Union (IUCN) and World Bank.

Munasinghe, Mohan, and W. Shearer, eds. 1995. *Defining and Measuring Biogeophysical Sustainability.* Tokyo and Washington, D.C.: United Nations University and World Bank.

Ostrom, L. 1990. *Governing the Commons.* Cambridge, U.K.: Cambridge University Press.

World Commission on Environment and Development (WCED). 1987. *Our Common Future.* Oxford, U.K.: Oxford University Press.

Warming, Jens. 1911. "Om grundrente af fiskegrunde." *Nationalokonomisk Tidsskrift:* 495–506. Translated in P. Andersen, 1983, "On Rent of Fishing Grounds: A Translation of Jens Warming's 1911 Article, with an Introduction." *History of Political Economy* 15(3):391–96.

Overview

2

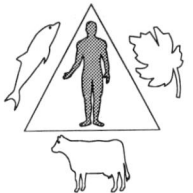

Property Rights and Environmental Resources

Susan Hanna, Carl Folke, and Karl-Göran Mäler

Abstract

IN THIS CHAPTER WE ARGUE THAT PROPERTY RIGHTS are fundamental to the use of environmental resources. Most environmental problems can be seen as problems of incomplete, inconsistent, or unenforced property rights regimes. Property rights regimes comprise *property rights*, the bundles of entitlements regarding resource use, and *property rules*, the rules under which those entitlements are exercised. They exist in a variety of combinations of ownership, locus of control, and the rights and duties of owners. Property rights regimes are necessary but not sufficient conditions for resource sustainability. The "tragedy of the commons" is an environmental outcome that results from an inadequate specification of property rights to environmental services.

This research was sponsored by the Beijer International Institute of Ecological Economics, the Royal Swedish Academy of Sciences, Stockholm, Sweden, with support from the World Environment and Resources Program of the John D. and Catherine T. MacArthur Foundation and from the Environment Department of the World Bank. The research was conducted as part of the research program Property Rights and the Performance of Natural Resource Systems, and has benefitted greatly from the contributions of its participants.

Also important is the consistency of property rights with social goals for equity, efficiency and sustainability, and the enforceability of resource use rules. No single type of regime can be prescribed as a remedy for problems of resource degradation and overuse. Certain components of property rights regimes are critical to their function, including design principles, the mechanisms by which they link the human and ecological systems, the mechanisms by which resources in different political regimes are coordinated, and the role of poverty. Policy addressing environmental problems must focus on general principles of property rights regimes and on the context in which they are placed. We conclude that interdisciplinary work of social scientists and natural scientists offers the greatest hope for the understanding of the interaction of humans with environmental resources through property rights regimes.

✧

Introduction

Picture a pasture open to all...the rational herdsman concludes that the only sensible course for him to pursue is to add another animal to his herd...the conclusion reached by each and every rational herdsman sharing a commons. Therein is the tragedy. Each man is locked into a system that compels him to increase his herd without limit—in a world that is limited. Ruin is the destination toward which all men rush, each pursuing his own best interest in a society that believes in the freedom of the commons. Freedom of the commons brings ruin to all. (Hardin 1968)

Although this famous quote can and has been criticized for loose terminology and historical inaccuracy (Dasgupta 1982; Cox 1985; McCay and Acheson 1987; Berkes and others 1989; Feeny and others 1990; Hanna 1990; Ostrom 1990; Bromley 1992), it conveys an important message: property rights matter. In Hardin's example, no one owns the grazing land. It is an open access resource to which hersdmen can bring any number of cattle to graze. At some point the addition of more cattle to the pasture will reduce the amount of food available for other animals and reduce the benefits herdsmen receive. Since there are no limits placed on the right to graze, each herdsman takes only his own benefits and costs into account and ignores the effect his actions have on others, creating the tragedy. He brings more cattle to graze than is socially optimal, and the pasture becomes overgrazed.

It is of course possible to structure rights to the pasture in ways other than those Hardin describes. The pasture land can be owned as private property, with grazing rights tied to land ownership. In such a case, each owner of grazing land is likely to be less myopic about the effects of grazing, since the services of the pasture land are his into the future. In deciding how many animals to graze on his land, the owner will take into account the future availability of food, grazing only the number that the land will support. If the owner is thinking about getting the most benefit from his land over time, the tragedy will be avoided. The owner can also decide to lease his grazing land to other herdsmen, setting the same limits on grazing which will maximize returns over time, or he may sell the rights to graze his land. In the leasing and selling options, the market allocates the grazing rights to users who have the greatest willingness to pay for them.

Property rights to the pasture may also be specified in a way that is not private but is still limited. One possibility is for a village to own the grazing land as community property, restricting use to village members. Just like the private owner, a village is likely to care about future as well as present benefits from the grazing land, and so will set limits on grazing to avoid exceeding the carrying capacity of the land. If the villagers are dependent on healthy animals from the pasture land for their survival, they are likely to ensure that grazing rights are limited and enforced. Some form of collective decisionmaking body will exist to form rules and monitor use.

A second public ownership possibility is for citizens of the state to own the grazing lands. In such cases, a state management agency as representative of the citizen-owners will make decisions about pasture management, setting limits on grazing which are consistent with social goals for the environment. In both cases, rights to resources are allocated by collective decisionmaking.

In both private and public ownership of the grazing land, circumstances may exist which shorten the time horizon and lead to the tragedy. Private owners may decide to mine the benefits of the land quickly to earn cash for other investments. Village owners may find that employment opportunities elsewhere lower the importance of the future productivity of the grazing land, and so decrease their enforcement efforts or loosen the rules of access. State owners may succumb to political pressure exerted by special interests, and allow higher levels of short-term use. In each of the ownership alternatives, what matters for environmental resources is that property rights are defined, that they reflect the social goals for resource use, and that they are enforced. In fact, most environmental problems can be seen as problems of incomplete, inconsistent, or unenforced property rights. Without a solution to the property rights problem, the environmental problem will remain.

The "tragedy of the commons" in the Hardin example is an environmental outcome that results from an inadequate specification of property rights to the environmental services of the pasture. Access to grazing services is open to all. The open-access outcome is an inefficient use of the pasture, because it leads to a lower level of meat and milk production than would be possible with a smaller number of cattle. Each herder creates negative external effects for other herders when he adds more animals. More resources than are necessary are being used in production, and those additional resources could be used for other production or for future production of meat and milk. The open access pasture is also suboptimal, because it is possible under a different arrangement to improve the well-being of some users without reducing it for others. Clearly, the pasture would be more productive over time if limits were placed on grazing rights.

Sometimes, however, even with well-specified property rights, environmental resource use is inconsistent with social goals. Environmental resources have stock and flow benefits which extend indefinitely over time. The time horizon over which humans make decisions about resources can be collapsed from the future to the present for a number of reasons. Uncertainties caused by political upheaval, health risks, or financial variability can create incentives to focus on present consumption. The myopic focus may lead to levels of resource that are higher than those which sustain the resource over time. Countering the tendency for short-sightedness is concern for one's descendants, which introduces ideas of intergenerational equity and intertemporal efficiency into the decision framework. Owners don't think about resources only for themselves, but also for their children and grandchildren (Young 1993; Mäler 1994; Norton 1994).

It is important to realize that under either situation of market allocation or collective allocation of rights to the resource, patterns of resource use which may evolve over time and be enforceable in relatively stable situations may be disrupted under conditions of technological, economic, or climate change. The introduction of new technology, development of wider market areas, or changes in ambient weather conditions may all lead to changes in behavior which alter the rates of resource use and limit the ability of enforcement efforts to contain them. Group allocation mechanisms may not be flexible enough to adapt rules quickly enough to guide behavior appropriately. On the other hand, market allocations may respond too quickly for protective regulations to adapt as they take advantage of new profit opportunities in the short-term.

Types of Property Rights Regimes

Property rights regimes have two components: *property rights*, which are bundles of entitlements defining owners' rights and duties in the use of a particular resource, and *property rules*, which are the rules under which those rights and duties are exercised (Bromley 1991). The collection of entitlements plus the rules under which they are used make up a regime of property rights which embody peoples' expectations about their claims to resources (Bromley 1989). Property rights regimes are a subset of a society's institutions, the organizational constraints which structure incentives and shape human interactions (North 1990).

Property rights regimes differ by the nature of ownership, the rights and duties of owners, the rules of use, and the locus of control. Table 2–1 presents a simple taxonomy of four types of property rights regimes with their associated rights and duties. (McCay and Acheson 1987; Berkes 1989; Bromley 1989; Feeny and others 1990; Ostrom 1990). The regime types are ordered loosely along a spectrum of ownership.

Private property, *res privatae*, assigns ownership to named individuals, guaranteeing to those owners control of access and the right to a bundle of socially acceptable uses (Black 1968). It requires of the owners that they avoid specified uses which are deemed socially unacceptable, such as fouling the water of streams. Common property, *res communes*, is owned by an identified group of people, which has the right to exclude nonowners and the duty to maintain the property through constraints placed on use (Ciriacy-Wantrup and Bishop 1975; McCay and Acheson 1987; Berkes and others 1989; Bromley 1989; Stevenson 1991). Such regimes are often implemented for common pool resources, those which are difficult to divide or bound (Ostrom 1990).

State property, *res publicae*, is owned by citizens of a political unit who assign rule-making authority to a public agency (Black 1968). The agency has the corresponding duty to ensure that rules promote social objectives. Citizens have the right to use the resource within the established rules. Open access, *res nullius*, has no ownership assigned, and is property open to all. The dynamics of open access are the basis for the "tragedy of the commons." Under a regime of open access, claims to resources are realized at the point of capture, and owners have no specified duty to maintain the resource or constrain use (Black 1968; Ciriacy-Wantrup and Bishop 1975; Berkes 1989; Bromley 1989; Stevenson 1991).

Property rights regimes must perform certain functions of limiting use, coordinating users, and responding to changing environmental conditions. These activities involve the transaction costs of coordination, information gathering, monitoring, and enforcement (Eggertsson 1990; Hanna 1994). Transaction costs are influenced by the particular structure and context of the property rights regime and the condition of the ecological system. As resources become more scarce, property rights regimes must account for more tradeoffs and spillover effects, and rules governing resource distribution and use increase in cost. It is possible to create a system which is so costly to implement that it overwhelms the

benefits to be gained from control. Movements to change property rights regimes are often driven by attempts to reduce transactions costs.

The performance of a property rights regime may be measured in any one or a combination of three dimensions: economic, social, and ecological. All dimensions are interconnected, interactive, and embedded in a system. One measure of performance for a property rights regime is economic efficiency. Efficiency measures focus on the extent to which the production of the "best" economic outcome is produced by means of the least-cost combination of inputs. A broader economic measure of performance would expand the notion of economic outcome to include the depletion and damage effects of environmental use (Daly and Cobb 1989). A social measure of performance focuses on the equity properties of the regime, reflecting social definitions of fairness in the distribution of benefits and costs. An ecologically based performance measure focuses on the extent to which stocks of natural capital are maintained. Unless resources are in surplus relative to demand, tradeoffs between these performance measures are inevitable.

In making tradeoffs, uncertainty works at cross purposes in natural and human systems. In natural systems, uncertainty dictates a precautionary approach to cover contingencies (Costanza 1987). In human systems, uncertainty creates incentives for accelerated rates of use due to the lack of assurance that resources not used in the present will be available in the future (Gardner and others 1990; Bromley 1991; Runge 1984). Such incentives create the need for an institutional framework that constrains human actions.

An early and widespread response to the "tragedy of the commons" metaphor was to propose that natural resources and their ecosystems be privatized, the argument being that only under sole ownership would people have incentives to protect the flow of services from resources into the future. Private ownership would protect the resource user from the "prisoner's dilemma" trap of overuse, which results from not knowing what fellow users will do. Underlying this argument was the assumption that only two types of ownership were possible for natural resources: private or open access.

Since the early proposals for privatization, a rapidly expanding body of research (cf. National Academy of Sciences 1986; McCay and Acheson 1987; Berkes 1989; Berkes and others 1989; Martin 1989; 1992; Pinkerton 1989; Berkes and Feeny 1990; Feeny and others 1990; Ostrom 1990; Bromley 1992) has undermined the argument for private property as the single solution for resource problems. As understanding of common property regimes and combined state/common property regimes has increased, it has become clear that in some contexts collective, decentralized regimes are a more appropriate structure for environmental resource management than private property regimes. Research to date has conclusively established three general principles:

1. Property rights regimes do not exist as two opposing types but rather as combinations along a spectrum from open access to private ownership.

2. Property rights regimes are not in themselves sufficient conditions for resource sustainability, but they are necessary conditions. Without specified rights to resource benefits, ownership is realized only upon capture. If the assurance to future claims to resource benefits is absent, no incentive exists to limit current use.

3. No single type of property rights regime can be prescribed as a remedy for problems of resource degradation and overuse. Both effective control and ineffective control can exist under any kind of regime. Effective property rights regimes are well-specified, context-specific, and enforceable.

If the property rights regime coordinates the human and natural systems in a complementary way, and if it contains feedback channels through which they interact, the result can be the maintenance of both ecological and human long-term objectives. If the natural and human systems are unrepresented in the property rights regime or if feedback channels between them are absent, the resulting pattern of resource use will only accidentally achieve both the ecological and human objectives. The more likely outcome is the short-term realization of human objectives, and the long-term realization of neither.

Research in property rights and environmental resources has established several components which are critical to the structure of property rights regimes and to their function. These components include the design principles on which property rights regimes are based, the linking mechanisms by which property rights regimes connect the human system to the ecological system, the coordinating mechanisms which exist for resources that cross jurisdictional boundaries, and the role of poverty in the use of environmental resources.

Design Principles of Property Rights Regimes

The design of property rights regimes must reflect the larger societal goals and objectives. The design task of a property rights regime, then, is to be congruent with societal objectives for economic performance, equity, and ecological maintenance. These objectives will be both explicit and implicit, formed by cultural traditions, social discourse, and economic dynamics. Objectives for long-term use of the resource must be specified within the property rights regime so that expectations of resource users and the society at large remain consistent (O. Young 1982; Gadgil 1987; Bromley 1989; Daly and Cobb 1989; Ostrom 1992; M. Young 1992; Gadgil and others 1993; Jodha 1993; McCay 1993).

Defining the various "interests," individuals or groups with a stake in the resource (Bromley 1989), is fundamental to property rights design. The specification of the "community" of interests is a first step in the specification of rights and obligations, and is often a complex process involving both traditional and emerging resource users (Ostrom 1990; Bromley 1992; Ostrom and others 1993; Young 1992). Associated with the definition of legitimate interests is the articulation of rules for participation of those interests in management. Various levels of user participation are possible, ranging from the passive receipt of government-imposed rules at one extreme, to active self-governance at the other (McCay 1993; Hance and others 1988; Ostrom and others 1993; Ostrom 1993). Also related to the definition of interests is the specification of property rules to ensure that rights and responsibilities are as congruent as possible. The task is to minimize the possibility of "free riding," a common phenomenon in environmental resource use when an individual receives resource benefits and avoids bearing proportional resource costs (Runge 1984; Young 1992).

A further design requirement is to ensure that the incentive structure of rules reflects the long-term sustainability goals for the ecological system. The time frames of human economic and social systems are typically much shorter than those of ecological systems, creating problems of congruency in design that must be resolved if sustainability is to be achieved. This can be dealt with explicitly through a specification of rights which create an expectation of long-term tenure and protection from the tyranny of short-term decisions (Jentoft 1989; Pinkerton 1989; Ostrom 1993). An additional complication is that the economic and ecological systems are measured with different currencies. While money is the currency of economies, physical quantities are the currency of environmental resources (Young 1992). This distinction becomes important in the choice of objectives for the property rights regime.

Related to temporal congruence is the issue of spatial congruence. It is important to ensure that a property rights regime has clearly defined boundaries, and that to the extent possible, those boundaries are consistent with the natural boundaries of the ecological system. The reason for boundary congruency is to bring the area of decisionmaking into line with areas of ecological interaction. Without this congruency, decisions taken within a property rights regime will have only a partial effect on the ecological system, and may conflict with decisions made about the remaining parts. Thus, for example, it is more effective to have fishery management on a watershed scale instead of stream-level scale. The boundary congruency concept underlies bioregional management (Costanza and Daly 1992; Berkes and Folke 1994; Gunderson and others 1994; Smith 1994).

Design includes the distribution of decisionmaking authority. A regime functions best when decision rules are consistent with ownership, for example, when collectively owned resources are managed through collective choice arrangements. Regardless of the type of regime, decisions which have the benefit of knowledge about local conditions and accommodate that knowledge are likely to be the most adaptable and enforceable (Ostrom 1990). Conflict between users and decisionmakers is inevitable, and rent seeking through lobbying is widespread (Tietenberg 1988). Equitable mechanisms for the resolution of conflict must be in place. Also needed is a reliable system of monitoring and enforcement, with graduated sanctions for violations of various degrees of seriousness (Ostrom 1990) which protect rights to claims.

Through all its attributes, the design of a property rights regime is a critical component of environmental outcome. So important is the design of a property rights regime that abrupt alterations in design may completely undermine the regime's performance. Numerous examples exist of development projects which were implemented to promote resource conservation but which replaced functioning, well adapted rights regimes with those not designed for the context. As one example, the replacement of many common property resource regimes in India with private property resulted in equitable community distribution systems being supplanted by extreme social and economic differentiation, increasing pressures for intensified resource use (Jodha 1993).

Linkages Between Ecological and Human Systems

Property rights regimes link ecological systems to human systems. The linkage they make is specific to context because they connect a particular human system, with its unique economic, legal, and social structure, to a particular ecological system, with its unique biophysical structure. The overriding characteristic of an effective linking mechanism is that it reflects the properties of the ecological and human systems it connects. Depending on the particular outcome produced, interactions may be modified through changes in the property rights regimes through which they are connected. Modification may be abrupt, as when existing regimes are replaced in their entirety. A more adaptive modification may result from the co-evolution of ecological systems and property rights regimes as they modify each other over time (Norgaard 1992; Gowdy 1994).

One way in which ecological and human systems are linked through property rights regimes is through various forms of capital. Natural capital is an ecosystem's complex array of plant and animal life, water and minerals (Costanza and others 1991). Physical capital—technology—is applied to the natural capital to extract a flow of resource benefits. Cultural capital includes all the factors which allow human adaptation to and modification of the natural environment (Folke and Berkes 1992). Institutional capital is a subset of cultural capital, and is defined as the stock of rules and underlying human organizational skills which coordinate human behavior in its interaction with natural resources (Hanna 1995). Human capital is the body of human knowledge and skills that allows transformation of natural resources into commodities.

From the human perspective, ecosystems are assets whose stock provides flow services over time. Resource management's greatest success has been the design of incentives to capture the flow of benefits from the ecosystem. Management's most difficult problem has been the design of incentives to sustain the stock of ecosystem assets. The management approach to the protection of the ecosystem's natural capital stock has often been to limit the application of physical capital, or to aim for sustained yields. These approaches have had only limited success. The adaptation of institutional capital has often not kept pace with the rate of change in natural and physical capital, and property rights regimes which have relied on this form of linkage have had to strain to stay within limits of natural capital. The focus on sustained yield has limited the willingness of users to vary yields as the ecosystem varies.

Another link between ecological and human systems is developed through local knowledge, also called traditional ecological knowledge or indigenous knowledge. There are many forms of knowledge about both ecological and human systems which are not generated scientifically but rather result from years of direct work experience. Customs and practices with respect to the environment are often operational expressions of traditional knowledge on the structure and function of the environmental resources.

Villagers in India, fishing skippers in the North Atlantic, and users of the coastal zones in the Pacific Islands all acquire and use knowledge in the course of their work, which links them to their environment (Pálsson 1991; Gadgil and others 1993; Berkes and others 1994; Ruddle 1994).

The concept of ecosystem resilience is important in relation to property rights systems and institutional capital. Resilience has been given two very different definitions in the ecological literature. The first definition focuses on stability at a presumed steady state, emphasizing resistance to disturbances and speed of return to the equilibrium point. The other definition of resilience, which we use here, is a measure of the perturbation that can be absorbed before an ecosystem is shifted into another state. In this definition, systems are complex and self-organizing, permeated by uncertainties and discontinuities, and have several possible equilibrial states (Holling 1986; Holling and others 1994).

As an example of a multiple equilibrial state, forest land cleared for agriculture in Amazonia, once abandoned, can develop into a savanna but hardly ever reverts to the original forest (Solbrig 1991; Young and Solbrig 1993). Different sets of interacting physical and biological processes and organisms control ecosystem functioning in forests and savannas. Such phenomena of threshold effects at the level of the whole ecosystem have been documented in savannas, boreal forests, fisheries and agriculture (Westoby and others 1989; Regier and Baskerville 1986, Trenbath and others 1990; Gunderson and others 1994).

A major challenge for the design and performance of property rights regimes is to ensure that decisionmakers (land owners, village councils, management agencies) have the appropriate incentives to take such equilibrium shifts into account and make the appropriate tradeoff between the social costs and benefits to society at large. This requires monitoring feedback from the ecological system when making decisions, allowing perturbations to enter the system at a scale that allows subsystem variability but does not challenge the underlying ecological and economic activity (Berkes and Folke 1994). Ecological systems will always have disturbances (Holling 1986). Sustained yield management which develops strategies to block out such feedback will allow such disturbances to accumulate, magnify, and enter on a much higher level, threatening the combined ecological and economic system (Holling 1994; Gunderson and others 1995).

Coordinating Mechanisms

Many of the world's most critical environmental problems have interregional or international dimensions that require coordination. Climate change and deterioration of environmental quality, ocean contamination, disruption of biogeochemical cycles, devegetation, desertification, and loss of genetic material are all problems identified by the UNEP's Earthwatch Program which spill across regional and national borders (Caldwell 1984). Indeed, political borders are completely arbitrary from the perspective of these problems (Mäler 1990). Environmental problems spread across borders in a number of ways: physically, as when a waterborne pollutant crosses borders; human transport, as when wastes are carried across borders; human concern, as when Northern Hemisphere residents worry about the survival of endangered species in the tropics; and economic side-effects, as when environmental damage or environmental policies affect markets (Mäler 1990). A large component of these dimensions are institutional: institutions can be both the cause and the solution of environmental problems (Keohane and others 1993).

Multiple geopolitical boundaries and legal systems add a great deal of complexity to the specification and coordination of property rights regimes. Transboundary environmental problems create external effects which may be either unidirectional, regionally reciprocal or global. A unidirectional externality exists when the source of the problem is different from the receiver, for example, upstream polluters causing damage to downstream water users. In a regionally reciprocal externality, a group of countries is both the source and the victim of the problem, as when European countries both cause and suffer from acid rain. Global externalities affect most countries and may be caused by a single country, by several countries, or by all countries (Mäler 1990). Because of the multiple jurisdictions, internalizing environmental benefits and costs is difficult (Dasgupta and Mäler 1992; Barrett 1993b; Young 1992). Coordination is difficult

because of the number of "games" being played simultaneously by different political entities. The multiple dimensions of conflicts adds complexity to their resolution (Barrett 1993a; Ostrom and others 1993).

Adding to the coordination difficulties is the number of inconsistent sustainability goals which may and probably do exist between different political entities (Jentoft 1989). For example, resources such as the atmosphere, stratosphere, and open oceans are shared as joint property by all nations, each of which may have different goals for the way they are used and protected. They are open access, rights to use them are difficult to define, and there is no international body in place to implement or enforce rules of conduct. The locus of authority lies within individual nations, leaving agreements between countries unenforceable at higher levels (Barrett 1990).

Solutions to environmental problems lie in voluntary cooperation among nation members of the global community. However, such solutions are surrounded by problems. Very high levels of transaction costs accompany international negotiations on the ownership and use of global environmental resources. One reason for this is the applicable doctrine of international law known as "equitable utilization." Because there is no agreed-upon standard for assessing equitable utilization, countries must negotiate rival interests on a case-by-case basis (Barrett 1993a). Incentives for individual countries to "free ride" on the agreements negotiated by others are strong.

In an effort to reduce the transaction costs of negotiation, international conventions on environmental problems have typically taken the form of framework conventions, shaping the environment in which negotiation takes place. Countries first decide on the negotiation process, then decide on more substantive matters. This procedure was successful in the 1985 Vienna Convention on Substances Harmful to the Ozone Layer. The Convention has been followed by a succession of protocols, for example, the Montreal Protocol on Substances which Deplete the Ozone Layer, which have substantially reduced the use of ozone-harming substances such as chloroflourocarbons (CFCs). Environmental protocols have established property rights to production and consumption of such harmful substances and allowed international trading of rights (Tietenberg 1990; Barrett 1993b). In limiting the domestic use and international trade of ozone-harming substances, the protocols have effectively transferred property rights over their manufacture from nations to the international community. In recognition of this transfer, mechanisms have been included to compensate poor countries for the phasing out of production (Barrett 1993b).

Addressing the problem of free riding has proven to be less tractable in the international sphere than at smaller scales. However, regional international agreements offer some promise in this regard. Cooperative arrangements such as the European Union and the North American Free Trade Agreement provide regional incentives to resolve environmental problems, and are limited enough in scale so that free riding by any individual country is more difficult. Embryonic attempts to establish regional property rights to the environmental resources can be observed in joint implementation agreements between countries, in which emissions reductions in one country are matched by reductions in another country. These agreements may eventually develop into international systems of tradable permits for pollutants, where individual countries own a specified number of permits and total numbers of permits are established by all member countries.

In addition to the negotiation and free-riding problems, international coordination has very real problems of scale. Property rights regimes are often nested within larger institutional jurisdictions, requiring compatible incentives at several levels (Young 1982; Ostrom 1990). Complicating the compatibility issue is the fact that both "scaling up" small-scale system properties to large-scale systems and "scaling down" international environmental agreements to local levels cannot be done proportionally (O. Young 1993).

Poverty and Environmental Degradation

Global population is projected to increase by nearly two-thirds over the next thirty years (World Resources Institute 1994). Expanding populations which exacerbate economic, social, and ecological impoverishment make all of the existing environmental problems more critical (Caldwell 1984). The increase has several components, including a desire for large families, unwanted fertility, and "population momentum," the tendency for population to increase for some time after fertility has stabilized (Bongaarts 1994). The environmental impacts of continued population growth will be felt through increases in energy demand, production, consumption, and waste. The implications of population growth for property rights regimes are also sobering. There is a limit to the extent that systems of property rights, however well-specified, consistent, and well-enforced, can protect environmental resources in the face of extreme population pressure. The need to understand the relationship between poverty, population, and the environment is critical.

Individual decisions about child-bearing are fundamental to the issue of population growth. In all countries, children are in some sense durable "consumer goods," which require expenditures and yield a flow of services over their lifetime. The services include those of love and affection, companionship, and extension of personal genetic material. In poor countries children provide additional services to the household: they contribute to household production and provide security for parents in old age. These two services provide poor households with a significant motivation for having children, a factor recognized in the literature (Cain 1982; 1983; Mueller 1976; Dasgupta and Mäler 1991; Nerlove and Myer 1991; Dasgupta 1992; Bongaarts 1994)

The motivation for fertility has its origins in the combination of private property rights to children's productive services and a paucity of basic services in rural areas of poor countries. Poor countries are for the most part biomass-based subsistence economies. Households typically do not have the easy access to sources of household energy and water that are standard for households in industrialized economies. Children perform services of collecting water and energy sources (fuelwood, dung, fodder) for the household, services which are necessary for survival and complementary to other productive activities. Several hours per day may be required for obtaining the minimum essential levels of water and energy sources, resulting in much higher relative costs for these basic factors than are faced by households in more industrialized economies. Children generally add more to household income than they cost to rear, creating a direct incentive for households to produce children as workers (Dasgupta and Mäler 1993). The number of basic activities required to survive means that each household needs many hands, and under certain circumstances the usefulness of each hand increases with declining resource availability. The further the distance to find fuel or water, the larger the number of gatherers required.

In resource-degraded areas, a high rate of fertility and population growth causes further damages to the environmental resource base, creating further need for large families, causing more damage to environmental resources, until some countervailing factor stops the spiral. The spiral may be stopped by public policy or by the feedback of lowered productivity of children. The problem is that by the time feedback is registered, many people have suffered. Such a spiral may be set off by a number of sources: government or private usurpation of community property rights to resources, labor immobility, breakdown of compliance with environmental rules, and the introduction of new technology (Dasgupta 1995; Gadgil and Rao 1995; Jodha 1995; Pradham and Parks 1995).

Conclusions and Policy Implications

This paper has presented an overview of property rights regimes, their structure, and their functions as links between humans and their environment. Types of property rights regimes are arrayed along a spectrum from open access to private property, with almost infinite variety in their components. No single type of property rights regime can be prescribed as a remedy for problems of environmental resource degradation and overuse. In addressing environmental problems, policy must not only focus on the establishment of property rights regimes, but also carefully consider the context in which property rights regimes are to be placed and the extent to which they are enforceable. General principles of property rights regimes are applicable across contexts, but the specific details of the human and ecological context are critical to success in particular applications.

Property rights regimes are a necessary but not sufficient condition for the efficient use of environmental resources. Without clearly specified property rights, environmental resources cannot be sustained over time, but property rights alone cannot ensure use levels that reflect social objectives. Property rights regimes must also meet certain design principles and perform critical functions of coordination and linkage between humans and the environment. Property rules must be enforced. Equally important, the linkages provided by property rights regimes are limited in their ability to constrain human action (Costanza and Daly 1990; Bromley 1992). Property rights regimes have failed in the past and are continuing to fail when overwhelmed with human pressure in the form of absolute population growth and increased per capita demand for resources.

Despite a growing body of knowledge on the design, linking, and coordination properties of property rights regimes, there are still important features which are unknown. The Beijer Institute's research program *Property Rights and the Performance of Natural Resource Systems* is investigating these areas through interdisciplinary teams of anthropologists, demographers, ecologists, economists, geographers, political scientists, and sociologists. In this research, we are finding great benefits from collaborations between natural and social scientists. The field of property rights research has been the traditional domain of social scientists. The focus has been on the human actors as "managers" of natural systems. The natural system itself has been left in the background as the provider of services and the recipient of impacts. Similarly, the field of natural resource management has been dominated by biological scientists. Their focus has been on a species of concern, usually a single species at a time. Humans are viewed as peripheral to the system's functions, as intruders. Evidence abounds that the failure to account for the full spectrum of natural system functions and human system complexity has hindered our capacity to sustain the resource base. Social scientists working with natural scientists have a unique opportunity to contribute to the pressing scientific and policy problems which surround the human interaction with natural systems through property rights regimes.

Bibliography

Barrett, S. 1990. "The Problem of Global Environmental Protection." *Oxford Review of Economic Policy* 6:68–79.

Barrett, S. 1993a. "Managing the International Commons." In G. Brown and V. K. Smith, eds., *Resource and Environmental Economics*. Cincinnati: South-Western Publishing.

Barrett, S. 1993b. "The Theory of Property Rights: Transboundary Resources." Beijer Discussion Paper Series Number 44, Beijer International Institute of Ecological Economics, The Royal Swedish Academy of Sciences, Box 50005, 104 05 Stockholm, Sweden.

Berkes, F., ed. 1989. *Common Property Resources: Ecology and Community-Based Sustainable Development*. London: Belhaven Press.

Berkes, F., D. Feeny, B. J. McCay, J. M. Acheson. 1989. "The Benefits of the Commons." *Nature* 340:91–93.

Berkes, F. and D. Feeny. 1990. "Paradigms Lost: Changing Views on the Use of Common Property Resources." *Alternatives* 17(2):48–55.

Berkes, F. and Folke, C. 1994. "Linking Social and Ecological Systems for Resilience and Sustainability." Background paper and Framework prepared for the workshop Property Rights and the Performance of Natural Resource Systems, August 29, 1994, Stockholm, Sweden.

Berkes, F., C. Folke, and M. Gadgil. 1994. "Traditional Ecological Knowledge." In C. A. Perrings, K-G.Mäler, C. Folke, C. S. Holling, and B.-O. Jansson, eds., *Biodiversity Conservation: Problems and Policies*. Dordrecht: Kluwer Academic Publisher.

Black, H. C. 1968. *Black's Law Dictionary, Revised 4th Edition*. St. Paul, Minnesota: West Publishing.

Bongaarts, J. 1994. "Population Policy Options in the Developing World." *Science* 263(11 Feb.):771–76.

Bromley, D. W. 1989. *Economic Interests and Institutions: The Conceptual Foundations of Public Policy*. Oxford: Basil Blackwell.

Bromley, D. W. 1991. *Environment and Economy: Property Rights and Public Policy*. Oxford: Basil Blackwell.

Bromley, D., ed., 1992. *Making the Commons Work: Theory, Practice, and Policy*. San Francisco: ICS Press.

Cain, M. 1983. "Fertility As an Adjustment to Risk." *Population and Development Review* 9(4):688–702.

Caldwell, L. K. 1984. *International Environmental Policy: Emergence and Dimensions*, Second Edition. Durham, North Carolina: Duke University Press.

Ciriacy-Wantrup, S. V., and R. Bishop. 1975. "'Common Property' as a Concept in Natural Resources Policy." *Natural Resources Journal* 15:713–28.

Costanza, R. 1987. "Social Traps and Environmental Policy." *BioScience* 37:407–12.

Costanza, R., ed., 1991. *Ecological Economics: The Science and Management of Sustainability*. New York: Columbia University Press

Costanza, R. and H. E. Daly. 1992. "Natural Capital and Sustainable Development." *Conservation Biology* 6(1):37–46.

Cox, S. J. B. 1985. "No Tragedy on the Commons." *Environmental Ethics* 7:49–61.

Daly, H. E., and J. B. Cobb, Jr. 1989. *For the Common Good*. Boston: Beacon Press.

Dasgupta, P. 1982. *The Control of Resources*. Cambridge: Harvard University Press.

Dasgupta, P. 1992. *An Enquiry into Well-Being and Destitution*. Oxford: Clarendon Press.

Dasgupta, P. and K-G. Mäler. 1991. "The Environment and Emerging Development Issues." *Proceedings of the World Bank Annual Conference on Development Issues 1990*.

Dasgupta, P. and K-G. Mäler. 1992. *The Economics of Transnational Commons*. Oxford: Clarendon Press.

Dasgupta, P. and K-G. Mäler. 1993. "Poverty, Institutions, and the Environmental Resource Base." Beijer Discussion Paper Series Number 27, Beijer International Institute of Ecological Economics, The Royal Swedish Academy of Sciences, Box 50005, 104 05 Stockholm, Sweden.

Dasgupta, P. 1995. "The Population Problem: Theory and Evidence." In S. Hanna and M. Munasinghe, eds., *Property Rights and the*

Environment: Social and Ecological Issues. Washington, D.C.: World Bank.

Eggertsson, T. 1990. *Economic Behavior and Institutions.* Cambridge: Cambridge University Press.

Feeny, D., F. Berkes, B. J. McCay. 1990. "The Tragedy of the Commons Twenty-Two Years Later." *Human Ecology* 18:1–19.

Folke, C. and F. Berkes. 1992. "Cultural Capital and Natural Capital Interrelations." Beijer Discussion Paper Series Number 8, Beijer International Institute of Ecological Economics, The Royal Swedish Academy of Sciences, Box 50005, 104 05 Stockholm, Sweden.

Gadgil, M. 1987. "Diversity: Cultural and Biological." *Trends in Ecology and Evolution* 2(12):369–73.

Gadgil, M., F. Berkes, and C. Folke. 1993. "Indigenous Knowledge for Biodiversity Conservation. *Ambio* 22(2–3):151–56.

Gadgil, M. and P. R. S. Rao. 1995. "Designing Incentives to Conserve India's Biodiversity." In Hanna, S. and M. Munasinghe, eds., *Property Rights in Social and Ecological Context: Case Studies and Design Applications.* Washington, D.C.: World Bank.

Gardner, R., E. Ostrom, and J. Walker. 1990. "The Nature of Common Pool Resource Problems." *Rationality and Society* 2(3):335–58.

Gowdy, J. M. 1994. *Coevolutionary Economics: The Economy, Society and the Environment.* Boston: Kluwer Academic Publishers.

Gunderson, L. H., C. S. Holling, and S. Light. 1995. *Barriers and Bridges to Renewal of Ecosystems and Institutions.* New York: Columbia University Press.

Hanna, S. 1990. "The Eighteenth Century English Commons: A Model for Ocean Management." *Journal of Ocean and Shoreline Management* 14:155–72.

Hanna, S. S. 1994. "Co-management." In K. L. Gimbel, ed., *Limiting Access to Marine Fisheries: Keeping the Focus on Conservation.* Washington, D.C.: Center for Marine Conservation and World Wildlife Fund. 233–42.

Hanna, S. S. 1995. "The New Frontier of American Fisheries Governance." Forthcoming in *Ecological Economics.*

Hance, B. J., C. Chess, and P. M. Sandman. 1988. *Improving Dialogue With Communities: A Risk Communication Manual for Government.* New Brunswick, New Jersey.: Environmental Communication Research Program, New Jersey Agricultural Experiment Station, Rutgers University.

Hardin, G. 1968. "The Tragedy of the Commons." *Science* 162:1243–48.

Holling, C. S. 1986. "Resilience of Ecosystems: Local Surprise and Global Change." In W. C. Clark and R. E. Munn, eds., *Sustainable Development of the Biosphere.* Cambridge: Cambridge University Press. 292–317.

Holling, C. S. 1994. "New Science and New Investments for a Sustainable Biosphere." In A. M. Jansson, C. Folke, R. Costanza, and M. Hammer, eds., *Investing in Natural Capital: The Ecological Economic Approach to Sustainability.* Washington, D.C.: Island Press.

Holling, C. S., D. W. Schindler, B. W. Walker, and J. Roughgarden. 1994. "Biodiversity in the Functioning of Ecosystems: An Ecological Primer and Synthesis." In C. Perrings, K.-G. Mäler, C. Folke, C. S. Holling, and B.-O. Jansson, eds., *Biodiversity Loss: Ecological and Economic Issues.* Cambridge: Cambridge University Press.

Jentoft, S. 1989. "Fisheries Co-management: Delegating Responsibility to Fishermen's Organizations." *Marine Policy* 13(2):137–54.

Jodha, N. S. 1985. "Population Growth and the Decline of Common Property Resources in India." *Population and Development Review* 11(2):247–64.

Jodha, N. S. 1993. "Property Rights and Development." Beijer Discussion Paper Number 41, Beijer International Institute of Ecological Economics, The Royal Swedish Academy of Sciences, Box 50005, 104 05 Stockholm, Sweden.

Jodha, N. S. 1995. "Environmental Crisis in the Himalayas: Lessons from the Degradation Process." In S. Hanna and M. Munasinghe, eds., 1995. *Property Rights in Social and Ecological Context: Case Studies and Design Applications.* Washington, D.C.: World Bank.

Keohane, R. O., P. M. Haas, and M. A. Levy. 1993. "The Effectiveness of International Environmental Institutions." In P. M. Haas,

R. O. Keohane, and M. A. Levy, eds., *Institutions for the Earth*. Cambridge: MIT Press.

Mäler, K.-G. 1990. International environmental problems. *Oxford Review of Economic Policy* 6(1).

Mäler, K.-G. 1994. Economic growth and the environment. In L. Pasinetti and R. Solow, eds., *Economic Growth and the Structure of Long-Term Development*. London: MacMillan.

Martin, F. 1989. *Common Pool Resources and Collective Action: A Bibliography*. Workshop in Political Theory and Policy Analysis, Indiana University, 513 North Park, Bloomington, Indiana.

Martin, F. 1992. *Common Pool Resources and Collective Action: A Bibliography, Volume 2*. Workshop in Political Theory and Policy Analysis, Indiana University, 513 North Park, Bloomington, Indiana.

McCay, B. J., and J. M. Acheson, eds. 1987. *The Question of the Commons: The Culture and Ecology of Communal Resources*. Tuscon: University of Arizona Press.

McCay, B. J. 1993. "Management Regimes." Beijer Discussion Paper Number 38, Beijer International Institute of Ecological Economics, The Royal Swedish Academy of Sciences, Box 50005, 104 05 Stockholm, Sweden.

National Academy of Sciences. 1986. *Proceedings of the Conference on Common Property Resource Management*. Washington, D.C.: National Academy Press.

Nerlove, M. and A. Meyer. 1993. "Endogenous Fertility and the Environment: A Parable of Firewood." In P. Dasgupta and K.-G. Mäler, eds., *Poverty, Institutions, and Environmental-Resource Base*. Development Research Programme Number 39, London School of Economics.

Norgaard, R. 1992. "Coevolution of Economy, Society and Environment." In P. Elkins and M. Max-Neef, eds., *Real Life Economics*. London: Routledge.

North, D. C. 1990. *Institutions, Institutional Change and Economic Performance*. Cambridge: Cambridge University Press.

Norton, B. G. 1992. "A New Paradigm for Environmental Management." In R. Costanza, B. G. Norton, and B. D. Haskell, *Ecosystem Health: New Goals for Ecosystem Management*. Washington, D.C.: Island Press.

Ostrom, E. 1990. *Governing the Commons: The Evolution of Institutions for Collective Action*. Cambridge: Cambridge University Press.

Ostrom, E. 1992. *Crafting Institutions for Self-Governing Irrigation Systems*. San Francisco: ICS Press.

Ostrom, E. 1993. "The evolution of norms and rights." Beijer Discussion Paper Number 39, Beijer International Institute of Ecological Economics, The Royal Swedish Academy of Sciences, Box 50005, 104 05 Stockholm, Sweden.

Ostrom, E., R. Gardner, and J. Walker. 1993. *Rules, Games, and Common-Pool Resources*. Ann Arbor: University of Michigan Press.

Pálsson, G. 1991. *Coastal Economies, Cultural Accounts: Human Ecology and Icelandic Discourse*. Manchester: Manchester University Press.

Pinkerton, E., ed., 1989. *Cooperative Management of Local Fisheries: New Directions for Improved Management and Community Development*. Vancouver: University of British Columbia Press.

Pradham, A. S., and P. J. Parks. 1995. "Environmental and Socioeconomic Linkages of Deforestation and Land Use Change in the Nepal Himalaya." In S. Hanna and M. Munasinghe, eds., *Property Rights in Social and Ecological Context: Case Studies and Design Applications*. Washington, D.C.: World Bank.

Regier, H. A., and G. L. Baskerville. 1986. "Sustainable Redevelopment of Regional Ecosystems Degraded by Exploitive Development." In W. C. Clark and R. E. Munn, eds., *Sustainable Development of the Biosphere*. Cambridge: Cambridge University Press. 75–101.

Ruddle, K. 1994. "Local Knowledge in the Folk Management of Fisheries and Coastal Marine Environments." In C. L. Dyer and J. R. McGoodwin, eds., *Folk Management of Marine Fisheries: Lessons for Modern Fisheries Management*. Niwot: University Press of Colorado.

Runge, C. F. 1984. "Institutions and the Free Rider: The Assurance Problem in Collective Action." *Journal of Politics* 46(1):154–181.

Smith, C. L. 1994. "Connecting Cultural and Biological Diversity in Restoring Northwest Salmon." *Fisheries* 19(2):20–26.

Solbrig, O. T. 1991. "Ecosystems and Global Environmental Change." In R. Correll, ed., *Global Environmental Change*. Berlin: Springer-Verlag. 173–94.

Stevenson, G. G. 1991. *Common Property Economics: A General Theory and Land Use Applications*. Cambridge: Cambridge University Press.

Tietenberg, T. H. 1988. *Environmental and Natural Resource Economics, Second Edition*. Boston: Scott, Foresman and Company.

Tietenberg, T. H. 1990. "Economic Instruments for Environmental Regulation." *Oxford Review of Economic Policy* 6(1):17–33.

Trenbath, B. R., G. R. Conway, and I. A. Craig. 1990. "Threats to Sustainability in Intensified Agricultural Systems: Analysis and Implications for Management." In S. R. Gliessman, ed., *Agroecology*. New York: Springer-Verlag.

Westoby, M., B. H. Walker, and I. Noy-Meir. 1989. "Opportunistic Management for Rangelands Not at Equilibrium." *Journal of Rangeland Management* 42:266–74.

World Resources Institute. 1994. *World Resources 1994–1995: A Guide to the Global Environment*. New York: Oxford University Press.

Young, M. D. 1992. *Sustainable Investment and Resource Use*. Man and the Biosphere Series Volume 9, Parthenon Press.

Young, M. D. 1993. "For Our Children's Children: Some Practical Implications of Inter-Generational Equity and the Precautionary Principle." Canberra, Australia: CSIRO Division of Wildlife and Ecology.

Young, M. D., and O. T. Solbrig, eds. 1993. *The World's Savannas*. Man and the Biosphere Series Vol.12, Paris: UNESCO.

Young, O. 1982. *Resource Regimes: Natural Resources and Social Institutions*. Berkeley: University of California Press.

Young, O. 1993. "The 'New Institutionalism' in International Relations." Beijer Discussion Paper Series Number 43, Beijer International Institute of Ecological Economics, The Royal Swedish Academy of Sciences, Box 50005, 104 05 Stockholm, Sweden.

Table 2–1: Types of Property Rights Regimes with Owners, Rights, and Duties

Regime Type	Owner	Owner Rights	Owner Duties
Private property	individual	socially acceptable uses; control of access	avoidance of socially unacceptable uses
Common property	collective	exclusion of nonowners	maintenance; constrain rates of use
State property	citizens	determine rules	maintain social objectives
Open access (nonproperty)	none	capture	none

Governance

3

Designing Complexity to Govern Complexity

Elinor Ostrom

Abstract

SINCE MANY BIOLOGICAL PROCESSES occur at small, medium, and large scales, governance arrangements that can cope with this level of complexity also need to be organized as multiple scales and linked effectively together. The importance of nested institutional arrangements with quasi-autonomous units operating at very small up through very large scales is stressed in this chapter. Design principles derived from a close study of long-surviving, self-governing institutions are presented, as are lessons derived for the future.

This chapter results from work on Social and Ecological System Linkages of the Property Rights Program of the Beijer International Institute of Ecological Economics, The Royal Swedish Academy of Science, and the International Forestry Resources and Institutions (IFRI) research program at the Workshop in Political Theory and Policy Analysis, Indiana University, supported in part by the Forests, Trees and People Programme of the Food and Agriculture Organization of the United Nations and the National Science Foundation (Grant SBR-9319835). The author wishes to thank Patty Dalecki for her perceptive editing.

A concern for biodiversity is a concern for the importance of sustaining complex systems at multiple spatial and temporal scales. Much of the literature on biodiversity stresses the global nature of the gene pool and the consequent need for international institutional arrangements to articulate worldwide concerns for the preservation of biodiversity for future generations. Many biological processes occur, however, at very small scales that vary dramatically in climate, elevation, structure, and importance from one niche to the next. An overemphasis on the need for large-scale institutional arrangements can lead to the destruction or discouragement of institutional arrangements at smaller to medium scales. It is at these smaller scales that local knowledge about specific complex interactions and concerns about natural capital can be applied in daily life (Jansson and others 1994).

The central theme of this chapter is that if complexity is the nature of the systems we have an interest in governing (regulating), it is essential to think seriously about the complexity in the governance systems that are proposed. Without a deep concern for creating complex, nested systems of governance, the very processes of trying to regulate behavior so as to preserve biodiversity will produce the tragic and unintended consequence of destroying the complexity we are trying to enhance (V. Ostrom 1991; V. Ostrom, Feeny, and Picht 1993).

W. Ross Ashby, an eminent biologist of an earlier era, wrote a book entitled *Design for a Brain: The Origin of Adaptive Behavior* (1960), in which he developed the "Law of Requisite Variety." Basically, the law of requisite variety can be stated thus: Any regulative system needs as much variety in the actions that it can take as exists in the system it is regulating. Translated into the discourse concerning biological diversity, the law of requisite variety can be stated as follows:

> Any governance system that is designed to regulate complex biological systems must have as much variety in the actions that it can take as there exists in the systems being regulated.

This is a tall order. It is one, however, to which we need to pay serious attention. Or, if we continue to stress the importance of simple, large-scale, centralized governance units that do not, and cannot, have the variety of response capabilities (and the incentives to use these capabilities) that complex, polycentric, multilayered governance systems can have, the goal of sustaining complex, multiscaled biological processes is unreachable (Gadgil and Rao 1994).

Among the institutions that humans utilize for generating highly desirable future goods are open, competitive markets. Open, competitive market arrangements for producing private goods—those that are easy to exclude from noncontributors and whose consumption is subtractive or rivalrous—have many advantages. One of them is that they create incentives for innovation and entrepreneurship. Those who are alert to the opportunities present at many different scales can enter tiny market niches to create benefits for others—and thus for themselves. In the environments in which markets work well, they are normally complex, polycentric, multitiered systems of individuals relating to one another in such a manner as to greatly enhance overall productivity. Efforts to achieve the same level of productivity by central direction have repeatedly failed, and failed dramatically.

It is well established, however, that markets do *not* perform effectively in relation to public goods where exclusion is difficult, and thus very costly, to achieve (Ciriacy-Wantrup and Bishop 1975; Heal 1994; E. Ostrom, Gardner, and Walker 1994). If one were to rely entirely on market institutions for exchanges of products drawn from living beings, sustaining a biologically diverse gene pool would be dramatically underprovided (Perrings, Folke, and Mäler 1992). Further, it is extremely difficult to develop property rights to many aspects of biodiversity (McNeely 1988). In some instances, we may not wish to allow any one entity to own key aspects of complex biological systems. Full ownership implies the complete power to control the access and use of a resource, and have the capacity to hold the resource for private use or to alienate or destroy the resource (Schlager and Ostrom 1993). Full ownership by one entity conveys the right to destroy biological diversity as well as the capability to enhance it.

Laura Jackson (1994), in an important paper, provides us with a deep insight into what can happen when one large corporation becomes the full owner of large tracts of land. The initial development of land for commercial purposes may be continued over time or abandoned, given the opportunities to maximize profits through shifting operations to locations where the accounting costs of production may be lower, and thus profits higher. Large private agricultural corporations, owned by distant shareholders and managed out of central offices, are not likely to enhance the biodiversity that exists in a particular ecological niche. Rather, incentives tend to press toward monoculture and the use of commercially available inputs rather than complex mixes of agricultural products that rely on intensive cultivation techniques. A similar argument is presented by McNeely (1988).

Jackson contrasts the level of biodiversity that exists in Iowa today under an agricultural system dominated by large, commercial farms with the level of biodiversity that existed in 1910 when the agricultural system was dominated by smaller family farms. The amount of land devoted to agriculture was the same in both periods. The key difference is in the complexity of the socioeconomic system. Biological diversity was higher in an era when large numbers of different cultivators had long-term stakes in the land they farmed. Jackson is working toward the restoration of complex, multitiered, ecological systems. She stresses that this type of restoration is not going backward—but rather to a better future. In this chapter, I will stress the importance of restoring (or creating) complex, multitiered, sociopolitical systems. This is definitely not going backward—rather it is an essential step to creating a better future.

Looking Backward as a Foundation for Looking Forward

To go forward into a future that preserves high levels of biodiversity, however, may require serious attention to institutional arrangements where those directly involved have successfully managed complex resource systems over long periods (McKean 1992). Many long-sustained, self-governing resource systems have been studied in depth by perceptive scholars such as Robert Netting, Thráinn Eggertsson, Daniel Bromley, Margaret McKean, Fikret Berkes, David Feeny, and others. The resources involved vary from irrigation systems to inshore fisheries, mountain grazing lands, and forests.

The most notable similarity among these systems is the sheer perseverance of these resource systems and institutions. The institutions can be considered robust and sustainable in that the rules have been devised and modified over time according to a set of collective choice and constitutional choice rules (Shepsle 1989). Most of the environments studied are complex, uncertain, and interdependent environments where individuals continuously face substantial incentives to behave opportunistically. In *Governing the Commons* (E. Ostrom 1990), I addressed the puzzle of how individuals using these systems sustained them over such long periods.

The specific rules-in-use differ markedly from one case to the next. Given the great variation in specific rules-in-use, the sustainability of these resources and their institutions cannot be explained by the presence or absence of particular rules. Part of the explanation that can be offered for the sustainability of these systems is based on the fact that the particular rules do differ. By differing, the particular rules take into account specific attributes of the related physical systems, cultural views of the world, and the economic and political relationships that exist in the setting. Without different rules, appropriators could not take advantage of the positive features of a local resource or avoid potential pitfalls that could occur in one setting but not others.

A set of seven design principles appears to characterize most of the robust institutions. An eighth principle characterizes the larger, more complex cases. A "design principle" is defined as a conception used either consciously or unconsciously by those constituting and reconstituting a continuing association of individuals about a general organizing principle. Let us discuss each of these design principles.[1]

Clearly Defined Boundaries

Individuals or households with rights to withdraw resource units from the common pool resource and the boundaries of the resource itself are clearly defined.

Defining the boundaries of the resource and of those authorized to use it can be thought of as a "first step" in organizing for collective action.

---

1. The next section draws on *Governing the Commons* (E. Ostrom 1990, ch. 3).

As long as the boundaries of the resource and/or the individuals who can use the resource remain uncertain, no one knows what they are managing or for whom. Without defining the boundaries of the resource and closing it to "outsiders," local appropriators face the risk that any benefits they produce through their own efforts will be reaped by others who do not contribute to these efforts. At the least, those who invest in the resource may not receive as high a return as they expected. At the worst, the actions of others could destroy the resource itself. Thus, for any appropriators to have a minimal interest in coordinating patterns of appropriation and provision, some set of appropriators have to be able to exclude others from access and appropriation rights. If there are substantial numbers of potential appropriators and the demand for the resource units is high, the destructive potential of all users freely withdrawing from a resource could push the discount rate used by appropriators toward 100 percent. The higher the discount rate, the closer the situation is to that of a one-shot dilemma where the dominant strategy of all participants is to overuse the resource.

Congruence Between Appropriation and Provision Rules and Local Conditions

Appropriation rules restricting time, place, technology, and/or quantity of resource units are related to local conditions and to provision rules requiring labor, materials, and/or money.

Unless the number of individuals authorized to use a resource is so small that their harvesting patterns do not adversely affect one another, at least some rules related to how much, when, and how different products can be harvested are usually designed by those using the resource. Well-tailored appropriation and provision rules help to account for the perseverance of the resources themselves. Uniform rules established for an entire nation or large region of a nation rarely can take into account the specific attributes of a resource that are used in designing rules-in-use in a particular location.

In long-surviving irrigation systems, for example, subtly different rules are used in each system for assessing water fees used to pay for water guards and for maintenance activities, but in all instances those who receive the highest proportion of the water also pay approximately the highest proportion of the fees. No single set of rules defined for all irrigation systems in a region would satisfy the particular problems in managing each of these broadly similar, but distinctly different, systems.

Collective Choice Arrangements

Most individuals affected by operational rules can participate in modifying operational rules.

Resource institutions that use this principle are better able to tailor their rules to local circumstances, since the individuals who directly interact with one another and with the physical world can modify the rules over time so as to better fit them to the specific characteristic of their setting. Appropriators who design resource institutions that are characterized by the first three principles—clearly-defined boundaries, well-fitting rules, and appropriator participation in collective choice arrangements—should be able to devise a good set of rules if they keep the costs of changing rules relatively low.

The presence of good rules, however, does not account for appropriators following them. Nor is the fact that the appropriators themselves designed and initially agreed to the operational rules an adequate explanation for centuries of compliance by individuals who were not originally involved in the initial agreement. It is not even an adequate explanation for the continued commitment of those who were part of the initial agreement. Agreeing to follow rules ex ante is an easy "commitment" to make. Actually following rules ex post, when strong temptations are present, is the significant accomplishment.

The problem of gaining compliance to rules—no matter what their origin—is frequently assumed away by analysts positing all-knowing and all-powerful *external* authorities that enforce agreements. In many long-enduring resources, no external authority has sufficient presence to play any role in the day-to-day enforcement of the rules-in-use. Thus, external enforcement cannot be used to explain high levels of compliance. In all the long-enduring cases, active investments in monitoring and sanctioning activities are very apparent. These lead us to consider the fourth and fifth design principles:

Monitoring

Monitors, who actively audit resource conditions and appropriator behavior, are accountable to the appropriators and/or are the appropriators themselves.

Graduated Sanctions

Appropriators who violate operational rules are likely to receive graduated sanctions (depending on the seriousness and context of the offense) from other appropriators, from officials accountable to these appropriators, or from both.

In long-enduring institutions, monitoring and sanctioning are undertaken primarily by the participants themselves. The initial sanctions used in these systems are also surprisingly low. Even though it is frequently presumed that participants will not spend the time and effort to monitor and sanction each other's performance, substantial evidence has been presented that they do both in these settings.

To explain the investment in monitoring and sanctioning activities that occurs in these robust, self-governing resource institutions, the term "quasi-voluntary compliance" used by Margaret Levi (1988, ch. 3) is very useful. She uses the term "quasi-voluntary compliance" to describe taxpayer behavior in regimes where most everyone pays taxes. Paying taxes is *voluntary* in the sense that individuals *choose* to comply in many situations where they are not being directly coerced. On the other hand, it is "*quasi*-voluntary because the noncompliant are subject to coercion—if they are caught" (Levi 1988, p. 52). Levi stresses the *contingent* nature of a commitment to comply with rules that is possible in a repeated setting. Strategic actors are willing to comply with a set of rules, Levi argues, when (a) they perceive that the collective objective is achieved; and (b) they perceive that others also comply. In Levi's theory, enforcement is normally provided by an external ruler even though her theory does not preclude other enforcers.

To explain commitment in many of the cases of sustainable community-governed resources, external enforcement is largely irrelevant. External enforcers may not travel to a remote village other than in extremely unusual circumstances. Resource appropriators create their own internal enforcement to (a) deter those who are tempted to break rules, and thereby (b) assure quasi-voluntary compliers that others also comply. The Chisasibi Cree, for example, have devised a complex set of entry and authority rules related to the coastal and estuarine fish stocks of James Bay, as well as the beaver stock located in their defined hunting territory. Fikret Berkes (1987) describes why these resource systems, and the rules used to regulate them, have survived and prospered for so long:

> Effective social mechanisms ensure adherence to rules which exist by virtue of mutual consent within the community. People who violate these rules suffer not only a loss of favor from the animals (important in the Cree ideology of hunting) but also social disgrace (Berkes 1987, p. 87).

The costs of monitoring are kept relatively low in many long-enduring resources as a result of the rules-in-use. Rotation rules used in irrigation systems and in some inshore fisheries place the two actors most concerned with cheating in direct contact with one another. The irrigator who nears the end of a rotation turn would like to extend the time of his turn (and thus, the amount of water obtained). The next irrigator in the rotation system waits nearby for him to finish, and would even like to start early. The presence of the first irrigator deters the second from an early start, and the presence of the second irrigator deters the first from a late ending. Monitoring is a by-product of their own strong motivations to use their water rotation turn to the fullest extent. The fishing site rotation system used in Alanya (Berkes 1992) has the same characteristic that cheaters are observed at low cost by those who most want to deter another cheater at that particular time and location. Many of the ways that work teams are organized in the Swiss and Japanese mountain commons also have the result that monitoring is a natural by-product of using the commons.

The costs and benefits of monitoring a set of rules are not independent of the particular set of rules adopted. Nor are they uniform in all resource settings. When appropriators design at least some of their own rules, they can learn from experience to craft enforceable rather than unenforceable rules. This means paying attention to the costs of monitoring and enforcing, as well as the benefits that those who monitor and enforce the rules obtain. A frequently unrecognized "private" benefit of monitoring in settings where information is costly is obtaining the information necessary to adopt a contingent strategy. If an appropriator who monitors finds someone who has violated a rule, the benefits of this discovery are shared by all using the resource, as well as providing the discoverer a signal about compliance rates. If the monitor does *not* find a violator, it has previously been presumed that private costs are involved without any benefit to the individual or the group. If information is not freely available about compliance rates, then an individual who monitors obtains valuable information from monitoring.

By monitoring the behavior of others, the appropriator-monitor learns about the level of quasi-voluntary compliance in the resource. If no one is discovered breaking rules, the appropriator-monitor learns that others comply and no one is being taken for a sucker. It is then safe for the appropriator-monitor to continue to follow a strategy of quasi-voluntary compliance. If the appropriator-monitor discovers rule infractions, it is possible to learn about the particular circumstances surrounding the infraction, to participate in deciding the appropriate level of sanctioning, and then to decide about continued compliance or not. If an appropriator-monitor finds an offender who normally follows rules but happens to face a severe problem, the experience confirms what everyone already knows. There will always be times and places where those who are basically committed to following a set of rules succumb to strong temptations to break them.

A real threat to the continuance of quasi-voluntary compliance can occur, however, if an appropriator-monitor discovers individuals who break the rules repeatedly. If this occurs, one would expect the appropriator-monitor to escalate the sanctions imposed in an effort to halt future rule-breaking by such offenders and any others who might start to follow suit. In any case, the appropriator-monitor has up-to-date information about compliance and sanctioning behavior on which to make future decisions about personal compliance.

Let us also look at the situation through the eyes of someone who breaks the rules and is discovered by a local guard (who will eventually tell everyone) or another appropriator (who also is likely to tell everyone). Being apprehended by a local monitor when the temptation to break the rules becomes too great has three results: (a) it stops the infraction from continuing and may return contraband harvest to others; (b) it conveys to the offender that someone else in a similar situation is likely to be caught, thus increasing confidence in the level of quasi-voluntary compliance; and (c) a punishment in the form of a fine plus loss of reputation for reliability is imposed.

The fourth and fifth design principles—monitoring and graduated sanctions—thus take their place as part of the configuration of principles that work together to enable appropriators to constitute and reconstitute robust resource institutions. Let me summarize my argument to this point. When resource appropriators design their own operational rules (design principle 3) to be enforced by individuals who are local appropriators or accountable to them (design principle 4), using graduated sanctions (design principle 5) that define who has rights to withdraw from the resource (design principle 1) and that effectively restrict appropriation activities given local conditions (design principle 2), the commitment and monitoring problems are solved in an interrelated manner. Individuals who think a set of rules will be effective in producing higher joint benefits and that monitoring (including their own) will protect them from being a sucker, are willing to make a contingent self-commitment of the following type: I commit myself to follow the set of rules we have devised in all instances except dire emergencies, if the rest of those affected make a similar commitment and act accordingly. Once appropriators have made contingent self-commitments, they are then motivated to monitor other people's behavior, at least from time to time, in order to assure themselves that others are following the rules most of the time. Contingent self-commitments and mutual monitoring reinforce one another, especially in resources where rules tend to reduce monitoring costs.

Conflict Resolution Mechanisms

Appropriators and their officials have rapid access to low-cost, local arenas to resolve conflicts among appropriators or between appropriators and officials.

In field settings, applying rules always involves discretion and can frequently lead to conflict. Even such a simple rule as "Each irrigator must send one individual for one day to help clean the irrigation canals before the rainy season begins" can be interpreted quite differently by different individuals. Who is or is not an "individual" according to this rule? Does sending a child below 10 or an adult above 70 to do heavy physical work meet this rule? Is working for four hours or six hours a "day" of work? Does cleaning the canal immediately next to one's own farm qualify for this community obligation? For individuals who are seeking ways to slide past or subvert rules, there are always ways in which they can "interpret" the rule so that they can argue that they meet it while subverting the intent. Even individuals who intend to follow the spirit of a rule can make errors. What happens if someone forgets about labor day and does not show? Or, what happens if the only able-bodied worker is sick, or unavoidably in another location?

If individuals are going to follow rules over a long period, some mechanism for discussing and resolving what is or is not a rule infraction is quite necessary to the continuance of rule conformance itself. If some individuals are allowed a free ride by sending less valuable workers to a required labor day, others will consider themselves to be suckers if they send their strongest workers who could be used to produce private goods rather than communal benefits. Over time, only children and old people will be sent to do work that requires strong adults, and the system will break down. If individuals who make an honest mistake or face personal problems that prevent them from following a rule cannot find mechanisms to make up their lack of performance in an acceptable way, rules can be viewed as unfair and conformance rates decline.

While the presence of conflict resolution mechanisms does not guarantee that appropriators are able to maintain enduring institutions, it is difficult to imagine how any complex system of rules could be maintained over time without such mechanisms. In the cases described above, these mechanisms are sometimes quite informal and those who are selected as leaders are also the basic resolvers of conflict.

Minimal Recognition of Rights to Organize

The rights of appropriators to devise their own institutions are not challenged by external government authorities.

Appropriators frequently devise their own rules without having created formal, government jurisdictions for this purpose. In many inshore fisheries, for example, local fishers devise extensive rules defining who can use a fishing ground and what kind of equipment can be used. As long as external government officials give at least minimal recognition to the legitimacy of such rules, the fishers themselves may be able to enforce the rules themselves. But if external government officials presume that only they can make authority rules, then it is difficult for local appropriators to sustain a rule-governed resource over the long run. At any point when someone wishes to break the rules created by the fishers, they can go to the external government and get local rules overturned.

Audun Sandberg (1993a, 1993b) provides an insightful analysis of what happens when the individuals using common pool resources for many centuries do *not* have recognized authority to create their own rules. The formal rules for the northern Norwegian commons were first written as law in the eleventh century and remained unchanged until 1993. They represent "more than 1,000 years of unbroken traditions of oral and codified Common Law" (Sandberg 1993b, p. 14). The rules, however, outlined only generalized rights and did not recognize any local governance responsibilities. Since most commons, and especially the northern commons, came to be conceptualized as the King's Commons, it was easy to conceptualize that the king was the only lawgiver with authority to change laws over time.

Through a long process, which started with the Protestant Reformation and accelerated around 1750, this eventually led to a conception in government that all forests and mountains in northern Norway that are not private property are considered state property (Sandberg 1993b, p. 19). The further effort of the state to then ration access to forests, grazing areas, fisheries, and other common pool resources to those engaged in full-time specialized employment has had an unintended effect of being disruptive to the mixed economic way of life of many Northerners who were part-time farmers, part-time fishers, part-time foresters, and part-time herders. Converting this sustainable way of life into a modern system that included heavy reliance on transfer payments to specialized farming, fishing, and reindeer ranching was probably not fully expected by anyone. Now, however, the economic and social base has been weakened substantially enough that simply assigning local authority to make rules related to the use of common pool resources would probably not be a sufficient way out of a major dilemma.[2]

Nested Enterprises

Appropriation, provision, monitoring, enforcement, conflict resolution, and governance activities are organized in multiple layers of nested enterprises.

In larger systems, it is quite difficult to devise rules that are well matched to all aspects of the provision and appropriation of that system at one level of organization. The rules appropriate for allocating water among three major branches of an irrigation system, for example, may not be appropriate for allocating water among farmers along a single distributary channel. Consequently, among long-enduring, self-governed resources, smaller-scale organizations tend to be nested in ever larger organizations. It is not at all unusual to find a larger, farmer-governed irrigation system, for example, with five layers of organization, each with its own distinct set of rules (Yoder 1994). In the Swiss Alps, day-to-day operational decisions have been made by local communities while larger governance units have had the responsibility to monitor local performance by doing periodic, careful site visits on a rotational basis (Glaser 1987). In the Italian Alps, the smallest units during the Middle Ages were Family Communities, which were groups of families who collectively owned and governed land the size of a hamlet. "Then came the Village Communities as such which were in turn grouped in Federations which could be of the first degree (generally comprising one single valley) or second degree (comprising a group of valleys...)" (Merlo 1989, p. 8).

---

2.   Merlo (1989) provides a detailed and sorry tale of a similar effort in Italy to destroy local communal institutions only to find that unanticipated consequences have led many to try to reestablish authoritative decisionmaking in local communities.

Looking Forward to a Future with Sustainable Levels of Biodiversity: Some Conclusions and Policy Implications

How are these design principles relevant for future policymaking that enhances the sustainability of biological resources? What one learns from a serious analysis of experience is that local users are effective managers of smaller-scale resource systems for many reasons. Thus, local users need to be included as one of the sets making future policy decisions related to biodiversity. An important reason is the immense diversity of local environmental conditions (for example, rainfall, soil types, hydrology, temperature, elevation, and the scale of plant and animal ecologies) that exist within most countries. Some resources are located near urban populations or a major highway system, and others are remote. Users managing their own resources learn about the unique aspects of a local ecology and can fit rules to these local circumstances. Given environmental variety, rule systems that regulate access, use, and the allocation of benefits and costs effectively in one setting are not likely to work as well outside this range of the environmental conditions. If many semiautonomous, local units are included in the regulatory effort, most access and harvesting rules can be matched effectively to local environmental conditions. Efforts to implement national legislation that would establish a uniform and detailed set of rules for an entire country are likely to fail in many of the ecological niches most at risk.

A second reason for the potential strength of local organizations in coping with problems of biodiversity losses is that the benefits local users may obtain from careful husbanding of their resources are potentially greater, when future flows of benefits are appropriately taken into account. Only when users have relatively secure tenure with respect to many of the biological resources near them, will they adopt a sufficiently low discount rate that future flows of benefits are given substantial weight. At the same time, the costs of monitoring and sanctioning rule infractions at a local level are lower than the costs of doing all monitoring and sanctioning from a national level. These advantages occur, however, only when local users have sufficient assurance that they will actually receive the long-term benefits of their own investments when costs and benefits are internalized.[3]

Although there is agreement that the potential for effective organization at a local level to manage smaller- to medium-sized biological resources exists in all countries, local participants do not uniformly expend the effort needed to organize and manage these resources, even when given formal authority. Some potential organizations never form at all. Some survive no more than a few months. In highly volatile worlds, some organize themselves more effectively and make better decisions than others. Others are dominated by local elite who divert communal resources to achieve their own goals at the expense of others (Arora 1994). In some cases, a local resource may be almost completely destroyed before local remedial actions are taken. These actions may be too late.

Other local organizations possess inadequate scientific knowledge to complement their own indigenous knowledge. Making investment decisions related to assets that mature over a long time horizon (25 to 75 years for many tree species) is a sophisticated task whether it is undertaken by barely literate farmers or Wall Street investors. Obtaining sufficient scientific knowledge and information to understand complex feedback mechanisms operating in complex ecologies is difficult even when resources are not extremely limited. Local organizations operating alone frequently cannot gain access to the kind of information essential to sustainable management.

Thus, the romantic view that anything local is better than anything organized at a national or global scale is not a useful foundation for a long-term effort to sustain biodiversity. Any organization or group faces a difficult set of problems if it tries to govern and manage complex multispecies-multiproduct resource systems whose benefit streams mature at varying rates. Relying only on small-scale organizations to

manage biological resources would not be an effective form of regulation where many of these resources range over very large scales. Further, without some redundancy in regulative capabilities, success and failure at a local level are not monitored, and no compensatory actions are taken to offset failure at a local level. Nested institutions may help to provide this essential redundancy.

A similarly romantic view is that "the problem is global and the solution international" (Task Force on Global Biodiversity 1989, p. 4). While the local romantics presume that indigenous peoples are conservative by nature, the international idealists presume that international agreements are relatively self-enforcing and are likely to work well. Putting all of one's faith in very large-scale organizations does not protect future generations from failures of organizations to achieve sustainable use patterns. And, if the larger-scale units destroy the viability of the smaller-scale units, then organizational failure is likely to be on a much larger scale than organizational failure at a local level.

The problem that we face is not pitting one level of organization against another as a solitary source for authoritative decisions. Rather, the problem is developing institutional arrangements at multiple levels that enhance the likelihood that individual incentives lead participants toward sustainable uses of biodiversity rather than imprudent uses. Given the diversity of biological scales involved, Ashby's law of requisite variety commends a variety of institutional arrangements at diverse scales. One key in understanding how to craft nested institutional arrangements at many levels is the analysis of how actions at one level change the incentives of actors at another level.

One threat to the long-term sustainability of local institutions, for example, is the availability of large quantities of funds from external authorities that appear to be "easy money." These can undercut the capabilities of a local institution to sustain itself over time. The problem of local units becoming dependent on external funding is not limited to the funding provided by international aid agencies. Sieber (1981) reviews some of the reverse effects created by domestic U.S. policy. The supposed aim of Nixon's "New Federalism" reform was to increase the autonomy of local units and strengthen the overall

---

3. Extensive literature on the consequences of the imposition of legal statutes by larger government units on the conservation of forest resources in India has consistently shown the adverse consequences of these efforts (see, in particular, Blaikie, Harriss, and Pain 1992; Gadgil and Guha 1992; Jodha 1992).

federal system. A study by Hudson (1980) reveals that the policy had an opposite effect in some cities, such as El Paso, Texas. "El Paso is now more dependent, politically and economically, on federal grants than it was prior to the New Federalism and local autonomy is significantly reduced" (p. 900).

When vast amounts of external funds replace locally generated resources, the financial connection between provision and use is lost. Individuals using "other people's money" are rarely as prudent as when they are using funds derived from themselves and their neighbors. Complex institutions to counteract the temptations to be less frugal with external funds can be devised, but they take substantial and sophisticated efforts that rarely are used by external donors or national governments. Whether the external funds so provided are directly invested in the effort for which they were mobilized or are diverted for individual use by politicians or contractors depends on the professionalism of those involved and on active efforts to monitor and sanction how these resources are used in the field. When the local users themselves are involved in the administration of activities using resources that were largely mobilized locally, they provide low-cost monitoring of how resources are being allocated for these activities. When external authorities and contractors are employed, expensive auditing systems are needed, but are rarely supplied. Consequently, a considerable portion of the mobilized resources is diverted to purposes other than those for which it was intended.

Further, the design of projects is oriented more toward capturing the approval of those who fund new projects rather than toward providing systems that solve the problems facing present and future users. To convince politicians that large chunks of a national budget should be devoted to the support of a new project, planners attempt to design projects that are "politically attractive." To convince external funding agencies that major environmental projects should be funded through loans or grants, the evaluative criteria used by these agencies in selecting projects has to play a prominent role in the design of projects. Projects designed by engineers, who lack experience as farmers or training as institutional analysts, are frequently oriented toward winning political support or international

funding. This orientation does not lead to the development of projects that serve most users effectively or encourage the investment of users in their long-term sustenance. Inefficiencies occur at almost every stage. At the same time, this inefficient process leads to projects that generate substantial profits for those who have political connections and strong political support for a government.

Processes that encourage looking to external sources of funding make it difficult to build upon indigenous knowledge and institutions (Gadgil, Berkes, and Folke 1993). A central part of the message in asking for external funds is that what has been accomplished locally has failed. Massive external technical knowledge and funds are needed to achieve "development" or to "save biodiversity." This can create a vicious circle. If those at a local level ask for funds repeatedly, those at a national level feel the need (or have an excuse) to exert more influence over what is happening at a local level. As central officials begin to finance and take a more active role, those at a local level may pull back even further, thus accelerating a process toward central dominance.

All types of opportunistic behavior are encouraged, rather than discouraged, by the availability of massive funds to subsidize the creation of large-scale projects. Corrupt exchanges between officials and private contractors are a notorious and widespread form of opportunism. Free riding on the part of those receiving benefits and the lack of trust between citizens and officials, as well as among citizens, are also endemic. Further, the potential rents that can be derived from subsidized game parks and reserves stimulate efforts to influence public decisionmaking as to where projects should be located and how they should be financed. Politicians, for their part, win political support by strategic decisions concerning who will receive or continue to receive artificially created economic rents.

Thus, while large-scale governments are an essential part of the mix of governance units, if these governments come to dominate decisionmaking through massive funding of activities or the imposition of force, the effectiveness of local organizations is reduced substantially. On the other hand, the *absence* of supportive, large-scale institutional arrangements may be just as much a threat to the sustenance of biodiversity as the presence of preemptive, large-scale government agencies. Obtaining reliable information about the effects of different uses of resource systems and resource conditions is an activity that is essential to long-term sustainability. If all local communities were to have to develop their own scientific information about the physical settings in which they were located, few would have the resources to accomplish this.

Let me use as an example of the essential role of larger units, the role that the U.S. Geological Survey has played in the development of more effective, local groundwater institutions in the United States. What is important to stress is that the Geological Survey does not construct engineering works or do anything other than obtain and disseminate accurate information about hydrologic and geologic structures within the United States. When a local set of water users want to obtain better information about a local groundwater basin, they can contract with the Geological Survey to conduct an intensive study in their area. Water producers pay a portion of the cost of such a survey. The Geological Survey pays the other portion. The information contained in such a survey is then public information available to all interested parties (see Blomquist 1992).

The Geological Survey employs a highly professional staff who rely on the most recent scientific techniques for determining the structure and condition of groundwater basins. Local water producers obtain the very best available information from an agency that is not trying to push any particular future project that the agency is interested in conducting. Many countries, such as India, that do have large and sometimes dominating state agencies, do *not* have agencies that provide public access to high-quality information about resource conditions and consequences. Recent efforts to open up groundwater exploration in India may lead to the massive destruction of groundwater basins rather than create a firm basis for long-term growth.

The absence of large-scale, low-cost, fair arenas for resolving conflicts that spill out beyond the bounds of a local community is also a threat to the creation of a viable, multilevel governance system. All groups face internal conflicts or intergroup conflicts that can destroy the fundamental trust and reciprocity on which so much effective governance is based. If the only conflict resolution mechanisms are either so costly or so biased that most self-governed local communities do not use them, conflicts can escalate and destroy even robust local institutions.

An important lesson for the future that one derives from looking backward is the importance of local institutions in the mix of institutions responsible for sustaining biological diversity over the long run. It is the institutional diversity that has, in many instances, helped to protect the biological diversity of the past. Institutional diversity provides the variety of policy responses that may begin to cope with the variety of actions that may be taken in complex biological systems. Without such diversity, it is almost impossible to imagine a single institutional arrangement sufficiently complex to obtain scientific and local information and respond adaptably to changing ecological systems over time.

While small-scale institutions are not a sufficient solution, they are a necessary part of the multilevel governance systems needed for the future. And, while there is no blueprint that can be used to create effective local institutions, design principles can be derived from the study of long-sustained, local institutions that have successfully sustained complex resources over time. These principles can be taught as part of extension programs. Associations of local units can be created to learn more from one another about how successes have been achieved or how to avoid some kinds of failures. Large-scale institutions are also a necessary part of effective governance systems, but are not themselves a sufficient solution. And, if large-scale institutions generate incentives that destroy the viability of local, resource-governing institutions, their activities can undermine the viability of future governance systems.

Bibliography

Arora, D. 1994. "From State Regulation to People's Participation: Case of Forest Management in India." *Economic and Political Weekly* (March): 691–98.

Ashby, W. Ross. 1960. *Design for a Brain: The Origin of Adaptive Behavior.* New York: Wiley.

Berkes, F. 1987. "Common Property Resource Management and Cree Indian Fisheries in Subarctic Canada." In B. McCay and J. Acheson, eds., *The Question of the Commons.* Tucson: University of Arizona Press, pp. 66–91.

———. 1992. "Success and Failure in Marine Coastal Fisheries of Turkey." In D. W. Bromley and others, eds., *Making the Commons Work: Theory, Practice, and Policy.* San Francisco: ICS Press, pp. 161–82.

Blaikie, P., J. Harriss, and A. Pain. 1992. "The Management and Use of Common-property Resources in Tamil Nadu, India." In D. W. Bromley and others, eds., *Making the Commons Work: Theory, Practice, and Policy.* San Francisco: ICS Press, pp. 247–64.

Blomquist, W. 1992. *Dividing the Waters: Governing Groundwater in Southern California.* San Francisco: ICS Press.

Ciriacy-Wantrup, S. V., and R. C. Bishop. 1975. "'Common Property' as a Concept in Natural Resources Policy." *Natural Resources Journal* 15(4) (Oct.):713–29.

Gadgil, M., F. Berkes, and C. Folke. 1993. "Indigenous Knowledge for Biodiversity Conservation." *Ambio* 22(2–3):151–56.

Gadgil, M., and R. Guha. 1992. *This Fissured Land: An Ecological History of India.* New Delhi: Oxford University Press.

Gadgil, M., and P. R. Seshagiri Rao. 1994. "On Designing a System of Positive Incentives to Conserve Biodiversity for the Ecosystem People of India." Paper presented at the Workshop on Design Principles. Beijer Institute, Stockholm, Sweden, August 27–28.

Glaser (Picht), C. 1987. "Common Property Regimes in Swiss Alpine Meadows." Paper presented at the Conference on Advances in Comparative Institutional Analysis. Inter-University Center of Postgraduate Studies, Dubrovnik, Yugoslavia, October 19–23.

Heal, G. 1994. "Markets and Biodiversity." Paper presented at the Conference on Biological Diversity: Exploring the Complexities, University of Arizona, Tucson, March.

Hudson, W. E. 1980. "The New Federalism Paradox." *Policy Studies Journal* 8:900–906.

Jackson, L. 1994. "How Can Land User Practices Facilitate the Maintenance of Biological Diversity? What Is the Role of Ecological Restoration?" Paper presented at the Conference on Biological Diversity: Exploring the Complexities, University of Arizona, Tucson, March.

Jansson, A., M. Hammer, C. Folke, and R. Costanza. 1994. *Investing in Natural Capital: The Ecological Economics Approach to Sustainability.* Washington, D.C.: Island Press.

Jodha, N. S. 1992. "Rural Common Property Resources: the Missing Dimension of Development Strategies." Discussion paper no. 169. Washington, D.C.: World Bank.

Levi, M. 1988. *Of Rule and Revenue.* Berkeley: University of California Press.

McKean, M. 1992. "Success on the Commons: a Comparative Examination of Institutions for Common Property Resource Management." *Journal of Theoretical Politics* 4(3) (July):247–82.

McNeely, Jeffrey A. 1988. *Economics and Biological Diversity: Developing and Using Economic Incentives to Conserve Biological Resources. International Union for Conservation of Nature and Natural Resources.* Gland, Switzerland: World Conservation Union (IUCN).

Merlo, M. 1989. "The Experience of the Village Communities in the North-Eastern Italian Alps." In M. Merlo and others, eds., *Collective Forest Land Tenure and Rural Development in Italy.* Rome: Food and Agriculture Organization of the United Nations, pp. 1–54.

Ostrom, E. 1990. *Governing the Commons: The Evolution of Institutions for Collective Action.* New York: Cambridge University Press.

Ostrom, E., R. Gardner, and J. Walker. 1994. *Rules, Games, and Common-Pool Resources.* Ann Arbor: University of Michigan Press.

Ostrom, V. 1991. *The Meaning of American Federalism: Constituting a Self-Governing Society.* San Francisco: ICS Press.

Ostrom, V., D. Feeny, and H. Picht, eds. 1993. *Rethinking Institutional Analysis and Development: Issues, Alternatives, and Choices.* 2d ed. San Francisco: ICS Press.

Perrings, C., C. Folke, and K. Mäler. 1992. "The Ecology and Economics of Biodiversity Loss: the Research Agenda." *Ambio* 21:201–211.

Sandberg, A. 1993a. "The Analytical Importance of Property Rights to Northern Resources." Working paper, Workshop in Political Theory and Policy Analysis, Indiana University, Bloomington.

———. 1993b. "Entrenchment of State Property Rights to Northern Forests, Berries and Pastures." Paper presented at the Miniconference on Institutional Analysis and Development, Workshop in Political Theory and Policy Analysis, Indiana University, Bloomington, December 11–13.

Schlager, E. and E. Ostrom. 1993. "Property-Rights Regimes and Coastal Fisheries: An Empirical Analysis." In T. L. Anderson and R. T. Simmons, eds., *The Political Economy of Customs and Culture: Informal Solutions to the Commons Problem*. Lanham, Maryland: Rowman and Littlefield, pp. 13–41.

Shepsle, K. A. 1989. "Studying Institutions: Some Lessons from the Rational Choice Approach." *Journal of Theoretical Politics* 1:131–49.

Sieber, S. D. 1981. *Fatal Remedies: The Ironies of Social Intervention*. New York: Plenum Press.

Task Force on Global Biodiversity, Committee on International Science. 1989. *Loss of Biological Diversity: A Global Crisis Requiring International Solutions*. Washington, D.C.: National Science Board.

Yoder, R. 1994. *Locally Managed Irrigation Systems*. Colombo, Sri Lanka: International Irrigation Management Institute.

4

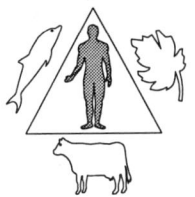

Distributed Governance in Fisheries

Ralph E. Townsend and Samuel G. Pooley

Abstract

FISHERIES MANAGEMENT, both in theory and in practice, is seeking ways to increase the involvement of the fishing industry and fishing communities in decisionmaking and administration. Some competing models of how to accomplish this greater involvement include cooperative management, comanagement, and rights-based management. It is difficult, however, to establish clear criteria to choose among the competing models to accomplish this greater governance involvement.

This research was supported in part by the National Oceanographic and Atmospheric Administration (NOAA), National Sea Grant Program, Department of Commerce, under Grant NA36RG0110-01 through the Maine/New Hampshire Sea Grant Program, Project R/FMD-237, and in part by the research program in Property Rights and the Performance of Natural Resource Systems of the Beijer International Institute of Ecological Economics, the Royal Swedish Academy of Sciences, Stockholm, Sweden, with support from the World Environment and Resources Program of the John D. and Catherine T. MacArthur Foundation and the World Bank. Ralph Townsend was supported by two National Marine Fisheries Service summer fellowships while part of this work was completed. The analysis presented herein does not represent the official position of the National Marine Fisheries Service.

These alternatives are analyzed within the framework of distributed governance: how rights and responsibilities are distributed among the central government, the industry, and local communities. Two levels of governance issues are identified: (a) how the external relationships among the central government, the industry, and local communities are structured; and (b) how the internal governance is structured within industry and local community institutions.

✧

Both the theory and practice of fisheries management are undergoing rapid and dramatic changes. The results from traditional, command-and-control regulation of fisheries is widely perceived as inadequate. An array of alternative approaches to management have been proposed, including rights-based management, comanagement, cooperative management, and corporate management. Often, the distinctions among these alternatives are difficult to define, even for those who have helped articulate these concepts. The concept of "distributed governance" is proposed here as a framework in which to compare and contrast these alternatives. Distributed governance examines how rights and responsibilities are distributed among and within the government, the fishing industry, and fishing communities.

Distributed Governance

Ostrom (1990) classified resource governance into four categories: open access, state control, communal governance, and private property. The Ostrom classification needs to be extended to recognize that governance can be shared among the state, local communities, and private interests in various ways. Governments, local communities and the private owners each bring different interests, abilities, and perspectives to the resource management process. It would be surprising if the most effective management incorporated the interests of only one of these three parties. That fisheries governance may increasingly involve a sharing of authority among these parties leads to our interest in distributed governance.

Because either a community or an industry must make collective decisions, distributed

governance also involves the internal governance structures of communities and private industry. How a community or industry group organizes itself is distinct from the external relationships of that group. Failure to separate internal and external structures has created unnecessary confusion over concepts of distributed governance in fisheries. For example, comanagement, an external structure, is often used as a term synonymous with cooperative governance, an internal structure. With a clear understanding of both internal and external structures, we can then analyze how the separate choices of internal and external structures interact.

In the analysis of the external relationships between government and the local industry or community, we will use the term "local fisheries management institution" (LFMI) as a generic term to cover the various institutions that might organize to represent local community or industry interests.

External Institutional Relationships under Shared Governance

In Western countries, central governments generally acquired all the authority for fisheries governance by displacing the governance void that was open access. But as government-centered fisheries regulation accumulated a relatively weak record, there has been widespread reassessment of the appropriate role for central governments. In turn, community-based or private property-based governance has increasingly come to be seen as superior to government-centered management.

The reasons for preferring a governance structure with active fisher and/or community involvement are easy to identify. Fishers or local communities may be able to devise and to administer regulatory institutions that are superior to externally imposed regulations. The local industry has extensive information about the resource and the harvest technology that may be very useful in designing effective rules. In a government-centered regulatory setting, that information is provided selectively by the industry to the manager. The manager faces the difficult task of separating true information from false or incomplete information. Once a set of rules is in place, the regulatory authority must enforce those rules. Locally imposed rules may have the advantage of greater local acceptance, and hence may face less opposition. Local cultural norms may support rules that are self-imposed to a greater extent than they support externally imposed rules.

On the other hand, there are at least two significant reservations about private or community governance. First, the central government has interests (such as the ecological interest in biodiversity) in fisheries resources that extend beyond those of the local community or industry. And second, there is no guarantee that the local community or industry will indeed organize itself into an effective governing institution.

These alternative perspectives suggest that some form of shared responsibility for fisheries management will prove more effective that any form of "pure" government, community, or industry governance. At least two concepts of external governance structures have already been identified: rights-based management and comanagement. A third alternative, which we call contractual management, will also be analyzed.

Rights-Based Management

Under rights-based management, the government bestows certain user rights directly upon the individual fisher. The term "rights-based management" is of relatively recent vintage; it has gained widespread use only since Neher, Arnason, and Mollett (1989). However, it is deceptive to think of rights-based management either as "new" or as equivalent to ownership rights. The fisher is a user of specified rights, not an owner of the resource. The primary forms of rights-based management are individual fisher quotas and individual fisher input allocations, both well-established fisheries management concepts.

The model of distributed governance under rights-based management is simple. The government assigns to the individual fisher only those responsibilities that can be exercised appropriately by an individual harvester. Any decisions that require collective decisionmaking are reserved for the government. The government assigns some decisions to competitive market forces, but assumes for itself a monopoly on any collective decisionmaking.

The primary forms of rights-based management are rights to harvest some volume of fish (for example, individual transferable quotas [ITQs]) or rights to use some set of inputs (for example, individual transferable inputs [ITIs]). Given these usufruct rights, the individual fisher makes decisions about the appropriate combinations of resources (including the usufruct rights) to use in the fishing process. Not only does the government determine the appropriate level of rights to allocate at each point in time, but it also has the sole responsibility for all other decisions that determine stock condition (such as closed seasons or minimum mesh sizes). The only responsibility that is distributed to individuals is the right to organize fishing activity within the constraints of the input or quota allocation.

The distribution of authority under an ITQ is quite clear, as is the empirical record for ITQs. Fishers do indeed respond to the grant of autonomy in fishing activity by organizing fishing more effectively. (For example, see the cases cited in Neher, Arnason, and Mollett [1989] and Townsend [1990].) But governments have been widely criticized for failing to achieve an equitable distribution of rights under ITQs. Enforcement of ITQs has also been a significant issue in many fisheries. The individual fisher has great incentive to avoid the restrictions on harvests by underreporting landings. This illegal activity is often cited (along with other evidence) to support the argument that ITQs do not create a "conservation ethic" among the ITQ rights holders. However, inasmuch as the government retains all responsibility for conservation decisions under ITQ management, it is not surprising that, in at least some ITQ fisheries, fishers feel no added responsibility for conservation.

The primary rights-based alternative to an ITQ is an input right. The basic relationship between the government and the fisher under input allocations is quite analogous to that under ITQ management. Input allocations generally create less desirable incentives for fishers (relative to ITQs), but enforcement of input allocations is often easier. An input right may be attractive when enforcement of ITQs is difficult. But when one or more inputs are subject to regulation, the fisher has incentives to substitute unregulated inputs for the regulated inputs. Thus, restrictions on boat length lead to wider boats with bigger engines, more electronics, more fishing gear, and larger crews. Generically, this problem is known as "capital stuffing," although the labor and variable inputs may be "stuffed" onto the vessel as well. Improvements in technology also tend to gradually defeat the effects of input restrictions. Given these incentives, the government must gradually reduce the levels of inputs, both to offset capital stuffing and to offset technology growth.[1] Thus, the division of responsibility between the government and the fisher is somewhat less perfect than under ITQ management.

Rights-based management is an important step in the distribution of governance authority. Instead of retaining all authority for decisionmaking, the government allows a narrow range of decisions to be made by individual fishers. The interest now is on creating governance structures that give a broader range of responsibilities to communities or to the industry. A primary suggestion in that direction has been comanagement.

Comanagement

Comanagement might be defined as any institutional arrangement that structures an external relationship for resource governance between a local fishery management institution (LFMI) and the government. The term comanagement has been used to span the spectrum from purely consultative arrangements to the coequal status accorded indigenous treaty rights (Rettig, Berkes, and Pinkerton 1989). This is clearly a broad spectrum—so broad as to cover essentially any form of distributed governance. Such a definition is also so broad as to be almost meaningless. However, the operational definition of comanagement has been narrower. Under comanagement, the government and an LFMI share ongoing responsibility for decisionmaking over all or most of the fisheries management decisions. This is clear in Pinkerton's (1989, p. 5) explanation of the functioning of comanagement:

Basically, by instituting shared decision-making among these actors, co-management

systems set up a game in which the pay-offs are greater for co-operation than for opposition and/or competition, a game in which the actors can learn to optimize their mutual good and plan cooperatively with long-term horizons.

That comanagement envisions a shared responsibility for most decisions is clear from Pinkerton's (1989, pp. 5–6) definition of "incomplete" comanagement:

Many co-management systems discussed in this volume could be called "incomplete" in the sense that not every management function is shared which theoretically could be.

Comanagement reconciles the differing interests of the government and the LFMI by ongoing, and to some degree, coequal involvement of both parties. As Pinkerton suggested above, the art of comanagement is to define a set of rules—a "game"—which leads to cooperative solutions.

An important question for comanagement is whether a balance of power between the government and the LFMI can be achieved and maintained. When coequal status is guaranteed constitutionally, an enduring balance of power may be possible. For example, under a treaty, a national government may be required to deal with the representatives of the indigenous population as coequals. But in the more general case, the governance rights of the LFMI are bestowed by the government. Not uncommonly, any authority granted to the LFMI is ultimately subject to government veto. Even if the veto authority is not explicit, the government retains an implicit veto through its right to change the rules at its sole discretion. Such a government veto, whether explicit or implicit, has a corrosive effect upon incentives. Failure to reach agreement with the government, or government exercise of its veto authority, can seriously weaken the internal authority and cohesion of the LFMI. Resisting the tendency for government oversight to devolve back to government regulation will require large expenditures of effort by the LFMI. The power of the LFMI is ultimately tied to the power of its members to subvert any regulations (as through noncompliance) or to exert political pressure in the broader political

---

1. For example, these adjustments can be accomplished through "taxes" that reduce effort proportionately or through devices like fractional licenses. See Townsend (1985) and Townsend and Pooley (1995).

system. But this power is not fundamentally different from the power of the local community or industry under command-and-control regulation.

Moreover, it is not obvious that all (or even most) decisions ought to be jointly determined by the government and the LFMI. Under rights-based management, the government identifies certain decisions for which all authority is given to individual fishers. Continuing in that vein, a more appropriate track may be to structure a set of rights and responsibilities that can be ceded entirely to the LFMI. The approach of defining unique rights and responsibilities for both the government and the LFMI we call "contractual management."

Contractual Management

Contractual management might broadly include any delineation of rights and responsibilities between a government and an LFMI. In a narrower and more meaningful conception, contractual management specifies the rights and responsibilities to be given to the LFMI as clearly as possible, with the government retaining only those rights and responsibilities that cannot be effectively delegated elsewhere.[2]

The missing incentive for efficient husbandry of fisheries under open access is the central justification for government control of fisheries. The central problem in government management of fisheries is that government itself can be an inefficient and ineffective decisionmaker. The ideal solution to the open access dilemma would be for government to create a decisionmaking institution that did have incentives for efficient husbandry of fishery resources and then to give that institution all appropriate authority. Government will function more efficiently as an architect of efficient institutions, rather than as an operator of a decisionmaking bureaucracy. It may, of course, not be possible to design institutions that appropriately internalize all incentives.

Thus, government may have an ongoing decisionmaking role. However, the objective is to transfer as large a part of the decisionmaking process as possible to an LFMI.

The decisionmaking about the use of a fishery resource has two impacts upon society: It affects the commercial harvests realized from the resource, and it affects the noncommercial benefits that society receives from the resource and from the environment that is altered by fishing. Open access fishing reduces economic benefits from the resource because it creates incentives for overexploitation of the resource that increases harvest costs and may reduce future harvests. Any fishing activity, under open access or not, may affect the broader environment by reducing biodiversity or damaging habitat, or through other negative environmental effects. If the adverse incentives of open access can be eliminated through appropriate institutional changes, the first source of social losses can be eliminated. However, even if the open access incentives are corrected, there still may be "spillover" effects (or "externalities") that impose social costs. It is this distinction between the open access incentives and broader environmental damages that delineates what responsibilities the government could give up under appropriate institutional redesign. If the government can create an LFMI that acts as a "sole owner," then the government can cede the responsibilities for managing commercial harvests (including all decisions about stocks) to the LFMI (Scott 1955). But the government will still have to be concerned with the impact of fishing upon environmental variables other than the stock of fish.

This distinction, between the incentives that a sole owner will appropriately internalize and the incorrect incentives that remain even for a sole owner, provides a basis for defining contractual management. First, contractual management must define a permanent, well-defined set of rights to the commercial harvests from the resource. Second, the right to harvest commercially may still have to be restricted to prevent excess environmental damage to resources other than the commercial stock. Because the interactions of commercial harvesting with other environmental resources will not be fully understood when the LFMI's rights are initially created, some mechanism for modifying these restrictions over time will be necessary. This second objective

---

2. We do not preclude using contracts between a government and an LFMI to accomplish more limited objectives. There may a variety of different applications of formal contracts between a government and an LFMI. For example, Canada has created local corporations or associations funded and operated by the industry to monitor ITQ landings. Although much narrower than our conception, these special-purpose institutions illustrate the flexibility of a contracting approach.

can be accomplished through a renewable operating contract that governs exercise of the LFMI's rights to harvest. Under this arrangement, ownership of the resource by the LFMI would be permanent, but certain conditions for use of the resource would be subject to periodic renegotiation and revision within a predetermined framework.

Through the operating contract, the government would retain the responsibility for certain broad public interests, such as biodiversity and ecosystem health. For example, the operating contract might regulate or prohibit fishing activities that are destructive of fragile environments, such as coral reefs. Interactions with threatened or endangered species might be regulated. This responsibility would be two-sided, in that the government would also have the responsibility to regulate external activities that negatively affect the resource. What the operating contract would *not* regulate would be commercial use of the resource. If the LFMI had the incentives of a sole owner, decisions about harvests and stock conditions would be left to the LFMI.[3]

The framework should also specify the extent to which compensation is due for changes in the operating contract. If, for example, the industry buys the initial rights at auction, the governing framework might specify that compensation will be paid if rights are restricted. If, on the other hand, the resource is simply given to some set of owners and members, then the framework may specify that no compensation will be paid for changes necessary to accommodate environmental interactions.

The operating contract renewal process should be structured so that the LFMI, as well as the government, has some power to influence the result. To create truly long-run incentives for the LFMI, it must face predictable outcomes from this negotiation process. For this objective to be met, one party (for example, the government) cannot have the preponderant power over contract renewal terms. Absent an ability to influence the renewal, an LFMI covered by a fixed-length contract faces inefficient "end point" incentives as the end of the contract approaches. In fisheries, an incentive to "mine" the resource would be created as the terminal date of the contract approached.

Neither the government nor the LFMI wants these end-point incentives to become dominant. To overcome this problem, the two parties would enter into negotiations for a contract renewal at the midpoint of the contract.[4] For example, at the beginning of year ten in a twenty-year contract, the two parties would negotiate for a new twenty-year contract. Both parties gain if a contract renewal is successfully renegotiated at this midpoint. The government obtains the benefits of any new environmental protections at midterm, instead of at the termination date. The LFMI gets the security of a new, longer planning horizon. Likewise, both parties have considerable leverage in the bargaining process. The government can implement new (and more onerous) requirements at the end of the contract if renewal negotiations fail. The LFMI can simply allow the existing contract to run to its terminal point, thus thwarting additional restrictions for the remainder of the contract. In a sense, both parties can use time as leverage in the negotiations. If contract negotiations go smoothly, the LFMI will never have a planning horizon of less than half the length of the contract. This planning horizon provides incentives for the LFMI to plan for the long-term status of the stocks.

The duration of the operating contract is an important, if somewhat arbitrary, aspect of this framework. The contract needs to be long enough to create long-term incentives for the LFMI, but short enough that new environmental information can be incorporated before excessive negative effects occur. A reasonable rule of thumb might be that the contract length should exceed the greater of the technological life of fishing vessels or two reproductive generations of the biological stock. In general, a time frame of ten to twenty years would seem to be appropriate for most fisheries.

This structure, with permanent rights subject to conditions in a staggered, renewable operating

---

3. If the stock has a noncommercial value, as in the existence value of salmon, then these noncommercial values might be a reason for government regulation. While very important for a few highly visible species, for most important commercial stocks these noncommercial existence values are probably small.

4. The idea of staggered contract renewal is from Young (1992).

contract, has an interesting analogy to terrestrial land rights. Land rights evolve over time, as when a town adopts zoning that restricts landowner rights. A stable legal system not only creates limits on how those rights can evolve, it also creates bounded and predictable paths for evolution of those rights. The purchaser of a piece of land may not know exactly how the rights to that land will evolve over time, but the purchaser knows that the evolution will occur within relatively well-defined bounds. In the case of fisheries, contractual management creates entirely new sets of rights for the LFMI. But precisely because these rights are new, no body of law guides the evolution of those rights in response to changing circumstances and knowledge. The staggered, renewable operating contract for the LFMI allows evolution of the rights, but in a framework that narrows the range of possible outcomes.

Internal Structures for Shared Governance

If fisheries management progresses to either comanagement or contractual management, a local fisheries management institution must exercise decisionmaking on behalf of the community and/or industry. How that LFMI is governed may affect how well it responds to the incentives created under either comanagement or contractual management. Therefore, the next task is to analyze the internal governance structures for LFMIs.

Three alternative internal governance structures have been closely associated with the concept of fisheries comanagement: self-organizing institutions (Ostrom 1990); cooperative management (for example, Jentoft 1989); and communal management. To these three, we add a fourth institution: corporate management (Townsend 1995). After examining each of these four internal governance structures, we will examine how internal structure is related to the external responsibilities granted to the LFMI.

Self-Organizing Governance

Instead of dictating an internal structure for an LFMI, the government could leave the organizational questions to the affected community. Such self-organizing institutions come with both advantages and disadvantages. On the one hand, locally self-organized institutions are clearly not puppets established by the central government, and they may have greater local credibility. On the other hand, there are no guarantees that such self-organizing institutions will arise spontaneously or that they will be resilient over time.

A significant literature has examined the conditions under which economic, political, and social institutions evolve to overcome open access problems (for example, Ostrom [1990]; Libecap [1989]; and Bromley [1992]). When no government acts to limit the losses due to open access, the ability of individuals collectively to organize institutions provides an important avenue for limiting or overcoming losses due to open access.

In the present context, however, the problem is generally not an organizational void in the authority to manage the open access resource. Governments generally have that authority; they simply have not been able to manage that authority effectively. Moreover, governments have the authority to rearrange institutions to a substantial degree to achieve their objectives of resource management. Governments have already created other institutions that may be valuable in structuring resource management, such as the legal code and the judicial system. And established governments have some ability to transfer their existing credibility and authority to new institutions that they create.

The question for the present is whether self-organizing institutions are superior to institutions that have been organized in part or in whole by the central government. Spontaneous and indigenously organized institutions may certainly have a credibility that centrally sponsored institutions lack. But self-organizing institutions also have significant limitations. Most obviously, there is no guarantee that a self-organizing institution will arise in any particular situation. If an organization does self-organize, it may not necessarily be representative of the entire set of local interests. And finally, a self-organizing institution may also self-disorganize, which would cause a renewed void in governance.

In general, the disadvantages of waiting for the arrival of a self-organizing organization to represent local interests seem significant. Using the institution-building capacity of central governments is an important theme throughout this analysis, and there seems little reason to abandon that capacity here. The government, of course, should be aware of the forces for self-organization so that it supports and gains strength from them, and does not frustrate and unnecessarily oppose them.

Communal Governance

The central government could designate specific local or regional governments as an LFMI. There is a large literature on communal governance of common property resources (for example, McCay and Acheson 1987; Berkes 1989; Bromley 1992). Most of this literature is addressed to governance that is entirely or primarily at the local level. A significant part of this literature is based upon experiences in developing countries, where the central government lacks the authority or resources to assert a broader interest in preserving open access resources. The present context is rather different, in that distributed governance is being proposed to reduce the existing authority of a central government and vest it in more localized interests.

In this context, the question is under what circumstances would it be more appropriate to vest local authority in a community rather than some type of industry organization? The primary issue must be whether the local community has a stake in the fishery that is broader than the fishing industry's economic interests. When fishing is a major part of a local economy or has special social significance to a local community, vesting authority in a community structure, rather than some sort of industry structure, may be appropriate.

The beneficial impact upon equity of communal governance is balanced by some organizational disadvantages. The broader community will have a less direct interest in management of the resource than the industry itself. In a large community, some of the open access incentives may re-emerge. For example, a local government that is interested in maximizing employment might be willing to expand fishing effort in response to local pressures to "share the wealth" from the resource.

There is a very interesting experiment in organized community governance being conducted in the Alaskan "community development quotas" under the U.S. federal Bering Sea pollock management plan (E3 Consulting, 1994.) That plan is essentially an ITQ allocation that is given to a group of six community development corporations. During the first two years, leases of quota allocations under this program earned the six development corporations $39 million, a very substantial infusion of capital. This community-based management is a radically new experiment, and its initial results offer interesting and provocative insights. Note, however, that the community has not shared in the responsibility for overall management decisions, which continue to rest with the federal management process.

Cooperative Governance

Cooperative governance is the most frequently suggested internal governance structure for an LFMI. Because a cooperative is an open, democratic institution which mirrors the democratic governance of Western political organizations, these governments rather naturally find cooperative structures appealing. To create a cooperative governance institution, the government would determine who would be designated as the members of the cooperative. While it is theoretically possible that cooperative memberships could be sold to yield a return to the government treasury, it seems more likely that memberships would be distributed on the basis of historical participation in the fishery. As Jentoft (1989) notes, it is unlikely that a fisheries management cooperative would have open membership (as is the norm for agricultural cooperatives and most current fisher cooperatives). Membership in the fisheries management cooperative would be limited in order to prevent resource depletion through continued entry into the cooperative.

If membership is closed, an important issue for the fisheries management cooperative is how to manage changes in membership. Would the members of the cooperative be free to sell their rights or to lease to third parties any fishing rights attached to their shares? Or would all transfers have to be approved by the cooperative? When exit from the fishery is necessary, would the cooperative be prepared to buy out some members? Could a member buy out another member and have two voting (and fishing) shares? What would happen if a court orders a share divided, as in the dissolution of a business partnership or a marriage partnership?

The answers to these administrative questions are not obvious. The simplest answers would seem to involve creating easily divisible, freely transferable rights, but cooperative rights that are divisible, freely transferable, and with cumulative voting rights are very close to corporate shareholder rights. Townsend (1995) has argued that cooperative and corporate management can be conceptualized as two ends of a spectrum of collective governance institutions. This leads us to consider corporate models of fisheries governance.

Corporate Management

Economists at least since Scott (1955) have argued that the most direct solution to the open access problem would be creation of private property rights. However, the concept of "private owner" seems to have been limited to literal sole owners, which are implausible in most fisheries. The idea that a set of sole owners organized under corporate governance would be a form of collective private property has been overlooked by the fisheries management literature.[5] Given the dominant role of corporations in our economies, it may seem surprising that the analysis of fisheries management has completely overlooked the institutional solution of corporate governance.

Under a corporate structure, the government would determine the initial ownership of shares of the fisheries governance corporation. The owners of the fisheries governance corporation would operate under governance rules typical of private corporations. The owners could make decisions either directly, by voting their shares on management issues, or indirectly, by electing a board of directors to make those decisions. Owners of shares in the corporation would be free to sell their rights or to lease to third parties

any fishing rights attached to their shares. Corporate shares could be given to some set of existing harvesters without any requirement for compensation to the government. Alternatively, the shares could be sold at auction, much as the government auctions leases for oil production on the continental shelf or now sells some radio spectrum for telecommunications applications.

Corporate governance may prove rather flexible in dealing with equity concerns in the privatization of fisheries. If there is a concern that local communities should have a stake in fisheries management, then local communities (or institutions within communities, such as port authorities) could be allocated shares in the fisheries governance corporation. Likewise, shares could be allocated to crew members and captains (or their pension fund), as well as to vessel owners. The ability the divide ownership in essentially unlimited ways makes it possible to deal very flexibly with equity concerns.

Finally, we would acknowledge that the term "corporate" has a somewhat pejorative connotation in many contexts. While the term is perhaps academically correct, it may be politically astute to establish corporate governance rules but with a "cooperative" title. An alternative title might be "fishery management foundation."

Governance Structure and the Scope of Authority

Any of these four governance structures could be vested with a range of management responsibilities, but the range of responsibilities that we could expect to be exercised appropriately probably varies among these different governance structures. Therefore, the degree of authority that the central government could grant to an LFMI varies with the internal governance structure.

If governance is to be most effective and efficient, two features should characterize distributed governance. First, clearly defined rights and responsibilities for each party to the governance structure minimize the potential for prolonged and costly disagreements among parties. Second, responsibilities for decisions should be distributed so that, wherever possible, the costs and benefits of any decisions are internalized within some cohesive decisionmaking unit.

An LFMI with well-structured incentives for resource use and conservation could be vested

---

5. The idea of structuring the internal governance of an LFMI corporately was suggested tangentially by Scott (1989). Jones, Pearse, and Scott (1980) suggested corporate organization of international fisheries agreements, but did not extend the idea to more traditional fisheries management problems. Townsend (1995) seems to provide the first direct analysis of corporate management as a collective governance alternative in fisheries.

with essentially all of the responsibilities usually associated with the management of commercial fisheries resources. These include how to regulate fishing, whom to allow to fish, and how to implement and enforce decisions. Such an LFMI could decide what management approach (such as ITIs or ITQs) would be most appropriate. The LFMI could decide when to invest in stock growth (by delaying harvest) and when to harvest. If the LFMI were responsible for costs of administration and enforcement, it would incorporate these cost considerations into its choice of management approach.

But which of the four internal governance structures create the strongest incentives for efficient resource use? Townsend (1995) has previously compared the incentives under cooperative and corporate organizations of fisheries governance. The important conclusions of that analysis were the following:

- The corporate structure with transferable share rights creates a well-defined, long-run interest in the resource.

- The market for the shares of the fishery management corporation creates an important bias in favor of conservation. Market transactions tend to place these assets in the hands of those with the greatest concern for the future. A fishery resource can yield different streams of benefits over the future. The resource will be most valuable to investors or members with a low discount rate (and hence the greatest concern for the future), so market sales will result in owners with far-sighted interests.

- Corporate governance creates stronger incentives for investing in the future than does cooperative governance. Under the democratic voting of cooperatives, the future benefits of any current costly decision (such as fishing less) will be uncertain because the allocation of benefits through future votes cannot be predicted. Corporate owners, on the other hand, have a claim to a share of any benefits that is proportional to share ownership. Because many fisheries face the task of investing in the stocks (through deferred harvests), corporate management creates clearer economic incentives for making those long-term decisions. Of course, as a nomi-

nally cooperative institution adopts rules that more closely approximate corporate governance, its incentives more closely approximate corporate incentives.

The thrust of Townsend's (1995) comparison of cooperative and corporate governance is that clearer individual rights increase the security with which economic actors can make decisions about the future. Individual rights are even less well defined under communal governance and self-organizing governance (as compared with corporate and cooperative governance). Thus, the incentives for long-run, conservation-oriented decisionmaking is even weaker under self-organizing or communal governance.

This analysis has important implications for a government that is considering contractual management. If an institution creates the appropriate long-run incentives for resource conservation, then the government can grant greater rights and responsibilities to that institution. If, on the other hand, a local governance institution has weak or uncertain incentives to manage the resource appropriately, then the government must reserve greater authority for itself. This explains why communal management tends to be associated with comanagement. When the central government cannot be assured that the destructive incentives of open access will not re-emerge under communal decisionmaking, it must reserve the authority to override local decisions. Similarly, the clearly delineated responsibilities of contractual management rather naturally fits with the well-defined rights of corporate governance. If the government is prepared to create the well-defined rights and incentives of corporate governance, then the government can give the owners of that corporation broad responsibility for management.

Conclusions and Policy Implications

Dissatisfaction with traditional fisheries regulations has led to great interest in distributed governance of fisheries. In examining the alternative models of distributed governance, we find that rights-based management distributes a very well-defined, but narrow, set of responsibilities to individual fishers. The dominant model of distributed governance seems increasingly to be comanagement that is based upon communal or cooperative governance within the LFMI. If successful, comanagement would distribute a broader set of responsibilities to local communities or industries, but these responsibilities would be shared with the central government. Contractual management incorporates the strengths of both rights-based management and comanagement. Like comanagement, contractual management would vest much wider authority in the LFMI. Like rights-based management, contractual management would create a clear delineation of rights and responsibilities between the LFMI and the central government.

The internal governance of an LFMI must be analyzed as a separate, but not unrelated, issue from the external relationships with the central government. Transferable corporate rights and corporate governance create stronger and clearer incentives for far-sighted investment in the resource than are created under cooperative or communal management. The creation of clearly defined internal rights under corporate governance reinforces the effect of creating clearly defined external responsibilities under contractual management. This analysis leads us to suggest that corporate governance that implements contractual management of fisheries is an important and powerful alternative for distributed governance in fisheries.

The model of distributed governance that combines the external structure of contractual management with the internal governance structure of corporate organization could find applications in the management of other common pool resources. These governance concepts emphasize the importance of (a) creating well-defined rights and responsibilities, and (b) vesting authority at a level where costs and benefits are internalized within the decisionmaking authority to the greatest extent possible.

Bibliography

Berkes, Fikret, ed. 1989. *Common Property Resource: Ecology and Community-Based Sustainable Development*. London: Belhaven.

Bromley, D. W., ed. 1992. *Making the Commons Work*. San Francisco: Institute for Contemporary Studies.

E3 Consulting. 1994. *Economic Impacts of the 1992/93 Pollock Community Development Quotas*. Prepared for Alaska Department of Fish and Game, Juneau, Alaska.

Jentoft, S. 1989. "Fisheries Co-management: Delegating Government Responsibility to Fishermen's Organizations." *Marine Policy* 13:137–54.

Jones, R. A., P. H. Pearse, and A. D. Scott. 1980. "Conditions for Cooperation on Joint Projects by Independent Jurisdictions." *Canadian Journal of Economics* 13:231–49.

Libecap, G. D. 1989. *Contracting for Property Rights*. New York: Cambridge University Press.

McCay, B. M., and J. M. Acheson, eds. 1987. *The Question of the Commons: The Culture and Ecology of Communal Resources*. Tucson: University of Arizona.

Neher, P. A., R. Arnason, and N. Mollett, eds. 1989. *Rights Based Fishing*. Boston: Kluwer.

Ostrom, E. 1990. *Governing the Commons: The Evolution of Institutions for Collective Action*. New York: Cambridge University Press.

Pinkerton, E., ed. 1989. *Co-operative Management of Local Fisheries: New Directions for Improved Management and Community Development*. Vancouver: University of British Columbia Press.

Rettig, R. B., F. Berkes, and E. Pinkerton. 1989. "The Future of Fisheries Co-management: A Multi-Disciplinary Assessment." In E. Pinkerton, ed., *Co-operative Management of Local Fisheries: New Directions for Improved Management and Community Development*. Vancouver: University of British Columbia Press, pp. 273–89.

Scott, A. D. 1955. "The Fishery: The Objectives of Sole Ownership." *Journal of Political Economy* 63:116–24.

Scott, A. D. 1989. "Conceptual Origins of Rights-Based Fishing." In P. A. Neher, R. Arnason, and N. Mollett, eds., *Rights Based Fishing*. Boston: Kluwer, pp. 11–38.

Townsend, R. E. 1985. "On 'Capital-Stuffing' in Regulated Fisheries." *Land Economics* 61:195-97.

Townsend, R. E. 1990. "Entry Restrictions in the Fishery: A Survey of the Evidence." *Land Economics* 66:359–78.

Townsend, R. E. 1995. "Fisheries Self-Governance: Corporate or Cooperative Structures?" *Marine Policy* 19:39–45.

Townsend, R. E., and S. G. Pooley. 1995. "Fractional Licenses: An Alternative to License Buy-Backs." *Land Economics* 71(1):141–43.

Young, M. D. 1992. *Sustainable Investment and Resource Use*. Carnforth, United Kingdom: Parthenon Press.

5

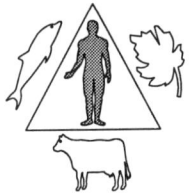

Efficiencies of User Participation in Natural Resource Management

Susan Hanna

Abstract

ONE OF THE CENTRAL DIFFICULTIES in the use of natural resources is the design of management systems that are effective, equitable, and efficient. A resource management system combines a set of regulatory tools within a particular resource context to achieve a management outcome. The process by which resource management is conducted affects its equity, effectiveness, and efficiency.

This chapter is the result of research sponsored by Oregon Sea Grant with funds from the National Oceanic and Atmospheric Administration, Office of Sea Grant, Department of Commerce, under grant no. NA85AA-D-SG095 (project no. R/PPA-39) and from appropriations made by the Oregon State Legislature. The U.S. Government is authorized to produce and distribute reprints for government purposes, nothwithstanding any copyright notation that may appear hereon. Parts of the research were sponsored by the Beijer International Institute of Ecological Economics, the Royal Swedish Academy of Sciences, Stockholm, Sweden, with support from the World Environment and Resources Program of the John D. and Catherine T. MacArthur Foundation and the World Bank. The research was conducted as part of the research program Property Rights and the Performance of Natural Resource Systems.

This chapter focuses on management efficiency and in particular on the role played by user participation in lowering management costs. The contribution of user participation to the efficiency of resource management is discussed in terms of the structure and function of user participation and its effect on management costs. User participation contributes positively to the cost-effectiveness of management processes when it lowers costs of information gathering, coordination, monitoring and enforcement. To make these positive contributions, user participation should be incorporated into the management process before resource conditions decline to the point of scarcity.

✧

One of the central difficulties in the use of natural resources is the design of management systems that are effective, equitable, and efficient. Effective management is difficult because of the recurring contradiction between the short-term interests of individuals and long-term objectives for resource sustainability. Individuals may promote their own well-being without regard to the collective good; collective objectives may be developed in ignorance of individual needs. Equitable management is difficult because of the diversity of interests and values involved. Efficient management is challenged by various sources of uncertainty that result in high transaction costs of information gathering, monitoring, and enforcement. It may happen easily that the benefits from resource management are exceeded by management costs.

A resource management system combines a set of regulatory tools within a particular resource context to achieve a management outcome. The process by which resource management is conducted affects both its equity and effectiveness. If the process is fair and effective, resources are sustained. If the process is considered unfair and is ineffective, resources are overused and degraded. A rich literature exists on the role played by various factors in contributing to management equity and effectiveness, such as design principles (Ostrom 1990), management structure (Young 1992), cultural context (McCay 1987), social sanctions (Gadgil 1985), self governance (Ostrom, Walker, and Gardner 1992), representation (Hanna 1994;

Jentoft and McCay 1995), local knowledge (Gadgil, Berkes, and Folke 1993; Ruddle 1993; Berkes, Folke, and Gadgil 1994), local control (Jodha 1990), adaptation to local context (Niamir-Fuller 1993), poverty (Dasgupta and Mäler 1993), income distribution (Munasinghe 1992), and political forces (O'Riordan 1988).

This chapter focuses on management efficiency and in particular on the role played by user participation in enhancing efficiency by lowering management costs. It is important to governments that management be efficient because resources available for management are limited. Resource management is directed toward particular objectives, and management efficiency depends on the cost-effectiveness by which those objectives are met. The least-cost combination of inputs to management creates the most technically efficient process. In the ideal, management will meet two efficiency conditions: it will cost the minimum necessary to achieve its objectives, and it will cost less than the benefits it creates. To make the best use of public resources, management systems should approach the efficiency ideal to the extent possible.

The major costs of conducting resource management are the costs to gather information, design regulations, coordinate participants, monitor conditions, and enforce regulations. These are called transactions costs (Matthews 1986). For a public resource agency or management organization, transactions costs are related to its coordinating function: data collection, analysis, design and implementation of regulations, communication, and conflict resolution. For individual resource users, the transactions costs of resource management are related to participation: the cost of work time lost to meetings, time required to acquire information and communicate to other users, and direct monetary expenditures for information, travel, and communication.

The efficiency of resource management does not stand alone but is linked to both equity and effectiveness. The concept of private and public interest is involved (Hirschman 1986). Management costs are directly related to how the various interests perceive management's effectiveness and fairness (Jentoft 1993). To be effective, resource management requires the compliance of resource users. Compliance with regulations increases and, hence, management costs decline when regulations are acceptable and considered legitimate by those interests being regulated. To be legitimate, the content of a regulation, the process by which it is made, the way it is implemented, and the effects of its distribution must be perceived as fair by resource users (Jentoft 1989). To be equitable, a resource management process must represent the range of user group interests and have a clear purpose and a transparent operation. In addition, an equitable process must address explicitly the distributional changes embedded in options under consideration. The extent to which participants' expectations are homogeneous, with respect to the process and its objectives, influences the perception of fairness and, hence, the equity and effectiveness of management.

User participation addresses the problems of management effectiveness, equity, and efficiency through the structure of incentives, the process of management implementation, and the distribution of management costs and benefits. The contribution of user participation to the efficiency of resource management is discussed below in terms of the structure and function of user participation and its effect on costs.

The Structure and Function of User Participation

Some management processes assign participation rights to a single entity, such as a resource management agency, which becomes the ultimate authority. Other processes broaden the decisionmaking authority to scientists and public agencies, taking supplemental nontechnical (local) knowledge from users (Ruddle 1993). Sometimes user groups are charged with limited decisionmaking powers (McCay 1993). Still other processes share power between government and resource users in comanagement (Jentoft 1989; Pinkerton 1989; Berkes, Geirge, and Preston 1991; Jentoft and McCay 1995).

Resource users are perhaps the most controversial of all potential participants in resource management. Assigning rights of decision making to resource users is often seen as a risky approach, based on the expectation that short-term interests of user groups will supersede long-term requirements for resource stewardship. What is at issue is the enduring conflict between the positive role of self-interest, as a motivator of economic action and increased efficiency, and the negative role of self-interest, as a motivator of greed and overuse. Olsen (1965) identifies two critical factors in the effectiveness of group action: the size of the group, and the use of social and psychological incentives to augment economic incentives for behavior. Small groups tend to be more effective in encouraging the active participation of all members in a thorough airing of the issues. Small groups which maintain face-to-face interactions also are more effective in the use of social pressures and incentives to construct consensus. Arrow (1974) addresses the group decision problem through the mechanism of organizations, noting that the purpose of organizations is to exploit the fact that decisions require the participation of many individuals. Organizations also serve as a communication center for ideas and information in an environment of uncertainty.

User participation in resource management is based also on mutual dependence on the services the resource provides. The question becomes how to exploit this mutual dependence for collective gain. Schelling (1960) has analyzed conflicts that contain an element of mutual interdependence—nonzero-sum games. According to Schelling (1960), instead of being "I-win-you-lose situations, these games represent conflicts in which some joint dependence requires cooperation, if only in the avoidance of mutual disaster." In addressing such interdependencies, Schelling identifies the important roles played by consistent expectations and the quality of communication. Also focusing on interdependency and expectations, Runge (1984) examines the role of individual choice in maintaining institutions that coordinate expectations and help individuals predict each other's behavior (the assurance problem). Interdependence creates feedback loops that reduce the uncertainty to individuals. This reduction in uncertainty, in turn, may lessen the urgency of individual inclinations to "free ride" by taking advantage of others' actions.

The Structure of User Participation

Decisions and information flow in different directions under different resource management processes. In general, decisions and information either originate at the top and flow downward or at the bottom and move upwards. In the standard hierarchy, the top includes management agencies or other legally authorized decisionmakers. The bottom includes user groups and other interests. The key difference between the two kinds of processes is the position of user groups relative to decisionmaking.

Top-Down Management

Top-down management processes have the least amount of user participation. Decisionmakers are designated by their institutional position: for example, as management-level staff of a public resource agency. Management information and decisions are centralized. Users are external to decision making, kept outside the decisionmaking process except in whatever ways they can bring political pressure to bear on decisionmakers.

A regulatory regime developed through a top-down process may reflect the relative weights of political pressures felt by decisionmakers, but may not reflect a sustainable compromise between conflicting goals and objectives. Regulations are imposed on users in an exercise of top-down authority. Those inside and outside the sphere of decision authority may possess different views of the nature of the resource management problem as well as different goals and objectives for the resource. Differences may persist throughout the period of regulatory development, leaving the management regime vulnerable to being bypassed by interests that feel disaffected by the process.

Bottom-Up Management

A bottom-up management process has a much larger degree of participation by resource users and other interests. Ideally, all categories of fishing interests are defined and represented. A structure exists and is followed for feeding advice into the decision process. These structures take different forms. Active consultations are arrangements in which formally defined decisionmakers allocate a portion of their decisionmaking responsibility to users through soliciting advice, with an explicit intent to follow the advice given. Comanagement involves formal power sharing between government and users and is a process, rather than a

tool, of management. The comanagement process defines stakeholders and incorporates them through their representation into various levels of resource management decisions. A comanagement process may design a management plan that incorporates any mix of tools deemed appropriate. Comanagement is realized through decentralized initiative and control, full participation in management by users, and the sharing of rulemaking and enforcement authority with users (Jentoft 1989; Pinkerton 1989; Berkes, Geirge, and Preston 1991).

In a bottom-up management process, decisionmakers are identified as a network of representative interests. Participants arrive at a consensus of the true nature of the problem and of common principles to structure the process. Through the participation of a wide variety of interests, multiple objectives are articulated that include ecosystem, economic, social, or cultural components. The process must be able to accommodate diverse individual styles while crafting cooperative solutions. The participatory process is not tied to a particular tool; it may incorporate any mix of tools deemed appropriate. The key attribute of a participatory, bottom-up management process is the position of resource users relative to the locus of authority.

The Function of User Participation

Resource management is a mix of three basic kinds of decisions: conservation, regulation, and allocation. Conservation decisions focus on limiting resource extraction to some level that will allow sustained use of the resource over time. Regulation decisions determine the mechanisms that control both the means and rate of extraction. Allocation decisions determine the division of the resource between various user groups. The relative importance of each of these kinds of decisions changes as natural resources develop. At each phase of development a new group of decisions is added as the nature of the binding constraint changes. The three kinds of decisions vary in the degree to which they are amenable to user participation (Hanna and Smith 1993).

Conservation Decisions

Conservation decisions are based on the biological assessment of resources. The level of resource extraction that can be sustained by a stock depends on resource status, resource dynamics, and environmental conditions. Biological assessments rely on extraction data and research survey data. Resource users may participate in data collection through the provision of records and occasional cooperative conduct of research surveys. Users also contribute a variety of nontechnical information derived from their knowledge of habitat, animal behavior, and environmental factors affecting resource abundance.

Regulation Decisions

Regulation decisions determine operating rules that include controls placed on the timing, area, and technology of resource extraction. Although the overall objective of a regulation decision is to maintain a conservation standard, such a decision often also has equity as an additional objective. The tendency for some users to prefer regulations that apply directly to operations, rather than to access, may be explained by the perceived fairness of such regulations to all users. In situations where the effects of regulations are uneven, supplemental regulations designed to mitigate effects often are devised. Because equity of impact is an important goal of resource management, regulation decisions are particularly amenable to user participation.

Allocation Decisions

Allocation, concerned with dividing a limited quantity of a resource between competing user groups, is the most conflict-ridden of the three kinds of management decisions. Allocation decisions may involve tradeoffs between interests representing different technologies, ethnic associations or scales of operation, and they pose difficult problems for user participation. The first problem is that by the time the need for an allocation decision arises, users have often developed expectations for use levels that reflect periods of high abundance. Because these expectations cannot be met in periods of restriction, participants enter a decision environment in which their expectations will be frustrated. Allocation decisions are zero-sum or even negative-sum, leaving participants to develop strategies to maximize their individual gains.

Despite their fundamentally distinct characters, conservation, regulation, and allocation decisions are closely linked, giving rise to another problem for user participation. As conservation needs increase, more restrictive regulations on resource exploitation are required. The design of regulations is enhanced by the on-the-ground knowledge of user groups. Equity aspects of allocations may be enhanced by the representation of all parties in the decision. However, user participation may also introduce weaknesses into the process. Because both conservation and regulation decisions underlie the allocation decision, one way to delay facing an unpleasant allocation decision is to attempt to weaken the integrity of the preceding conservation and regulation decisions. User groups sometimes react to changes in allocation by questioning the validity of the process used to establish the target quota or the system of regulations. In such circumstances, user participation can undermine the management process.

User Participation and Costs

Transactions Costs

Transactions costs of resource management result from the need to describe a fishery and to design, implement, monitor, and enforce a set of regulations. Some transactions costs remain fixed regardless of the type of process used to make decisions, for example, costs related to the provision of the scientific information used in biological assessments. Other transactions costs vary with the process used to make decisions and the quality of data collected. Costs of information gathering, coordination between user groups, and program implementation and enforcement can vary according to the quality of data and the process adopted. Four resource management stages in which variable transactions costs are incurred are the description of the resource context, regulatory design, implementation, and enforcement.

Describing the resource context is an assessment process, with resource users as its focus. Information requirements include a description of resource users, processors, markets, and the analysis of social and economic characteristics of all resource interests. This information is most complete when gathered through a combination of routine government data collection and advice from users. The fact that social scientists often are scarce or even absent from the staffs of resource management agencies means that data to support such assessments often are not collected or used.

The program design phase of management builds on the information describing the resource context and is dependent on the quality of contextual information provided. The quality of the resource description determines whether the design of a management program accurately or inaccurately reflects its social and economic environment.

The implementation of a regulation is a critical test of a regulation's fit to its context. It is at the implementation stage that the impact of regulations on user groups and on the resource becomes clear. Effective regulations must control user behavior in economic, social, and cultural dimensions. The history of resource management is replete with regulatory failure at the implementation stage, owing to an incomplete accounting of the components of resource context and the corresponding failure to anticipate regulatory impacts.

Monitoring and enforcement of a regulation is a final area of transactions costs. Monitoring compliance with regulations will be excessively costly if monitoring systems are not designed to be consistent with resource dynamics or user operations. The same condition applies to the enforcement of regulations. Resource extraction activities often take place over a large geographic area, so the effective enforcement of regulations requires some degree of cooperation of those who are regulated. Regulations must also fit within the structure of operations.

User Effect on Costs

The way user participation is structured critically affects the transactions costs of management. Management costs are incurred in four stages: two *ex ante* stages (description of the resource context and program design) and two *ex post* stages (program implementation and program enforcement). The type of management process used affects the distribution of these costs. A top-down process is often associated with low *ex ante* and high *ex post* transactions costs. A participatory process is associated with high *ex ante* and low *ex post* transactions costs (Hanna 1994).

The least-cost structure for the description of the resource context is top-down, using a small number of in-house agency staff, secondary data, and no consultation with user groups. In contrast, using a participatory structure to establish context generates social and economic information of greater quality and quantity through a combination of agency staff, secondary data, and user groups. The incorporation of users as technical experts requires greater amounts of time and money spent in coordination and information dissemination. A participatory structure is a more costly approach to establishing resource context.

Program design through a top-down structure involves a small number of experts working together to develop a system of regulations. A bottom-up, participatory structure is associated with higher levels of *ex ante* transactions costs because a broader sphere of experts is brought into the design and development stages. A participatory process includes resource users as co-designers. Users are often heterogeneous, representing different scales of operation and occupational styles. Investment in the human capital required to craft effective participation of a diverse group is time-consuming, and coordination and organizational costs are correspondingly high. Because user participation includes interactions among users and between users and management agencies, it often is conflict-ridden. The top-down approach, using fewer people, relatively homogeneous styles of working, and a limited number of options, is a faster, lower-cost path to program development.

In sum, for the first two stages of regulatory development, top-down approaches have lower transactions costs than bottom-up participatory approaches. Once the implementation stage is reached, however, the balance of transactions costs shifts. Implementation involves the application of regulations within the resource context. The low-cost resource description and regulatory design of the top-down approach lead to higher costs at the implementation stage through inadequate accounting of the resource structure and the increased probability of a mismatch between regulatory tools and resource operations. Poor program design and awkward program implementation may add further to the costs associated with the top-down approach as they play out in noncompliance, high monitoring costs, and high enforcement costs. In contrast, the active participation of users in a participatory process, compensating to some extent for the inadequacies in social science data, increases the probability of smooth implementation.

The benefits of user participation are realized in lower *ex post* transactions costs, because resource structure and operations are reflected in regulations more likely to be enforceable. Incrementalism may seem expensive at the time regulations are being developed but may pay off with fewer setbacks in implementation. The large leaps forward associated with top-down approaches carry the illusion of being low cost but may be followed by large and expensive reverses if regulations are poorly designed and are rejected by users. The net result depends on both the ecological and human context and the extent to which those contexts lead to greater *ex ante* or *ex post* costs.

Costs are also affected by the different incentives faced by users under top-down and bottom-up management. The top-down approach excludes users until the end of the process, creating an incentive to sabotage. Uncertainty about the goals of the process may shorten time horizons of users, encouraging short-term actions at the expense of long-term sustainability. In contrast, the participation of users at the regulatory design and development stage creates a stake in the outcome and reduces uncertainty about process goals. User participation can promote stewardship through creating an assurance of control over outcomes. The benefits of top-down approaches are frontloaded, whereas the benefits of the user participation approach are endloaded, with the potential for long-lasting returns.

Net Efficiency Effects: Conclusions and Policy Implications

Resource management typically brings together resource users, resource agency representatives, scientists, and other interests. Underlying the entire process is the question of which combination of these interests will contribute most to management efficiency. This chapter has focused on cost-effectiveness as a measure of efficiency and on the role that user participation has on influencing cost-effectiveness. User participation can make either a positive or negative contribution to management costs depending on the distribution of management activities.

User participation contributes positively to the cost-effectiveness of management processes when it lowers information costs through the provision of supplemental nontechnical knowledge. It may also lower coordination costs when the number of users is small or, if large, well-represented. User participation lowers monitoring costs when user participation increases management legitimacy and leads to higher levels of compliance. It also contributes to lower enforcement costs when user knowledge leads to regulations that are appropriate to the context.

To make these positive contributions, user participation should be incorporated into the management process before resource conditions decline to the point of scarcity. User participation may work against cost-effective management in cases where local knowledge adds little to the information base, where the number of users is diverse and unrepresented, or where the resource base is degraded to the point that short-term incentives to cheat on rules overwhelm the longer-term benefits of compliance. Perhaps the most sobering lesson from existing resource management systems is that user participation in management processes increases in difficulty as resource scarcity increases. Once management decisions become a negative-sum gain, where every decision becomes loss-loss, user cooperation for collective goals becomes more costly to maintain, leading to processes which break down in disharmony and disarray.

On balance, the efficiency enhancing effects of user participation in resource management depend both on its cost reducing effects and the ultimate balance between its costs and benefits. When user participation lowers *ex post* transactions costs of management and when the savings in *ex post* costs exceed the increases in *ex ante* costs, user participation contributes to cost-effectiveness. Conversely, when users help lower *ex post* costs but the particular resource context creates larger *ex ante* costs, user participation makes no particular contribution to the efficient use of resources in the management process.

To the extent that user participation creates regulatory legitimacy, it further can reduce transactions costs. Regulations that represent all interests and are perceived to be legitimate have an increased probability of compliance, leading to lower enforcement costs. Legitimate regulations also are more apt to shape behavior in ways that are compatible with long-term sustainability needs. Equity also contributes to efficiency. When user participation results in regulations that are equitable in their impact, compliance increases and costs of monitoring and enforcement decrease.

There are enough potential efficiency gains from user participation to warrant its serious consideration in resource management systems. A further reason for its consideration is that, regardless of the management structure adopted, users will be involved in management in some way. The management process can be structured to allow users to be proactive or to be reactive. If users are not involved at the design and implementation stages, they are likely to be involved at later stages through various acts of noncompliance. The relevant question is which process will minimize the transactions costs of management.

References

Arrow, K. J. 1974. *The Limits of Organization*. New York: W. W. Norton and Company.

Berkes, F., P. J. Geirge, and R. J. Preston. 1991. "Co-management: The Evolution in Theory and Practice of the Joint-Administration of Living Resources." *Alternatives* 18(2):12–18.

Berkes, F., C. Folke, and M. Gadgil. 1994. "Traditional Ecological Knowledge: Biodiversity, Resilience and Sustainability." In C. Perrings, K.-G. Mäler, C. Folke, C. S. Holling, and B.-O. Jansson, eds., *Biodiversity Conservation: Policy Issues and Options*. Dordrecht, Netherlands: Kluwer Academic Publishers.

Dasgupta, P., and K.-G. Mäler. 1993. "Poverty, Institutions, and the Environmental-Resource Base." Beijer International Institute of Ecological Economics Discussion Paper Series No. 27.

Gadgil, M. 1985. "Social Restraints on Resource Utilization: The Indian Experience." In J. McNeely and D. Pitt, eds., *Culture and Conservation: The Human Dimension in Environmental Planning*. Dublin: Croom Helm.

Gadgil, M., F. Berkes, and C. Folke. 1993. "Indigenous Knowledge for Biodiversity Conservation." *Ambio* 22(2–3):151–56.

Hanna, S. S., and C. L. Smith. 1993. "Resolving Allocation Conflicts in Fishery Management. *Society and Natural Resources* 6(1):55–69.

Hanna, S. S. 1994. "Co-management." In *Limited Access Management: A Guidebook to Conservation*. Washington, D.C.: World Wildlife Fund and Center for Marine Conservation.

Hirschman, A. O. 1986. *Rival Views of Market Society and Other Recent Essays*. New York: Viking Penguin.

Jentoft, S. 1989. "Fisheries Co-management: Delegating Government Responsibility to Fishermen's Organizations. *Marine Policy* 13(2):137–154.

———. 1993. *Dangling Lines*. St. Johns: Institute of Social and Economic Research, Memorial University of Newfoundland.

Jentoft, S., and B. McCay. 1995. "User Participation in Fisheries Management: Lessons Drawn from International Experience." *Marine Policy* 19(3):227–46.

Jodha, N. S. 1990. "Depletion of Common Property Resources in India: Micro-Level Evidence." In G. McNicoll and M. Cain, eds., *Rural Development and Population: Institutions and Policy*. Oxford: Oxford University Press.

Matthews, R. C. O. 1986. "The Economics of Institutions and the Sources of Growth." *Economic Journal* 96 (Dec.):903–10.

McCay, B. J. 1987. "The Culture of the Commoners: Historical Observations on Old and New World Fisheries. In B. J. McCay and J. M. Acheson, eds., *The Question of the Commons: The Culture and Ecology of Communal Resources*. Tucson: University of Arizona Press, 195–216.

———. 1993. "Management regimes." Beijer International Institute of Ecological Economics Discussion Paper Series No. 38.

Munasinghe, Mohan. 1992. "Biodiversity Protection Policy: Environmental Valuation and Distribution Issues." *Ambio* 21(3):227–36.

Niamir-Fuller, M. 1993. "Indigenous Natural Resource Management Systems among Pastoralists of Arid and Semi-Arid Africa." In D. Warren, D. Brokensha, and L. Slikkerveer,

Cultural Dimension of Development. Forthcoming.

Olsen, M. 1965. *The Logic of Collective Action.* Cambridge, Mass.: Harvard University Press.

O'Riordan, T. 1988. "The Politics of Sustainability." In R. Turner, ed., *Sustainable Environmental Management: Principle and Practice.* London: Belhaven Press.

Ostrom, E. 1990. *Governing The Commons: The Evolution of Institutions for Collective Action.* Cambridge, England: Cambridge University Press.

Ostrom, E., J. Walker, and R. Gardner. 1992. "Covenants With and Without a Sword: Self-Governance is Possible." *American Political Science Review* 86(2):404–17.

Pinkerton, E., ed. 1989. *Co-operative Management of Local Fisheries: New Directions for Improved Management and Community*

*Development.*Vancouver, Canada: University of British Columbia Press.

Ruddle, K. 1993. "Local Knowledge in the Folk Management of Fisheries and Coastal Marine Environments." In C. L. Dyer and J. R. McGoodwin, eds., *Folk Management in the World's Fisheries. Boulder, Colo.:* University of Colorado Press.

Runge, C. F. 1984. "Institutions and the Free Rider: The Assurance Problem in Collective Action." *Journal of Politics* 46(1):154–81.

Schelling, T. C. 1960. *The Strategy of Conflict.* Oxford, England: Oxford University Press, 1977 reprint.

Young, M. 1992. *Sustainable Investment and Resource Use: Equity, Environmental Integrity and Economic Efficiency.* Man And The Biosphere Series Volume 9. UNESCO: Parthenon Publishing.

6

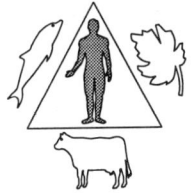

The Management of Transboundary Resources and Property Rights Systems: The Case of Fisheries

Veijo T. Kaitala and Gordon R. Munro

Abstract

THIS CHAPTER IS CONCERNED with the optimal management of those transboundary fishery resources that are found in both the coastal state Exclusive Economic Zone and the adjacent high seas, and which are categorized as highly migratory fish stocks and straddling fish stocks. The high seas portions of the stocks are exploited by both coastal states and distant water fishing nations. The problem of managing such resources, which was deemed to be of minor importance a decade ago, is now seen as severe and has become the focus of a major UN intergovernmental conference. The problem is made particularly difficult by virtue of the fact that property rights to the high seas portions of the resources are ill defined. The ill-defined property rights can easily lead to a breakfown in cooperative management of the resources. The analysis makes it absolutely clear that noncooperative management of transboundary fishery resources is virtually certain to lead to overexploitation. All these difficulties have been exemplified by the recent Canada-Spain "fish war" off Newfoundland.

Property rights and the absence thereof lie at the very heart of the economic problem of managing capture fishery resources. The property rights issue becomes particularly difficult and complex when the fishery resources are transboundary in nature. While transboundary fishery resources have always existed, the transboundary fishery management problem has been greatly magnified by the New International Law of the Sea and Extended Fisheries Jurisdiction, which has given rise to the regime of coastal state 200-mile Exclusive Economic Zones (EEZs). Most fishery resources are mobile. Consequently, when coastal states established EEZs, and extended their jurisdiction over fishery resources from a hitherto maximum of 12 miles to 200 miles, it was inevitable that some of the fishery resources encompassed in the 200-mile EEZs would be found to cross the boundaries of the zones.

International lawyers now make a distinction between two nonmutually exclusive classes of transboundary fishery resources. The first consists of fishery resources that cross a coastal state EEZ boundary into the EEZ of a neighboring coastal state. These are referred to as shared fishery resources. The second class consists of fishery resources that cross an EEZ boundary into adjacent high seas.

The management of the first class, shared fishery resources, has been recognized as a major resource management problem from the dawn of Extended Fisheries Jurisdiction and the 200-mile regime and is reasonably well understood. The management of the second class, involving the high seas, on the other hand, has become a serious problem only in recent years and is not at all well understood. This chapter is concerned mainly with the problem of managing the second class of transboundary fishery resources and the link that this problem has to property rights systems.

The problem is sufficiently great and widespread that the United Nations convened a major intergovernmental conference to address the issue—the UN Conference on Straddling Fish Stocks and Highly Migratory Fish Stocks (hereafter referred to as the UN Fish Conference). The conference has held four substantive sessions and looks forward to at least one more.

Because the problem of managing transboundary fishery resources that are found in both coastal state EEZs and the adjacent high seas has its origins in the management of marine capture (as opposed to aquaculture) fishery resources in general, a review of the basic economics of the management of such resources is in order. The review is simplified by focusing on fishery resources confined to a single EEZ.

A Review of the Basic Economics of Fisheries Management

Economists view a fishery resource as they would any other natural resource, namely as a form of natural capital (Clark and Munro 1994). The resource, like conventional capital, is capable of yielding to society a stream of economic benefits through time. Moreover, fishery resources are renewable, that is they are capable, within limits, of growth. This means, on the one hand, that for given resource levels, they can be harvested on a sustainable basis by setting the harvest rate equal to the net natural growth rate. On the other hand, it means that one can invest in the resource by setting the harvest rate below the growth rate. Obviously, one can also disinvest in the resource by setting the harvest rate above the growth rate.

The gross value of the harvest from a fishery resource, minus the cost of harvesting, is commonly referred to by economists as the "resource rent." Optimal economic management of a fishery resource would require that any harvest be taken in the least costly manner. Less obviously, it would call as well for a program of resource investment and disinvestment that would stabilize the resource or biomass at a level at which the present value of the stream of resource rent through time from the fishery was maximized. This optimal resource, or biomass level, is denoted by X^*, which is determined by the application of a straightforward investment rule: the future gains in terms of increased stream of resource rent arising from incremental investment in the resource are balanced by the cost of investment in the form of forgone resource rent arising from reduced current harvesting. (For a detailed discussion, see Clark 1990 or Munro and Scott 1985.)

Fishery resources, which serve as the basis for marine capture fishery, are difficult to manage because they are, by and large, mobile and unobservable prior to capture. As a consequence it has been difficult, or perhaps more to the point costly, to establish effective property rights to the resources. Hence, such fishery resources traditionally have been common property. Under common property conditions fishers are given little or no incentive to conserve the resource. The theory of the economic management of fishery resources predicts that, if a commercially valuable common property fishery resource is exploited on an open-access, wholly unregulated basis, the resource will be driven down to a level—conceivably zero—at which the resource rent is fully dissipated. In the literature this level is referred to as "bionomic equilibrium" (Gordon 1954). The bionomic equilibrium level is denoted as X^∞. It will always be true that:

$$X^\infty < X^*$$

unless the rate at which society discounts the future, the "social rate of discount," is equal to infinity. Hence, an uncontrolled, unregulated common property fishery will result in excessive disinvestment in the fishery resource from society's point of view.

The predictive power of the economic fisheries management theory has proven to be high indeed. There are numerous examples of ineffectively regulated fisheries leading to gross overexploitation of the resource. Much of fisheries economics is devoted to analyzing means of addressing the common property problem in fishery resource management.

After this brief review of the basic economics of fisheries management, which emphasized the common property nature of the resource, a review of the background to the problem of managing of transboundary fishery resources is considered next.

Background

Prior to the 1970s, coastal states had jurisdiction over fishery resources no more than twelve miles from shore. The vast bulk of marine fishery resources were found in the high seas and as such constituted international common property. The common property problem was thought to exist in a particularly virulent form in international fisheries because many nations, let alone many fishers, competed in exploiting the resources.

In some instances attempts were made to regulate international fisheries by establishing international management bodies. An example is the International Commission for the Northwest Atlantic Fisheries (ICNAF), which governed international fisheries in the northwest Atlantic from Greenland to the Carolinas. Serious doubts began to emerge about the efficacy of such bodies, however. Canada, for example, complained vigorously in the early 1970s about the inadequate management measures of ICNAF. These doubts were to have a significant impact upon the UN Third Conference on the Law of the Sea.

Since the end of World War II coastal states have asserted jurisdiction over marine resources off their shores. In order to impose some degree of order over these attempts to extend jurisdiction, the United Nations convened the Law of the Sea Conference. The first conference was held in 1958 and a second in 1960. Neither addressed fishery resources, other than those found on the sea bed. A third and all encompassing conference was proposed in 1967. After several years of preparation the UN Third Conference on the Law of the Sea was convened in late 1973 and held its concluding session in December 1982. The conference brought forth the Law of the Sea Convention (UN 1982), which came into force as international treaty law on November 16, 1994.

Whereas the first and second Law of the Sea conferences had little to say on fisheries, the greatest achievement of the third conference was in the area of fisheries. It met the international common property problem head on. Under the Law of the Sea Convention arising from the conference, coastal states were enabled to establish 200-mile Exclusive Economic Zones (EEZs) off their shores. The coastal states effectively have full property rights to the fishery resources contained within their EEZs (McRae and Munro 1989). Implementation of Extended Fisheries Jurisdiction—the EEZ regime—has now become all but universal. It was estimated in 1982 that 90 percent of the world's harvest of marine fishery resources would be based upon fishery resources encompassed, or to be encompassed, by coastal state EEZs (Kaitala and Munro 1993; FAO 1993).

Thus, the UN Third Conference on the Law of the Sea brought about the transformation of a massive amount of marine renewable resource wealth from the status of international common property to that of coastal state property. Not surprisingly, there had been extensive resistance during the conference to this move from so-called distant water fishing nations, which can be defined as those nations whose fishing fleets operate far beyond home waters (for example Japan, Spain, Thailand). Indeed, the 200-mile outer boundary of the EEZ, often scorned as making little biological, economic, or legal sense, was the result of a compromise worked out between coastal state and distant water fishing nation interests within the conference.

This is not the place to assess the benefits, or lack thereof, of the Extended Fisheries Jurisdiction (EFJ). It is, however, the place to point out that EFJ brought with it its own set of resource management problems, one of which involved the management of transboundary fishery resources. Because even shellfish are mobile at some stage of their development, it was inevitable, as noted previously, that when coastal states came to establish EEZs, many would find that some of the fishery resources encompassed by the EEZ did in fact cross the EEZ boundary.

Legal specialists distinguish between transboundary fishery resources that are shared by two or more coastal states and those that cross the EEZ boundary into adjacent high seas. It was recognized from the time of the UN Third Conference on the Law of the Sea that the management of shared fishery resources would pose a major problem. Numerous cases existed throughout the world, such as salmon shared by the United States and Canada in the Pacific Northwest and tropical tuna resources shared by Latin American states in the eastern Pacific.

One important aspect of shared fishery resources is that the property rights of coastal states sharing such a resource are made reasonably clear by the Law of the Sea Convention (McRae and Munro 1989). That portion of a shared resource in the EEZ of a given coastal state constitutes the property of that state. The lack of ambiguity of property rights with respect to this set of transboundary resources has greatly facilitated the establishment of cooperative resource management regimes.

The fact that the management of shared fishery resources was deemed to have been a major problem, from the time of the commence-ment of the UN Third Conference on the Law of the Sea, had the result that economists began studying the optimal management of shared fishery resources during the 1970s. The economics of management of shared fishery resources is now reasonably well developed and understood. (See for example Kaitala 1985; Kaitala and Pohjola 1988; Munro 1979, 1990.)

By way of contrast the management of the second class of transboundary fishery resources, those found in both the EEZ and the adjacent high seas, was deemed to be a minor problem at the time of the Third Conference on the Law of the Sea. There were at least two reasons for this. First, because it was estimated that 90 percent of the world's harvest of marine, nonaquaculture fish would be accounted for by fishery resources encompassed by the rapidly spreading EEZs (Kaitala and Munro 1993), those fishery resources remaining in the high seas seemed to be of no great importance.

Second, it was thought that the portions of this second class of transboundary fishery resource found in the adjacent high seas would be harvested largely by distant water fishing nations. If a distant water fishing nation were to begin harvesting the high seas portion of this form of transboundary resource, it could do so on a commercially viable basis, only if it was granted access to the coastal state EEZ, or so it was believed. Under the Law of the Sea Convention, distant water fishing nations do not have automatic access to an EEZ. On the contrary a coastal state is granted broad powers in setting terms and conditions of access to its EEZ. Thus, the coastal state was expected to be in a powerful bargaining position, which would enable it to monitor effectively the activities of a distant water fishing nation in the adjacent high seas as well as the EEZ (Munro forthcoming). If one were to take this argument seriously, then it could be maintained that, although coastal states might not have any clear legal property rights to portions of the transboundary resources in the adjacent high seas, they would have de facto property rights to the resources.

Several consequences followed from the seeming unimportance of this transboundary resource management issue. First, economists studiously ignored the problem. Second, and of greater immediate importance, the drafters of the Law of the Sea Convention produced a section on high seas fisheries (Articles 116–120) that was and is manifestly inadequate. The relevant articles are a model of imprecision and vagueness. In particular, the rights, duties, and obligations of coastal states and those of distant water fishing nations, with respect to fishery resources in the high seas adjacent to the EEZ, are exceedingly unclear (Miles and Burke 1989; Kaitala and Munro 1993). The high seas fisheries section of the convention was subsequently referred to as the "unfinished business" of the Third Law of the Sea Conference. In summary the de jure property rights to the high seas portions of these transboundary fishery resources were decidedly unclear.

Since the mid to late 1980s, the status of the problem of managing high seas fishery resources has been transformed from minor to major to severe. Case after case of overexploitation of such high seas fishery resources has been revealed. It has been argued that the problem has come to constitute a threat to the Law of the Sea Convention itself (Kaitala and Munro 1993).

The Food and Agriculture Organization of the United Nations (FAO) suggests several reasons for the transformation (FAO 1992b). First, the distant water fishing nations have found that their access to the EEZs has steadily eroded, often for reasons flying in the face of basic economic principles. Second, distant water fishing nation fleet capacity has shown surprisingly little decline over the past decade. As a consequence, increased pressure on high seas fishery stocks seemed inevitable.

Third and perhaps most important, the comfortable coastal state assumption that they could effectively monitor distant water fishing nation activity in the high seas adjacent to the EEZs proved to be demonstrably false. As one example, Canada has experienced what can only be described as a resource management catastrophe in its Atlantic coast groundfish fisheries. One factor contributing to the catastrophe has been gross overexploitation of the groundfish stocks found in the high seas adjacent to Canada's Atlantic coast EEZ (Munro 1992; Kaitala and Munro 1993).

The comfortable coastal state assumption carried important implications, namely that if valid the coastal state had, in effect, de facto property rights to the segment of the resource in the adjacent high seas. With the assumption

proving to be invalid, these de facto property rights were shown to be empty. In light of the aforementioned inadequacies of the Law of the Sea Convention as it pertains to high seas fishery resources, we are left with the conclusion that the high seas portions of the transboundary resources did in fact remain as international common property.

Coastal states such as Canada could, of course, attempt to deal with troublesome stocks in the high seas adjacent to their EEZs through a unilateral extension of jurisdiction. Certainly, there have been threats of such extension of jurisdiction. There are difficulties, however, with this solution. We have already noted that the 200-mile boundary of the EEZ is the result of a compromise in the Third Conference on the Law of the Sea. If coastal states were to begin violating this compromise, there would be the risk that the Law of the Sea Convention could be seriously undermined.

Additionally, extension of coastal state jurisdiction would mitigate the problem but could not be expected to eliminate it entirely. Canada, for example, could probably deal with its problem through a fairly modest extension of jurisdiction. The FAO, however, reports on stocks found in the EEZ and adjacent high seas that may extend as much as 900 miles offshore (FAO 1993). No one at this stage is seriously contemplating an extension of coastal state jurisdiction to such distances.

The increasing severity of the high seas fishery management problem and the concomitant threat of coastal state unilateral extension of jurisdiction caused the United Nations to take action and convene the UN Fish Conference to address the "unfinished business" of the Third Law of the Sea Conference. If all goes well a convention or agreement will be forthcoming from the conference, which will buttress, or supplement, the existing Law of the Sea Convention. The foundation for such a convention or agreement now exists in the form of a draft agreement, which appeared initially as a conference negotiating text during the first substantive session of the conference in July 1993. The text underwent several revisions and emerged as a draft agreement in the August 1994 session (UN 1994). The draft agreement is certain to undergo further revisions in the sessions scheduled for 1995.

In its discussion of fishery resources to be found in both the EEZ and the adjacent high seas, the UN Fish Conference makes a distinction between highly migratory stocks and straddling stocks. Highly migratory stocks refer to the tuna species, which because of their highly migratory nature move naturally from the EEZ to the adjacent high seas. The highly migratory stocks are particularly important for major groups of developing coastal states, such as the states of the Indian Ocean, several Southeast Asian coastal states, the Pacific Island Nations of the western and central Pacific, and Latin American coastal states of the eastern Pacific, from Mexico to Peru.

Straddling stocks is essentially a catchall term for all other relevant fishery resources. Examples are jack mackerel stocks off Peru and Chile and groundfish stocks in the Doughnut Hole in the Bering Sea, on the Grand Bank of Newfoundland, and in the Loop Hole in the Barents Sea. Straddling stocks are ubiquitous throughout the world.

The distinction between highly migratory stocks and straddling stocks is based largely on historical and political factors. During the UN Third Conference on the Law of the Sea, one major distant water fishing nation argued strenuously that highly migratory stocks should not be subject to coastal state jurisdiction, but should rather be managed by international bodies. This position was vigorously opposed by many developing coastal states. Echos of this debate are to be heard in the current UN Fish Conference.

On the other hand, the FAO makes the point that it is difficult to make a clear distinction between highly migratory stocks and straddling stocks on biological grounds. Some highly migratory stocks move only short distances, and some straddling stocks, such as jack mackerel, are distributed over many hundreds of miles (FAO 1993). In light of this fact we shall hereafter refer to straddling stocks alone. It should be understood that all comments that follow, pertaining to straddling stocks, apply with equal force to highly migratory stocks.

One final comment on the UN Fish Conference is in order. One question on which there is unanimity within the conference is whether the management regime for the portion of the straddling stock in the adjacent high seas should be allowed to differ from the management regime for the portion of the straddling migratory stock within the EEZ. All parties are agreed that it would be nonsensical to have anything other than a single management regime for the straddling stock in question.

Where there has not been unanimity in the past is relevant to the question of who should determine the management regimes for the high seas portions of the aforementioned stocks. Distant water fishing nations have maintained that they should play a significant role in establishing such management regimes. If coastal states were to be granted sole power in establishing the management regimes, this would constitute "creeping coastal state jurisdiction" beyond the existing 200-mile limit.

If distant water fishing nations play a significant role in determining the management regimes for the high seas portions of straddling stocks, then they will influence the management regimes of the portions of the straddling stocks *within* the EEZ as well. This follows from the proposition that the management regime for the high seas portion of a straddling stock must be consistent with that for the EEZ portion of the stock. Coastal states have viewed such influence as a threat to the sovereignty that they have with respect to living resources within the EEZ, as granted to them by Article 56 of the Law of the Sea Convention.

As a consequence, the lines of division within the UN Fish Conference have been between coastal states on the one hand and distant water fishing nations on the other, with a few nations, such as the United States, finding that they have interests in both camps. It is worth stressing that the lines of division are not between developed and developing countries. Not all distant water fishing nations are developed countries; some developed countries have no distant water fishing interests whatsoever.

Consider the following example. suffice. Canada is a developed country with no distant water fishing interests, and within the conference it has been a leader in the coastal state camp. Japan is a developed country that has been a leader in the distant water fishing nation camp. Canada finds that it has allies in the conference in such developing countries as Argentina, Chile, Indonesia, and the Philippines, to name a few. Thailand, which also is a developing country and an important distant water fishing nation, finds itself sympathetic to the views being expressed in the conference by Japan.

Approaches to the Economics of the Management of Transboundary Fishery Resources

The development of the economics of the management of those transboundary fishery resources (straddling stocks) to be found in both coastal state EEZs and the adjacent high seas is still at an early stage because of the relatively recent emergence of the problem. It will be seen that we turn for assistance to the more fully developed economics of the management of shared fishery resources.

The UN Fish Conference has progressed to a degree that it is beginning to provide a reasonable framework within which to develop the economics of the management of straddling stocks. Two documents that have come from the conference are critical. They are the draft agreement (UN 1994), to which reference has been made previously, and a draft convention presented at the first substantive session of the conference in July 1993 by a group of coastal states, including Canada, Chile, New Zealand, and Peru (UN 1993).

From the draft agreement it is clear that the conference will recommend that straddling, highly migratory fish stocks be managed locally through regional organizations that by necessity would have both coastal states and distant water fishing nations as members. An existing prototype of such an organization is provided by the Northwest Atlantic Fisheries Organization (NAFO), successor to the International Commission for the Northwest Atlantic Fisheries, which governs the management of fishery resources in the high seas adjacent to Canada's Atlantic coast EEZ.

The issue thus becomes what should be the nature of optimal economic resource management programs for the regional organizations to be established. Although the focus in the conference has been on the high seas, it is agreed by all in the conference that one sensibly cannot have a management regime for the portion of the straddling stock inside the EEZ that differs significantly from the management regime for the portion of the resource in the high seas. Thus, a regional organization, once established, will have to serve as the framework within which the management regime for the entire transboundary fishery resource is determined.

In contrast to the economics of the management of straddling stocks, the economics of the management of shared stocks is reasonably well developed. An appropriate way to proceed is to ask how far the analysis of the economics of shared stock management will carry us in developing the economics of straddling stock management. The economist's model applied to the management of shared fish stocks is a blend of the standard dynamic model of the fishery and the theory of dynamic games. (See the survey article: Munro 1990.)

It is appropriate and indeed essential, in analyzing the management of shared fish stocks, to allow for the possibility that the management goals of coastal states sharing a resource will differ. Many factors could result in such differences. We chose for our analytical purposes one such factor, namely differences in cost of labor plus capital applied to harvesting the resource, commonly referred to as fishing "effort." Suppose that with respect to a shared stock there are but two relevant coastal states, C1 and C2, and suppose in addition that C1 is the low fishing effort cost state. Suppose further that C1 and C2 are similar in all other respects.

If C1 were to control the resource outright there would be an optimal resource stock level as seen from C1's perspective, denoted as X_{C1}^*. There will be a corresponding bionomic equilibrium stock level for C1, denoted as X_{C1}^∞. What holds true for C1 also holds true for C2. Thus, we can think of X_{C2}^* and X_{C2}^∞ as well.

It can be shown by applying the standard dynamic economic model of the fishery that the difference in fishing effort costs will lead C2 to be the more conservationist of the two joint owners of the resource, that is:

$$X_{C1}^* < X_{C2}^*$$

It can also be shown that:

$$X_{C1}^\infty < X_{C2}^\infty$$

The first question to be addressed is what are the economic consequences, if any, of noncooperative management of the shared resource. We use a dynamic version of the noncooperative game developed by Nobel Laureate John Nash (1951).

The solution to the Nash noncooperative game is as follows: The shared fishery resource will be stabilized at X_{C1}^*, if $X_{C1}^* < X_{C2}^\infty$. If $X_{C1}^* > X_{C2}^\infty$ on the other hand, the resource will be stabilized at X_{C2}^∞. If fishing effort costs should be equal, then the resource would be stabilized at the common bionomic equilibrium X^∞. Thus, except in the special case in which $X_{C1}^* < X_{C2}^\infty$, the result is a type of outcome associated with what is perhaps the most famous of all competitive or noncooperative games, the Prisoner's Dilemma. The participants or players are driven to adopt strategies that all recognize as highly undesirable. Noncooperative management can be expected to result in the overexploitation of the resource from the point of view of both competing countries and thus lead to an outcome not dissimilar to an open-access, unregulated fishery within a single EEZ. Thus, noncooperative management of a shared fishery resource leads to the collapse of effective property rights with respect to the resource.

The theory has strong predictive powers. For example, the factor that drove the American and Canadian negotiators through fifteen tortuous years of negotiation leading to the signing of the Canada-U.S. Pacific Salmon Treaty in 1985 and has kept the treaty afloat since that time was and is the fear of a destructive "fish war" if cooperation should break down (Munro and Stokes 1989).

When one enquires into the consequences of noncooperative management of straddling stocks, the analysis is the same as was applied to the shared fish stock case. Instead of two coastal states exploiting a resource, assume that the exploiters are a coastal state and one or more distant water fishing nations. Noncooperation can easily lead to a Prisoner's Dilemma outcome, the equivalent of an open-access, common property type of fishery, and overexploitation of the stock (Kaitala and Munro forthcoming). Once again, the theory has strong predictive powers. For example, reference has been made to Canada's fishery problems in the high seas adjacent to its Atlantic EEZ. The plundering of groundfish stock in the Doughnut Hole in the Bering Sea, the near fish war between Norway and Iceland in the Loop Hole in the Barents Sea,

are but two of several other examples. Thus, cooperative management does indeed matter. It was of course the growing concern with overexploitation of high seas fishery resources that induced the United Nations to convene the UN Fish Conference.

With the economic case for cooperative management now established, the cooperative economic management of shared stocks should be considered. At this stage we use the highly simplifying (and restrictive) assumption that if the players succeed in establishing a cooperative agreement it will be binding through time. With this assumption, we join the standard dynamic economic model of the fishery with Nash's theory of cooperative games (Nash 1953).

The whole point of a cooperative agreement is that both players or joint owners of the resource will hope to succeed in achieving an outcome superior to what they would achieve under conditions of competition. Hence, in the theory of cooperative games a key reference point is the so-called threat point, which consists of the net economic returns or payoffs that the players would receive under noncooperation. If there is to be a solution to the cooperative game, then each player must receive a payoff not less than its threat point payoff. A second and equally obvious requirement for a solution to the cooperative game is that it be Pareto efficient, in the sense that it is not possible to make one player better off except at the expense of the other.

If these two basic conditions are met the coastal states sharing the resource can, as joint owners of the resource, come together to manage the resource in such a way as to prevent overexploitation of the resource and to assure sustainable economic benefits from the resource for both or all resource owners. Of course bargaining will have to take place for the division of the returns.

One complication that can arise is that the joint owners will have different management goals. For example, if we continue to assume that there are but two coastal states involved as joint owners of the resource, C1 and C2, and if we continue to suppose that C1 had lower fishing efforts costs than C2, then we would have the result, as noted, that $X_{C1}^* < X_{C2}^*$. Country 1 would wish to pursue a more liberal harvesting regime than C2.

Such differences in management goals can complicate the bargaining process enormously and, as a result, can threaten the cooperative management program. There is, however, a means for circumventing this difficulty. It involves the use of so-called side payments, essentially transfers between the players or joint owners. The implication of the existence of side payments in the context of fisheries is that a joint owner's return from the fishery is not determined solely by that joint owner's harvest of the resource.

With the existence of side payments the optimal joint management program becomes that of maximizing the global net economic returns from resources, or resources rent, and then dividing the resources rent among the players. When the players have differing management goals it invariably means that one player, or joint owner, places a higher value on the resource than the other (Munro 1987). Thus, maximizing the resource rent from the resource through time means ensuring that the management preferences of the joint owner placing the greatest value on the resource are allowed to hold sway (Munro 1987). In our example this would mean establishing a management regime in which the management preferences of the low fishing effort cost country, C1, are dominant. Indeed, C1 would to all intents and purposes buy out C2. Bargaining would then ensue over the division of the global net economic returns.

In formal terms the theory predicts the outcome of the bargaining as follows. First, denote the global net economic return from the fishery (in present value terms) achieved from following the optimal management policy prescribed by C1 as W. Denote the threat point payoffs as T_{C1} and T_{C2} respectively. Then, the surplus, S, or the net economic benefit to be enjoyed through cooperation, is simply:

$$S = W - T_{C1} - T_{C2}$$

The Nash bargaining solution (Nash 1953) leads to the outcome that under the cooperative management regime each player will enjoy a payoff equal to its threat point payoff plus ½ S. Because the refusal of either player to cooperate would destroy the opportunity for cooperation, each player is seen as making an equal contribution to cooperation and thus deserving an equal share of the surplus.

So important is the concept of cooperative resource management and so important is the accompanying and poorly understood concept of side payments, that we digress briefly to present an example to illustrate that the concepts are much more than exercises in esoteric theory. At the turn of the twentieth century an important renewable resource being exploited in the North Pacific was fur seals. The resource was shared and exploited by four countries: Canada, Japan, Russia, and the United States.

The exploitation took place initially on a noncooperative basis. The Prisoner's Dilemma model predicted accurately, and the seal herds were subject to severe overexploitation. The threat of ongoing overexploitation and possible extinction led the four countries to meet in 1911 and establish a cooperative management regime through the Convention for Preservation and Protection of Fur Seals (FAO 1992a).

The four countries' harvests were not identical. Canada and Japan harvested seals at sea, whereas Russia and the United States harvested seals on the Pribilof Islands. The Canadian and Japanese harvesting operations were carried out at a much higher cost than those of the Americans and Russians. Hence, a basis for dispute over management goals existed.

A cooperative resource management regime with side payments was established. The management preferences of the low-cost harvesters, Russia and the United States, were allowed to determine the nature of the resource management regime. Indeed, Canada and Japan not only accepted the management preferences of Russia and the United States, they reduced their harvesting of fur seals to zero. In return Canada and Japan received a percentage of the harvested skins, side payments, every year.

The management regime proved to be not only profitable for all four participants but effective in terms of conservation of the resource as well. At the time of the signing of the convention in 1911, the number of fur seals in the northeast Pacific was estimated to be 125,000. Over the following thirty years the herds increased in number to 2,300,000 (FAO 1992a).

Turning to the cooperative economic management of straddling stocks, we find that the analysis of the cooperative management of shared stocks carries us only part of the way. There are two reasons for this, one minor, the other major. The minor reason is that in the typical economic model of cooperative management of shared fishery resources it is assumed that there are but two players, by no means an unreasonable assumption. Such an assumption, however, is unreasonable when studying straddling stock management where typically one coastal state will confront several distant water fishing nations. With the number of players exceeding two, one has to consider the possibility of subcoalitions, which can complicate the analysis considerably and in practical terms exacerbate the difficulty of achieving a stable cooperative management regime.

The major reason is that the number and nature of the participants are unlikely to be constant through time. It is this reason that will be seen to distinguish most clearly the shared and straddling stock case.

To begin to understand why this should be so, suppose that the regional organization responsible for the management of a particular straddling stock fishery has three participants, one coastal state, C, and two distant water fishing nations, D1 and D2. Suppose further that neither D1 or D2 will exit the fishery and that it is not possible for new distant water fishing nations to enter the fishery at any time in the future.

If neither D1 or D2 will leave the fishery, we can suppose as well that there is nothing to prevent them from operating in the fishery in perpetuity. Now suppose further for the sake of simplicity that the fishing effort costs of C, D1, and D2 are identical and that, although side payments are feasible, subcoalitions are not. The situation would be all but identical to a shared stock management problem. Indeed, we could designate the surplus from cooperation as:

$$S = W - T_C - T_{D1} - T_{D2}$$

and conclude that in a cooperative agreement each player would receive a payoff equal to its threat point payoff plus 1/3 S.

The distant water fishing nations D1 and D2, as well as C, would have at least de facto property rights to part of the resource. The resource would in effect be jointly owned, with the consequence that each of the three participants would have security with respect to their share of the stream of future economic benefits from the resource.

If we were to relax the assumption pertaining to subcoalitions, the cooperative arrangements would become more complex. Essentially, however, this would be a minor consideration.

In fact, the following assumptions are wholly invalid: (1) distant water fishery nations currently operating in a straddling stock fishery will never exit, and (2) new distant water fishing nations will never enter the fishery. The fleets of distant water fishing nations are nothing if not mobile. Hence, there is nothing to prevent a distant water fishing nation from causing its fleet to exit the fishery. Of even greater importance there is nothing to prevent fleets of distant water fishing nations, which have never participated in the fishery in the past, from appearing on the horizon and demanding access to the fishery.

The term for such distant water nations that have not participated in the fishery in the past and now demand access is "new entrants." Given the importance of new entrants, it is important to explain the term and its implications with greater precision. Suppose that a regional organization is established to manage a particular straddling stock. Let the coastal states and distant water fishing nations that established the regional organization be designated as the "charter members." A distant water fishing nation, which hitherto had not exploited the resource, seeks access to the fishery and thus membership in the organization. Such a distant water fishing nation would constitute a new entrant. Under the current interpretation of the Law of the Sea Convention, the charter members of the regional organization would be denied the right to bar fully any such new entrant. A prospective new entrant could be barred only if it refused to abide by the management regime established by the regional organization (Kaitala and Munro 1993).

If the only requirement that bars prospective new entrants from the fishery is that they agree to abide by the prescribed resource management regime, then the risk is obvious. If the charter members establish a potentially successful resource management regime, this will attract new entrants, each of which may agree to abide by the prescribed regime but also will demand a share of the resource rent. It can be demonstrated (Kaitala and Munro unpublished) that the following outcome is only too likely, namely that at least one charter member, in calculating its economic benefits from cooperation and anticipating a stream of new entrants, will estimate that its payoff from cooperation will fall below its initial threat point payoff. Hence, it will refuse to cooperate and the cooperative arrangement will prove to be stillborn.

Essentially, the lack of effective restrictions on new entrants will undermine the property rights to the resource of the charter member distant water fishing nations, if not the coastal state or states. The consequence will be that the cooperative resource management regime itself, in turn, will be effectively undermined.

The UN Fish Conference does, however, hold out some hope that the new entrant issue could be addressed. Reference has already been made to two documents emerging from the conference, the draft agreement (UN 1994) and a draft convention prepared by a group of leading coastal states (UN 1993). The latter document addresses the issue directly and proposes three possible solutions to the new entrant problem, two of which have prima facie validity. We would assert that the draft agreement would not prevent any regional organization from attempting to implement either solution.

There is no intention on the part of the authors to suggest that the solutions they discuss are the only solutions. Rather, the solutions should be seen as a starting point. The fact that they were accepted for discussion by the UN Fish Conference does indicate that they were not deemed infeasible and that they should be given serious consideration. In any event, the proposed solutions are (UN 1993):

1. Permit new entrant access to a regional organization, but insist that it go through a waiting period before enjoying benefits from the fishery. Thus, the charter members would enjoy a period over which they would not have to share the benefits of cooperation with new entrants.

2. Provide that charter members declare the straddling stock fishery to be fully utilized and announce that a prospective new entrant may participate in the fishery and become a member of the organization only upon an existing member relinquishing its

share and hence membership in the organization.

The first proposed solution implies that a new entrant upon application becomes a member of the regional organization and thus a player in the game. The analysis suggests that as a player the new entrant will receive a payoff equal to its threat point payoff plus an equal share of the surplus arising from cooperation. The payoff is measured in present value terms; hence, the waiting period, as long as it is not indefinite, is immaterial. Thus, this solution is no significant improvement over open and unimpeded access for new entrants. The perceived benefits or privileges for charter members are illusory.

The second proposed solution holds much more promise. We deem it highly unlikely that any current member of a regional organization would relinquish its share or membership free of charge. There is, however, presumably nothing to prevent an existing member from selling its share or membership.

The share or membership thus becomes a form of property right to be held in perpetuity or sold. Indeed, the share bears some similarity to the popular scheme of individual transferable quotas (if held in perpetuity) for fishers or companies in nontransboundary fisheries. The possibility of new entrants thus does not directly threaten to destroy the benefits of cooperation to the charter members of the regional organization. Consequently, the prospects for achieving a successful cooperative regime are considerably greater than under the first proposed solution.

The existence of saleable memberships, however, does create formidable analytical difficulties. The difficulties are being addressed, but they have not been fully resolved (Kaitala and Munro unpublished).

Consider for example the following apparently simple situation. In spite of what we said about reasonable assumptions concerning the numbers in a regional organization, we now suppose that there are only two charter members of the regional organization, C and D1. C's fishing effort costs are lower than those of D1. A new entrant, D2, appears. Its fishing effort costs are greater than that of C but lower than those of D1. Hence, D1 is given an incentive to sell out to D2. If the sale takes place a new cooperative agreement will have to be negotiated. The expected global return from the resource will be unchanged but the threat point certainly will shift. It is reasonable to expect that $T_{D2} > T_{D1}$ and that T_C will be less than it would have been had D1 remained as the partner (Kaitala and Munro unpublished). Hence, C will most assuredly lose if D1 sells out to D2.

D1 will not be unaware of the fact that C would lose if the sale were to take place. Consequently, rather than sell out to D2, D1 may remain in the regional organization but use the threat of a sell out to extract during the negotiations a greater portion of the resource rent. In other words the presence of D2 may effectively alter D1's threat power. As of yet these issues remain to be explored in depth. We can be certain, however, that the introduction of bluff and blackmail complicates the negotiations immensely and makes the achievement of a stable cooperative management regime far more difficult.

All of these difficulties aside, the discussion up to this point leads inexorably to one conclusion. If the straddling type stocks are to be effectively managed, the relevant high seas adjacent to a coastal state EEZ will become high seas in name only. For a given straddling stock the coastal state and a limited number of distant water fishing nations will have to establish de facto, if not de jure, property rights to the portion of the resource in the adjacent high seas.

Conclusion and Policy Implications

Over the past decade a serious management problem concerning international renewable resources has emerged. The resources are transboundary fishery stocks, which are found in both coastal state Exclusive Economic Zones (EEZs) and the adjacent high seas. The resources are specifically highly migratory fish stocks (tuna) and so-called straddling stocks. The problem is now worldwide and is of direct relevance to developing and developed coastal states alike. The United Nations has convened a major intergovernmental conference to address the issue. The conference has held four substantive sessions and is looking forward to at least one more.

It is clear that the conference will call for the management of the fishery resources on a local basis through regional organizations. Each

regional organization will have as members one or more coastal states plus distant water fishing nations engaged in exploiting the high seas portion of the relevant resource.

If a given regional organization does not succeed in developing an effective cooperative resource management regime, then the consequences will be straightforward. Noncooperative management of these transboundary resources leads straight to overexploitation. The United Nations convened the conference precisely because of the growing and alarming evidence that noncooperative management was leading to serious overexploitation of the resources in question.

Developing effective cooperative management regimes for fishery resources found in both coastal state EEZs and the adjacent high seas will be difficult, considerably more difficult than developing effective cooperative management regimes for so-called shared fish stocks. The reason is simple and uncomplicated: Whereas property rights with respect to shared fish stocks are reasonably well defined, they are ill defined with respect to the high seas portions of straddling type stocks.

It follows, therefore, that developing effective cooperative management regimes for a straddling type fish stock will involve establishing an effective property rights system for the entire resource. The relevant adjacent high seas will have to become high seas in name only.

Our analysis indicates clearly that establishing an effective property rights system requires in the first instance that the new entrant problem be addressed. If unresolved, the search for an effective property rights system for straddling type stocks will prove futile and the resources will be managed under conditions of noncooperation, with all that implies.

Addendum

The first draft of this chapter was written shortly before the dramatic eruption of the fisheries dispute between Canada on one hand and Spain and the European Union (EU), of which Spain is a member, on the other. It is incumbent upon us to add a commentary because the Canada-Spain incident is of direct relevance to certain key issues raised in the chapter. Because one author is a citizen of

Finland, a European Union member country, and the other author is a citizen of Canada, we hope that we can present a balanced view.

The dispute is centered on a groundfish species, turbot or Greenland halibut, found on the Grand Bank of Newfoundland. The stock in question is found in both the Canadian EEZ and a high seas portion of the Grand Bank, popularly known as the Nose of the Bank. The stock is thus an unambiguous straddling stock. It has been exploited by Canadian vessels and by the vessels of two distant water fishing nations, Portugal and Spain, both of which are members of the European Union.

The high seas portion of the turbot stock, as well as the high seas portion of other Grand Bank straddling stocks has, since 1979, been under the management of an international body, the Northwest Atlantic Fisheries Organization (NAFO). NAFO has as members Canada and relevant distant water fishing nations, the most important of which is the EU.

Portuguese and Spanish fleets have fished on the Grand Bank for centuries. Neither country was, however, a charter member of NAFO. It is in fact the case that Canada's fishery relations with both countries have been subject to severe strain since Canada implemented Extended Fisheries Jurisdiction in 1977. Portugal and Spain became participants in NAFO, only as a consequence of their acquiring membership in the EU in 1985.

In its early years NAFO was a reasonably successful management body, with the resource management policy being dominated by Canada. One could have described NAFO as a moderately effective cooperative game. The game, however, degenerated into a competitive game after 1985. The fact that this degeneration followed Portuguese and Spanish entry into the EU is not entirely coincidental.

In any event the EU from 1985 onward maintained that the Canadian-inspired resource management plan was excessively conservationist. Canada subsequently complained bitterly that the EU was exceeding the harvest quotas allocated to it under NAFO and that its activities were destructive to the resources. One problem was that the NAFO quotas were nonbinding. All that a member state had to do to ignore its assigned quota was to lodge a formal objection (Kaitala and Munro, 1993).

The destructive competitive game continued to be played out until both sides recognized the serious depletion of the stocks in question. A peace agreement was signed in December 1992 in the form of a Memorandum of Understanding between Canada and the EU (Kaitala and Munro 1993). The agreement must now be seen as having been a temporary truce.

In February-March 1995 Canada charged that Spain was harvesting turbot straddling stock on the Nose of the Bank in excess of quotas allocated to the EU under NAFO. Moreover, the Canadian charge continued, the Spanish were engaged in illegal harvesting practices, such as the harvesting of immature fish. The Canadian charge was then followed by police action, when Canadian authorities apprehended a Spanish trawler and forced it to make port in St. John's, Newfoundland, where it remained in custody until it was finally released under bail.

The incident illustrates our point about the uncertainty created by the existing Law of the Sea Convention with regards to the rights, duties, and obligations of coastal states versus distant water fishing nations in the adjacent high seas. One school of thought, which has found its most eloquent proponents in Professors William Burke and Edward Miles of the University of Washington (Miles and Burke 1989), argues that although coastal states do not have full jurisdiction to fishery resources beyond the 200-mile limit they do have superior rights for conservation purposes, with respect to the high seas portions of straddling stocks (Miles and Burke 1989). At one point Miles and Burke state categorically that, "Article 116 [Law of the Sea Convention] establishes that the coastal state has the superior right, duty, and interest in straddling stocks beyond the EEZ" (Miles and Burke 1989, p. 343). Distant water fishing nations reject this argument, often with vehemence (Kaitala and Munro 1993).

Assuming a Miles and Burke position, Canada maintained that as a coastal state it was taking entirely justifiable police action to prevent the willful overexploitation of a straddling stock of importance to the economic well-being of its fishing industry. Spain and the European Union responded by insisting that in seizing a Spanish vessel on the high seas, well beyond the boundary of the Canadian EEZ, Canada was in clear violation of international law. Indeed, the

Spanish-EU argument continued, Canada's action was tantamount to piracy.

The charges and counter charges of overharvesting, the capture of immature fish, and other acts destructive to the fishery resource, are precisely what the analysis would lead us to expect when a straddling fish stock is managed in a competitive, noncooperative manner. Indeed, if one wishes to find an example of a real world noncooperative transboundary fishery game, with all that that entails and implies, one need look no further than the Canada-Spain turbot war.

Bibliography

Clark, C. W. 1990. *Mathematical Bioeconomics: The Optimal Management of Renewable Resources, Second Edition*. New York: Wiley Interscience.

Clark, C. W., and G. R. Munro. 1994. "Renewable Resources as Natural Capital: The Fishery." In A. Jansson, M. Hammer, C. Folke, and R. Costanza, eds., *Investing in Natural Capital: The Ecological Economics Approach to Sustainability*. Washington D.C.: Island Press. pp. 343–61.

Food and Agriculture Organization of the United Nations (FAO). 1992a. *Marine Fisheries and the Law of the Sea: A Decade of Change*. Rome: FAO Fisheries Circular no. 853.

———. 1992b. *World Fisheries Situation*. International Conference on Responsible Fishing, Cancun, May 6–8, 1992.

———. 1993. *World Review of High Seas and Highly Migratory Fish Species and Straddling Stocks*. Rome: FAO Fisheries Circular no. 858.

Gordon, H. S. 1954. "The Economic Theory of a Common Property Resource: The Fishery." *Journal of Political Economy* 62:124–42.

Kaitala, V. T. 1985. *Game Theory Models of Bargaining and Contracting in Fisheries Management*. Institute of Mathematics, Helsinki University of Technology.

Kaitala, V. T., and G. R. Munro. 1993. "The Management of High Seas Fisheries." *Marine Resource Economics* 8:313–29.

———. Forthcoming. "The Economic Management of High Seas Fishery Resources: Some Game-Theoretic Aspects." In C. Carraro and J. A. Filar, eds., *Game-Theoretic Models of the Environment*. Boston: Birkhauser.

———. Unpublished. "Conservation and Management of High Seas Fishery Resources: The Problem of New Entrants." First draft.

Kaitala, V. T., and M. Pohjola. 1988. "Optimal Recovery of a Shared Stock: A Differential Game with Efficient Memory Equilibria." *Natural Resource Modeling* 3:91-119.

McRae D. M., and G. R. Munro. 1989. "Coastal State 'Rights' Within the 200 Mile Exclusive Economic Zone." In P. Neher, R. Arnason, and N. Mollett, eds., *Rights Based Fishing*. Dordrecht, Netherlands: Kluwer Academic Publishers. pp. 97–112.

Miles, E. L., and W. T. Burke. 1989. "Pressures on the United Nations Convention on the Law of the Sea of 1982 Arising from New Fisheries Conflicts: The Problem of Straddling Stocks. *Ocean Development and International Law* 20:343–57.

Munro, G. R. 1979. "The Optimal Management of Transboundary Resources." *Canadian Journal of Economics* 12:355–76.

———. 1987. "The Management of Shared Fishery Resources under Extended Jurisdiction." *Marine Resource Economics* 3:271–96.

———. 1990. "The Optimal Management of Transboundary Fisheries: Game Theoretic Considerations." *Natural Resource Modeling* 4:403–26.

———. 1992. "Evolution of Canadian Fisheries Management Policy Under the New Law of the Sea: International Dimensions." In A. C. Cutler and M. W. Zacher, eds., *Canadian Foreign Policy and International Economic Regimes*. Vancouver: University of British Columbia Press. pp. 284–310.

———. Forthcoming. "The Management of High Seas Fishery Resources." In *Proceedings of the Seventh Conference of the International Institute of Fisheries Economics and Trade*. Taipei.

Munro, G. R., and A. D. Scott. 1985. "The Economics of Fisheries Management." In A. V. Kneese and J. L. Sweeney, eds., *Handbook of Natural Resource and Energy Economics*. Vol. II. Amsterdam: North-Holland. pp. 623–76.

Munro, G. R., and R. L. Stokes. 1989. "The Canada-United States Pacific Salmon Treaty." In D. McRae and G. Munro, eds.

Canadian Oceans Policy: National Strategies and the New Law of the Sea. Vancouver: University of British Columbia Press. pp. 17–38.

Nash, J. F. 1951. "Noncooperative Games." *Annals of Mathematics* 54:289–95.

———. 1953. "Two Person Cooperative Games." *Econometrica* 21:128–40.

United Nations (UN). 1982. *United Nations Convention on the Law of the Sea*. UN Doc. A/Conf. 61/122.

———. 1993. "United Nations Conference on Straddling Fish Stocks and Highly Migratory Fish Stocks." Draft convention on the conservation and management of straddling fish stocks on the high seas and highly migratory fish stocks on the high seas. UN Doc. A/Conf. 164/L11/Rev. 1.

———. 1994. "United Nations Conference on Straddling Fish Stocks and Highly Migratory Fish Stocks." Draft agreement for the implementation of the provisions of the United Nations Convention on the Law of the Sea of 10 December 1982 relating to the conservation and management of straddling fish stocks and highly migratory fish stocks. UN Doc. A/Conf. 164/22.

Equity and Stewardship

7

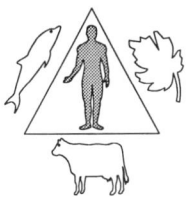

Building Equity, Stewardship, and Resilience into Market-Based Property Rights Systems

Michael D. Young and Bonnie J. McCay

Abstract

Market-based property rights systems, usually in the form of an exclusive and tradable license, lease, quota, or permit, are now being used in the management of natural resources for the control of water and air pollution, to influence water use, and to control land use.

This research was sponsored in part by the Beijer International Institute of Ecological Economics, The Royal Swedish Academy of Sciences, Stockholm, Sweden, with support from the World Environment and Resources Program of the John D. and Catherine T. MacArthur Foundation and the World Bank. The research was conducted as part of the program Property Rights and the Performance of Natural Resource Systems. The work was also supported by the National Sea Grant College Program, the National Science Foundation, and the New Jersey Agricultural Experiment Station.

Many of the ideas expressed in this chapter were developed during workshops convened by the Beijer Institute to discuss the design of property-rights systems of resources management. The invaluable contributions made by other members of the project team is acknowledged with deep appreciation and with apologies for any misrepresentations. The full team included Alan Christopher Finlayson, Peter Parks, Kelly Robinson, and Bonnie McCay from Rutgers University, New Jersey; John Gatewood, Lehigh University, Bethlehem, Pennsylvania; Susan Hanna, Oregon State University, Corvallis, Oregon; Gísli Pálsson, University of Iceland, Reykjavik, Iceland; Ralph Townsend and James Wilson, University of Maine, Orono, Maine; Tom Tietenberg, Colby College, Maine; and Michael Young from the CSIRO Division of Wildlife and Ecology, Canberra, Australia. We thank each and every member of the team, but reserve responsibility for errors of fact and interpretation.

Recognizing the importance of efficiency as a criterion for such management regimes, such systems are evaluated with a focus on the criteria of equity, resiliency, and stewardship, and suggestions are offered about ways these can be built into the design of adaptive and flexible management regimes. Particular emphasis is given to dual property rights systems, zero revenue auctions, community returns, and to bottom-up and nested structures of decisionmaking and governance.

✧

Introduction

Market-based property rights systems, usually in the form of an exclusive and tradable license, lease, quota, or permit, are now being used in the management of conditionally renewable natural resources like fisheries, forests, wildlife, and grazing land. They are also advocated and used to control water and air pollution, to influence the use of renewable resources like water, and to control land use.

The use of market-based property rights systems for common pool resources is new, only a decade or so old in most instances. They involve major institutional change and are therefore often controversial. In this chapter, the aim is to demonstrate, primarily by example, how market-based property rights systems can be adapted to incorporate social and environmental objectives. The examples given are those known from the authors' work and the work of their Beijer workshop colleagues. The examples are weighted heavily toward the fisheries of the North Atlantic; Australia's ranching, forestry, kangaroo shooting, and fishing industries; and national and global systems of pollution control.

In a subsequent paper, we and our colleagues consider the intellectual frameworks involved in designing and understanding market-based property rights systems, which have their roots in neoclassical economics and institutionalism and presume the privileged position of the state and its administrators and technical experts, including scientists, in common pool resource management. In this chapter, we take that framework for granted, dealing instead with the ways that market-based property rights systems can

better incorporate objectives such as equity, resiliency, and stewardship.

Reasons for Administrative Attraction and Resistance to Market Mechanisms in Common Pool Resources Management

The markets created by "free market environmentalism" provide important adjuncts to command-and-control methods of environmental management on the one hand and communal or corporate management of "the commons" on the other. Well-designed market-based property rights systems combine the advantages of top-down regulatory instruments with those of markets and democratic institutional processes. For example, command-and-control instruments may be used to make certain practices illegal and to monitor the system, enforce the rules, and sanction offenders. They also may be used to create markets. Democratic institutional processes can be involved at many stages, including making decisions about allocation rules, how much can be traded, and what production techniques can be used. The systems may be designed to provide corporate governance by the users (Townsend and Pooley 1995). Finally, markets are used to find the most cost-effective way of pursuing the remaining opportunities. Constrained by institutional restrictions, the result is a Pareto efficient reallocation and use of resources.[1]

A quota, for example, is essentially a command that only that quantity may be taken, emitted, or used. Making the quota tradable means that the locus of control for allocation and business decisionmaking purposes shifts to the industry or other units, such as public utilities and municipalities.[2] If implemented astutely, members of the industry involved can be given a much greater sense of ownership of the resources management strategy being pursued than is possible with a pure command-and-control regulatory regime.

---

1. Pareto efficiency, as constrained by the regulatory system, is achieved because participants trade voluntarily.

2. The terms industry and community are used loosely to cover a broad range of possible actors, although the importance of a more precise definition is recognized.

One of the major political attractions of market-based property rights systems is that, like pure command-and-control or local-level regulations, they may be able to deliver an ecological objective, but unlike the others they transfer difficult resource allocation decisions to the marketplace. This means that administrators only are asked to set the strategic direction of policy and not to choose among competing resources users. Depending somewhat on how they are designed, they force administrators to take a strategic and anticipatory approach to management. Commitments, once made, cannot be easily revised, and opportunities to make special exceptions and provide political favors are lessened by the fact that the commitments must apply consistently.

An added advantage is that market-based property rights systems do not involve taxes and can even increase individual and community wealth. Thus, for example, individual transferable quotas (ITQs) in fisheries are intended to help capture economic rent that is otherwise dissipated in open-access or other property regimes with less exclusive and well-defined rights. Although there has been an increase in the use of market approaches in forest, fishing, grazing, pollution control, and other systems, this increase has been slow and halting. In practice, few policymakers have been prepared to adopt them. In our opinion, the reasons for this reluctance are closely aligned with failure to adequately build features promoting resilience, stewardship, and equity into recommendations for adoption. From an administrator's perspective, many of the systems proposed, because of their simplicity, appear too prone to failure. Perhaps this is because many of the people who advocate the addition of market mechanisms to regulatory systems do not know or wish to reveal how hard the transition can be and what social and economic consequences will emerge.

We also perceive that the case for market-based approaches has been presented thus far from an inappropriately narrow perspective, that of economic efficiency. Rather than focus on efficiency, we emphasize the capacity of such systems to enable administrators to deliver multipolicy objectives at lower cost and with confidence, less risk, and more freedom from political interference.

Fundamental Design Guidelines

Value

Because market-based property rights systems rely on the incentive of guided self-interest more than command-and-control systems do, their effectiveness is a function of the value of the tradable rights. Rights to fish, graze animals, cut trees, or dump pollutants into waters or the air, become commodities. Accordingly, value is a key feature of design and it can be increased by making the rights:

- Transferable as much as possible so that opportunities to profit from the aspirations of others are maximized.

- Mortgageable and bankable with security. The security should be equivalent to that given to a land title; rights and any conditions that attach to them should be recorded on a central register, which would be the only way to complete any dealing associated with the right.

- Divisible or separable as much as possible so that the right is easily divided into its components and/or sold in small as well as large quantities. Irrigation rights, for example, will be more valuable if they are not tied to a specific land parcel and can be moved from agricultural to urban sectors. Heavy metal emission rights will be more valuable if mercury rights can be separated from chromium emission rights.

Property rights are best thought of as bundles of rights, and one of the "sticks" in the bundle is whether or not changes in the value of the rights, because of changes in regulations, may be compensable. Individual transferable quota (ITQ) systems in fisheries typically do not have formal compensable renewal rights; rather, participants rely on the likelihood that courts will accept their claims to perpetual property rights against attempts by government agencies to make changes because of unforeseen circumstances, as shown vividly in the New Zealand ITQ case, when the species orange roughy was found to be far more vulnerable to overfishing than suspected (Major 1994; Monk and Hewison 1994).

Partly because of what happened in New Zealand, the governments of the United States and Canada have been wary of creating common pool resources property rights that allow holders to claim compensation for changes in government regulatory policies. One technique is to define rights as "privileges" and to specify the condition that the government may make changes in the system at any time. This practice works against the role of privatized or individual property rights in giving the holder a stake in the long-term, and also can make it difficult to make rights mortgageable and bankable.

However, the New South Wales fishery management system, recently approved in Australia (Young 1995), includes compensability. An advantage of making any change in permitted use subject to compensation is that it may enhance the accountability of administrators, who typically retain roles in determining allowable catches, harvests, or emissions, as well as in monitoring, enforcing, and other functions. It forces administrators to take a strategic approach, as opposed to an ad hoc, incremental approach. Currently. governments are wary of creating such property rights systems because of the possibility of costly lawsuits, but the payoffs from increased accountability can be worth the risks.

More generally, because market-based property rights systems are so new, there is very little common law or experience for guidance, and thus questions that bear upon expectations and compensation are more safely handled by explicit contractual agreements. Depending on the nature of those agreements, a marketable property rights system has the potential of affecting the distribution and locus of responsibility.

Value can be increased also by using dual property rights systems that split annual allocations, or use rights, from the underlying right to receive future allocations. This enables annual rights to be traded (at the margin) without influencing investment security, mortgage, and liability arrangements. In a new fishery share system being introduced in the Australian state of New South Wales (Young 1995), the long-term property rights—fishery shares—are held separately from the yearly allocation, so that the latter may be transferred without having to transfer or sublease the entire property right. This is designed to provide both security over long-term rights, believed important to developing a sense of stewardship, and adaptiveness to changing circumstances.

Similar systems are envisioned for emissions permit trading systems in Canada (Godby and others 1995). Otherwise, in fisheries at least, this approach is very novel. Subleasing is common in the well-known New Zealand ITQ system, but rights under this system cannot be mortgaged. A de facto analog, cast as "temporary" versus "permanent" transfer, exists in the surf clam and ocean quahog (hereafter "sea clam") ITQ fishery in the United States and the under 65-foot mobile gear fishery for cod, haddock, and pollock in Atlantic Canada (hereafter "Canadian ITQ fishery") (McCay 1994b; Apostle, McCay, and Mikalsen 1994; O'Boyle, Annand, and Brander 1994).

Equity

Notions of equity vary from culture to culture, community to community, and profession to profession. One pragmatic approach is to search for overlapping consensus principles among the many notions of equity that exist (Rawls 1987; Young 1992). For Western industrialized nations and their rural and urban communities, overlapping consensus about equity is likely to support the following equity-based design principles:

- Prevent the aggregation of rights to a select few without compensation of those disaffected at both the industry and community level, or at least slow the rate of change so that communities have time to adjust;

- Distribute risk burdens so that the worst off are less exposed than those who stand to profit from the new system;

- Support structures that favor employees and others disadvantaged by the aggregation of power often associated with the introduction of market-based property rights;

- Reduce incentives to adopt monopolistic and oligopolistic practices; and

- Establish mechanisms that provide a return to local communities.

Some market-based property rights systems have had inequitable consequences in the above terms. In Iceland, for example, ITQs for cod have caused control of the industry to shift to fewer large operators, some of whom have shifted their processing factories to the capital city or the southern coast (Pálsson and Helgason 1995). The result is greater profit for the factory owners but less income for those who remain in the towns that used to process cod. As a result, some coastal towns and regions have lost fishing and fish processing jobs.

Comparatively recent ITQ systems in the United States and Canada have also caused very rapid decline in boats and jobs in the relevant fisheries. The U.S. surf clam and ocean quahog fishery entered an ITQ regime in 1990; two years later, only 53 percent of the vessels and about two-thirds of the crew were still engaged in the fishery (McCay and Creed 1994a, 1994b). Ownership of ITQs and vessels became much more concentrated than before as owners economized by consolidating harvesting on fewer vessels, and many marginal or small-scale firms sold out. The Canadian under-65-foot dragger fleet began fishing within an ITQ system for cod, haddock, and pollock in 1990. By the end of 1993, there were about half as many vessels fishing for those species as there had been in 1990 (Liew 1995), and ownership of ITQs became more concentrated in fewer communities and fewer hands despite programmatic measures to reduce consolidation processes (Apostle, McCay, and Mikalsen 1994; Creed, Apostle, and McCay 1994).

To a large extent, the above problems are "intended," in that ITQs, like other market-based property rights resources management systems, are usually designed for economic efficiency, or to reduce inefficiencies created by command-and-control regulation, as well as a lessened administrative burden. Both goals are readily satisfied by reductions in numbers of firms, individuals, jobs, and so forth, particularly when the ecological systems are under stress because of over-use. The goal of economic efficiency can clash with goals such as maintaining rural communities, a major reason for reluctance to develop full-fledged market-based property rights systems. (See Crowley and Palsson 1992 for the Canadian situation.) Incorporating design principles that would prevent or minimize such effects can only be achieved by increasing administrative costs and, in most cases, reducing economic efficiency, defined according to the market's (Pareto) view of equity.

The above can be achieved only by increasing administrative costs and, in most cases, reducing economic efficiency, defined according to the market's (Pareto) view of equity. Nevertheless, because social concerns about equity are often so strong, market-based property rights systems have been implemented with special features that seek to preserve community perceptions of equity, at least during the initial period of structural adjustment. Some of these systems are discussed below. It needs to be recognized, however, that over time many of these equity preservation measures lose their effectiveness and may even be abandoned as operators find innovative means to get around the restrictions.

Limits on Holding

One mechanism used to achieve more equitable outcomes is to place a limit on the maximum size of a holding that may be held by one party. It is usually implemented by requiring all transfers to be approved and by legislating that permission may be refused only when aggregation limits are exceeded. In many cases, the limits are more restrictive than those required to comply with antitrust laws. An example is the Canadian mobile gear ITQ system, where no one can hold more than 2 percent of the total quota for a given species (O'Boyle, Annand, and Brander 1994; Apostle, McCay, and Mikalsen 1994).

Similarly, to reduce the possibility of monopoly formation, New South Wales kangaroo wholesalers are prevented from owning more than 75 percent of the processing rights in one area (Young 1992). In contrast, the U.S. sea clam fishery ITQ system was designed with no such restriction, relying on federal antitrust laws.

Limits on holdings are notoriously easy to circumvent. They often can be avoided by subleasing rights and investing through third parties. Nonetheless, they can be viewed as extremely important, at least as symbolic expressions of the importance of an equitable distribution of ownership.

Protecting Socially Valued Groups and Life-styles

Transferability can be restricted to certain classes of people in order to achieve social goals, including protecting small businesses or families from corporate takeover. In the Canadian ITQ fishery, for example, only bona fide fish harvesters are allowed to hold quotas, reflecting concern that fish buyers would buy up ITQs, placing fishermen at a bargaining disadvantage. The measure reflected a more broadly applied policy of separating processors from ownership of fishing vessels, expressing the value of owner-operator small firms in the fish harvesting sector. Similar rules for similar reasons apply to the new ITQ fisheries for halibut and sablefish in the North Pacific (Berman and Leask 1994). However, in the U.S. ITQ fishery for sea clams, anyone can hold a quota, but foreign nationals are not allowed to own vessels used in the fishery. This is a pre-existing general protectionist law.

Distribution of Control Between Labor and Capital

A related issue concerns vertical integration and the position of labor in the allocation and trade of property rights. In a fishery, for example, processors are likely to want to acquire a direct stake in ITQs in order to maintain consistent supply, thereby reducing the risks of temporal variability and product perishability. This may clash with vessel owners' wishes to maintain control of ITQ to maintain a bargaining position, or for other reasons, as well as with their concern about the effects of "absentee ownership."

Generally, output control systems transfer power to rights holders and reduce the negotiating power of those who work for them. Fishery ITQ systems typically award the initial allocation of shares to owners of productive capital; it is usually difficult for others to acquire shares because of the large value immediately created. Where payment is through shares of the catch, the sharing formula often changes, reflecting the shift in power, and there may be a movement toward payment in wages rather than shares.

The extent to which workers are encouraged to participate in the share market is a relatively unexplored policy and design issue. The prop-erty rights system can be divided so that power is distributed amongst producers, workers, and processors. Thus, to shoot and sell a kangaroo in New South Wales, shooters must obtain a royalty tag, plus an occupiers tag from the land holder, and wholesalers must obtain a restricted processing license. To be effective, however, it is critical that rights of both workers and owners are limited, so that each party is forced to negotiate the best way to share the economic rent embodied in the system. Before contemplating the addition of such attributes to a system, it needs to be recognized that one consequence is a reduced incentive for the principal right holder to innovate. Moreover, owners can often find a means to destroy much of the worker's initial power. The most common mechanism is to force workers to enter into contracts that effectively eliminate or even worsen their initial negotiating position.

Competing Rights of Native Peoples.

One consequence of creating commodities in rights to fish has been the activation of claims of native peoples to fishing rights or the right to revenue from fisheries. The lesson was costly for New Zealand, which was first to embrace ITQs in fisheries as a major policy but later had to compensate commercial fishermen for parts of the annual quota that had to be allocated to the Maori nation (Major 1994). In Alaska, similar claims exist, even for offshore fisheries never directly relevant to native communities. The Community Development Quota program for the species pollock was created to bring native communities into the fisheries allocation system, allowing them to lease fishing rights in exchange for revenues (Ginter 1995). Similar issues may be found in the position of developing nations with respect to tradable permits for sulfur and other pollutants.

Slowing The Rate of Structural Adjustment.

The transition to a market-based property rights system can be very difficult, calling for measures to slow the process. One approach is to allow temporary (within season) transfers of rights but not permanent transfers. In Australia, for example, irrigation rights were first made transferable on a temporary basis and limited to the immediate area so that local businesses would not be adversely affected. In the Icelandic and Canadian fisheries, in the early years of market-based property rights management, the permanent shares allotted to vessel owners could not be transferred, but the yearly allocations of catch quotas could (Pálsson and Helgason 1995; Crowley and Palsson 1992). Usually, however, an underground system of permanent transfers quickly evolves, and industry begins to pressure government to change the system.

Redistributing Adjustment Cost Burden

Often participants, who see a need for a new system, are reluctant to share in the cost of transition to a new system because of free-riding or uncertainty. Structures can be devised that force a subset of participants to start the process and exempt others. Thus, under the 1992 Global Change Convention, developing countries are required only to monitor carbon dioxide and other greenhouse gas emissions rather than to reduce those emissions. Similarly, under the Canadian fishery ITQ program, smaller-scale fishers using fixed gear were exempted, and mobile gear fishers were given the option of staying in a competitive fishery focused on another species, with a by-catch for the regulated species (O'Boyle, Annand, and Brander 1994).

This approach can also make it much easier to set up a new system and avoid high administrative and enforcement costs. Icelandic fishers who catch less than 6 tons of cod per annum do not have an ITQ. Canadian fishers who use fixed gear (gill nets and long lines) as opposed to mobile gear (drag nets and seines) do not have ITQs. Under Los Angeles' RECLAIM project for tradable emissions permits, firms that emit less than 4 tons of SO_x or NO_x per annum are managed under a non-market regulatory system (Robinson 1993). Young (1995) has proposed that households be excluded from a tradable sewage waste pollution scheme in Melbourne.

Small Numbers and Zero Revenue Auctions

Lowering administrative and enforcement costs by excluding large numbers of small-scale participants from the plan worsens the problem of small numbers found in many market-based property rights systems. A fishery, for example, may involve fewer than fifty boats and a handful of processing factories; a forest, one or two saw

mills. A stream may be polluted from only ten town sewage plants. In such an environment, the conditions necessary for an effective market do not exist. Structural rigidities are common and oligopolies and monopolies emerge.

Mechanisms can be introduced to deepen the market and give it the characteristics of one that has many players, even though the number that play may be few. One mechanism is to hold all rights centrally and auction them on a regular basis. Another, worthy of more attention, is the zero revenue auction. Zero revenue markets were first introduced in the United States, where they are used to improve air pollution rights systems. They require the rights holders to regularly return a proportion of their holdings to an auction, or tender pool, for reallocation. At the auction, each rights holder is given a first right of refusal. The rights holder is forced to choose between the highest offered price and buying it back. If bought back, no money changes hands, hence the term "zero revenue." It is, essentially, a zero-sum game, designed to force all actual and aspiring participants to evaluate all options in a transparent manner.

Zero revenue auctions guarantee each person, at a price, a periodic opportunity to acquire additional rights and enter the industry. They also reduce barriers to entry and, hence, opportunities to form monopolies and oligopolies. They make the value of the rights transparent and, hence, the industry's assessment of the future value of the rights system. In addition, they speed adjustment by forcing all rights users to value their rights and periodically decide whether or not they should sell or use them. Zero revenue auctions also give workers an opportunity to invest in "their" industry. The down side is that they can only be used for rights that can be allocated in an a-spatial manner. They are, however, well suited to water resources, fisheries, and pollutants in water, air ways, and some forests.

Community Interests

One of the main criticisms of many market-based property rights schemes is that they appear to involve privatization of resources owned by the larger community. From an equity position, it can be argued that at least some of the economic rent embodied in the system should return to the community. Mechanisms used to do this range from simply leaving this challenge to the taxation system and normal political processes, through charges on gross revenue, to establishing a mechanism that guarantees a direct return to the community.

A community return has been proposed for the New South Wales fishing industry and is used in certain Canadian forests (Young 1995; 1993a). The community return system operates by requiring rights holders to surrender part of their holdings to a process that resembles a zero revenue auction, except that at least part of the revenue received is returned to the community. Such a mechanism can be operated at a community level so that the rents go directly to a community or pass to central government. (Note that the term "community" is used in very general terms, as a unit of organization somewhere between an individual or firm and the nation-state; it can mean a locally defined unit, such as a municipality or township, or a unit defined by an industry, such as ranchers in a region, or even a cooperative or corporate structure.)

Stewardship

Stewardship refers to the intentions and behaviors of resources users with respect to maintaining the productivity and ecological characteristics of a resource or ecosystem. Essentially, it is a measure of the degree to which resources users prefer potential long-term benefits to short-term, opportunistic gains. It pertains to individual behavior and motivations, and it also pertains to the capacity of individuals to engage in collective action for long-term benefits.

Resource Security and Privatization

In economic theory, which assumes that markets reflect social aspirations for a resource, the simplest way to achieve perfect stewardship is to give resources users exclusive rights to use a resource in perpetuity as private property. Long-term resource security maximizes the weight that self-interested individuals give to future considerations. In contrast, short-term arrangements, such as an annual license, give users little guarantee that they will benefit directly from conserving future productivity.

However, unfettered privatization is not a sufficient condition to ensure stewardship in dynamic living systems. As Colin Clark (1973) long ago showed, where the natural rate of increase is less than the discount rate, the optimal private strategy is to drive stocks to a level where either extinction occurs or the marginal cost of extraction equals the marginal value product. Even if rights to harvest whales were privatized or granted to a maximizing sole owner (Scott 1955), it is likely that, without intervention, several species now would be extinct.

The question, then, is how to specify rights to maximize the incentive for resources stewardship. The options are many and choices are complex. A general rule, reflected in the very notion of market-based property rights, is to mimic attributes found in private property. One does not own the fish, but one may own a right to take a specified share of the allowable catch of fish. One does not own the atmosphere or stratosphere, but one may own and trade a share of the volume of sulfur that society will allow into the atmosphere.

Generally, a strong sense of stewardship can be built into a market-based property rights system by building institutional mechanisms that:

- limit opportunities to use a resource to those who own it (exclusive access rights, and a provision that entry can be achieved only by buying that right from an existing user)

- reduce the number of people who have a direct interest in a specific part of the resource (so, for example, a logging company that has exclusive rights to a forest area is more likely to avoid degrading future production potential than one that shares rights to the timber in a forest with ten other companies)[3]

- reduce the number of factors that are external to the private incentive structures faced by users

- build feedbacks into the system so that rights holders face aggregate incentives that pro-

---

3. Area rights, however, may induce a company to adopt silvicultural and logging practices that maximize expected timber yield. In some cases, such as when the forest contains valued wildlife, the outcome may be suboptimal.

mote stewardship in a resilient manner and, in particular, that give them a strong incentive to maintain system credibility and solve problems as soon as they arise

We discuss next alternative allocation methods, the institutional mechanisms that change the incentives faced by resources users, and then more direct measures that tend to be associated with rewards and penalties.

Sharing the Cake

Two general ways to allocate resources rights are to give exclusive areas to separate people and to give people a transferable share of the future revenue stream. For most natural resources, which retain a common-pool element in the sense that there is extractability, the share model is appropriate. Shares can be issued in their own right or allocated via quasi-mechanisms, such as an individual transferable quota, gear unit, or permit. A share-based approach that guarantees each participant a proportion of the potential revenue stream, based upon the number of shares held, retains the flexibility necessary to add resilience to the model and to adjust to new circumstances and new information. Share-based models are appropriate for both input-control systems, output-control systems, and mixed input-output control systems (Young 1995, Townsend and Pooley 1995).

Share models also offer governments an economically safe way to alter or remove a right without having to compensate for mismanagement. In essence, this is what a private corporation does. It promises to share the profits according to the number of shares held, but uses a series of separate institutional processes to determine how large those profits will be. Great care must be used whenever quasi-share models are introduced, as they are not easily revised. When this option is pursued, we recommend that the right be issued as a proportional right and never as an absolute quantity, a lesson learned the hard way by the government of New Zealand, where fixed tonnage quotas of fish were issued and subsequently found to be unsustainable. Adjustment to a proportional quota system cost the New Zealand government millions in compensation (Major 1994).

Interim Allocation Models

A problem with many share-based systems is that the necessary information is scarce, unreliable, and costly to obtain. Interim systems can be put in place to generate the necessary data while accomplishing some management goals, but care must be taken to ensure that these interim arrangements do not worsen the problems. For example, in air pollution management, firms within the United States moved first to a "bubble" arrangement, whereby they traded emissions permits within their own plants and then between adjoining plants, eventually to the entire airshed. If not grandfathered at the start, however, allocation would need to be made on the assumption that each firm uses the best available technology. Otherwise, they have an incentive to pollute in order to obtain a larger allocation. Fishing has similar problems: it has become common for fishers to "fish for quota" in anticipation of the creation of market-based property rights management systems where initial allocations are made on the basis of historical performance.

Devolving Control and Responsibility

Changing the values and incentives for stewardship is often a challenge for collective action and organizational reform. As adverse experience with top-down models of management accumulates, more attention is given to the involvement of resources users and how the involvement is structured (Jentoft and McCay 1995). Bottom-up and comanagement models have the potential of restructuring incentives for groups of people to solve their own problems.

One example comes from Australia. Faced with widespread land degradation, the federal government has created a "landcare" program that enables community groups to employ professional facilitators. Because such people can only be employed by local groups, the process is bottom-up and is designed to change social attitudes regarding land and, in particular, to develop peer group pressure mechanisms that discourage resources degradation. Such resources care movements could easily be extended to other resources, such as fisheries and forests, and used to bring congruence between social and private incentives.

Another mechanism is found in the New South Wales fishery that issues renewable ten-year shares in each fishery with attached usage conditions for each share. Within nested constraints set by state-wide policy, fishers can prepare their own look-up tables that specify the relationship between shares and boat length, for example, and which species should be put under quota. Subject to agreement, they can also vary aggregation limits and divide the fishery into two parts (Young 1995).

The comanagement movement for fisheries and watersheds and forests in North America is another example (Pinkerton 1994; Felt and others, forthcoming). Significantly, such processes offer an opportunity to develop detailed programs that, working through local people, address spatial detail in a manner impossible for regional or national administrators. Where a resource is spatially heterogeneous, it seems reasonable to support a decentralized system in which local institutional arrangements are primary. The following hypothesis also seems appropriate: the greater the control that local people have over their own destiny, the greater the probability there is of stewardship.

At issue and open to empirical testing is whether the use of market-based property rights as a management tool reduces or enhances this sense of control. The potential for linking market-based property rights with such restructuring of authority and responsibility has been suggested (Scott 1993) and shown in the ability of a comanaging body in a Canadian ITQ fishery to gain acceptance of more selective fishing gear and practices in that industry (Creed, Apostle, and McCay 1994; Apostle, McCay, and Mikalsen 1994).

On the other hand, there are also incentives to "highgrade" (discard all but the most valuable species or ages and sizes) and, more generally, to seize opportunities to cheat. These incentives may be anticipated by careful specification of a right. Where fishers can maximize profits by throwing back low value fish, with the consequence that a resource is wasted and information necessary to monitor populations with precision is lost, size quotas and special pricing arrangements can be introduced. In New South Wales, for example, low- grade and over-quota fish can be landed and sold, providing that 75 percent of the revenue received is surrendered.

A significant variable, important to the design of the systems and relevant in this context, is whether the market-based rights regime encompasses the natural reality of the resources. If, as is the case in the Canadian ITQ fishery, a large percentage of the allowable catch is taken by fishers outside the ITQ system (the local fixed gear fleet, a Canadian offshore fishery, and foreign fishing fleets working outside 200 miles), then it becomes difficult to justify one's own conservationist behavior.

Positive Incentives for Stewardship

A mechanism that should improve compliance with conservation rules is one that designs formal renewal of rights into the market-based property rights system. The guarantee of a renewal of rights can be limited to those who comply with the conditions and obligations that attach to a right. This "sustainability guarantee" (Young 1992) also creates an incentive for users to solve problems and self-monitor so that they can demonstrate compliance. A sustainability guarantee also enables administrators to reduce the incentive for financiers to force resources users to run down an asset in order to meet short term financial commitments.

Administrative charges can also be used to encourage stewardship by reducing the incentive for people to falsify records. One simple example of this is the separation of annual entitlements from long-term rights, so that resources users can trade their short-term entitlements without affecting their long-term interests. By issuing tags for sea clams in the United States and for kangaroos in Australia, for example, the cost of compliance is kept low. The tags follow the harvest from vessel to processor or consumer, making it relatively easy to verify compliance.

Negative Incentives

The more traditional way to bring congruence between stewardship and private incentives is to develop a complex web of penalty structures that discourages people from operating outside the bundle of rights and obligations they hold. Mechanisms used to do this include:

- Placing the onus on resources users to monitor and prove compliance (require that fishers do paperwork before off-loading);

- Making noncompliance a very transparent and highly visible activity, so that the degree of peer group pressure for compliance is high (which is very effective in international forums);

- Specifying rights on a proportional share basis, so that the industry recognizes that the more it can reduce the size of the black market the more the value of its rights will increase;

- Requiring users to hold a minimum number of shares and making these shares liable for forfeiture (the rights portfolio then operates in a manner similar to an environmental bond);

- Specifying fines at replacement cost;

- Developing a consistent set of rights for all.

One of the major advantages of market-based property rights to common-pool resources is that it becomes easier to assign not only rights but also penalties and hence responsibilities. With clear assignment of property rights, rights holders can be assigned their fair share of enforcement costs, as is done in the Canadian ITQ fisheries. Moreover, penalties for infringements of the rules can be more effective where permits have marketable value. In addition, the costs of information can also be more readily borne by rights holders (see Scott 1993). In one of the Canadian ITQ fisheries, the privileged class of exclusive rights holders has gone one step further to provide much of the funding required for research by government professionals.

The environmental bond analogy would make the rights holder's shares subject to forfeiture (Young 1995). It requires that each participant in the system holds, or is able to get access to, a substantial number of shares. (In the dual property rights system, these are the more secure, longer-term shares in the fishery or other activity, as opposed to specific allotments.) For example, if fishers have obtained allotments of, say, 300 tons by leasing or other means, at least 100 tons must be either in their "right," or their own shares, or lodged by someone else. Then, if they breach the system, these shares as well as the fishers' own may be subject to forfeiture. All fines are specified in terms of the number of shares that are lost. This means that all people interested in the investment, including bankers, have a strong interest in ensuring compliance with conditions that attach to the right. A related approach is used in the U.S. sea clam ITQ system: the owner of the shares—which could be a bank—is liable for infractions on the part of anyone using those shares to fish, including hired captains and crew and lessees.

Resilience

In ecology, resilience refers to the capacity of a disturbed ecosystem to maintain or restore its key structures and processes. Adapted to include socioeconomic considerations, resilience refers to the capacity of an institutional system to continue to function as expected in the face of new and different circumstances. The characteristics sought are the capacity to continue to achieve social objectives in the light of new prices and technology, allow and encourage structural change and innovation, permit new knowledge to emerge, and enable the system to evolve as these characteristics occur.

Experience would suggest that market-based property rights systems that are not designed to keep pace with changes in technology and social objectives eventually break down and require a major review. In Australia, for example, it has been necessary to review pastoral leases and change the conditions under which they are managed approximately every twenty years. The key theme is the search for a system that manages change without compromising efficiency, equity, and resources stewardship. A prime indicator of success is the degree to which the modifications made reduce the value of the right.

Mixing Term and Perpetual Rights

Resilience can be maximized by issuing rights for a fixed period and then developing an institutional mechanism to review the conditions that attach to the rights. This respects the fact that industry will be more efficient if it is protected from sudden and unexpected changes in government attitudes and social objectives. A framework for a system that achieves this is set out in Figure 7–1.

Resilience can be built into a market-based property rights system at a minimum loss in value by:

- Guaranteeing that the bundle of entitlements, obligations, and conditions will not change for a fixed term;

- Setting the term so that it is longer than the time period over which most investments are written off; this is largely a function of the discount rate. Terms longer than ten to fifteen years are difficult to justify;

- Guaranteeing shareholders the periodic and perpetual right to receive the offer of a replacement right well before their current right expires;

- Organizing a periodic review of the entitlements, obligations, and conditions that attach to the right;

- Limiting the conditions and obligations, at the periodic review, that can be changed without payment of compensation;

- Giving shareholders, when they are dissatisfied with offers made following the review, the option to remain under existing conditions until the term expires.

In short, any market-based property rights system will benefit from a structure that facilitates an adaptive approach to management. Many existing systems do not incorporate such a formal review process. The RECLAIM project in Los Angeles, for example, assumes that the NO_x reductions planned for 2025 will be appropriate and achievable. ITQ systems in fisheries typically do not have formal compensable renewal rights. Instead, participants rely on the likelihood that courts will accept their claims to perpetual property rights against attempts by government agencies to make changes owing to unforeseen circumstances, as shown vividly in the New Zealand ITQ case, when the species orange roughy was found to be far more vulnerable to overfishing than suspected (Major 1994; Monk and Hewison 1994).

Unfortunately, review processes create uncertainty that diminishes value and generally discourages investment and, as discussed below, stewardship. The challenge, then, is to design the review process so that its likely outcomes are as predictable as possible and, perhaps more important, so that it is seen to be as reasonable as possible. Regular reviews force anticipatory planning and strategic management. The institutional process is one of negotiated rule making. Reviews can be made more effective by:

- Mandating a review "sunset" so that, if the issue can not be resolved within a fixed period, all rights are automatically extended for a further term (so that the incentive to come to an agreement is greater than to filibuster);

- Appointing industry and community representatives to the review panel;

- Using facilitators to assist in the process;

- Conducting the review in a transparent manner;

- Synchronizing reviews within a region and rotating the reviews through regions, so that all can prepare well in advance and watch other regions for indicators of the direction and likely extent of change.

Between review periods, contingency plans remain necessary to deal with unexpected and unanticipated crises. To reduce uncertainty, predetermined triggers should be specified within the conditions that attach to the rights system. For equity reasons and also to encourage efficient investment, when a crisis develops, unused entitlements should not be taken from a rights holder without compensation. In the Canadian ITQ fishery, in 1994, the government decided in mid-season to close fishing because of changes in stock assessments, but provided no compensation for ITQ holders. This jeopardized continuation of the regime and sharply devalued ITQ rights. Note, also, that some parts of the rights package can be specified separately. Fish quotas, for example, can be determined by separate quota setting committees, which can meet as and when necessary.

Resilience is also encouraged by making the bundle of rights as separable and decomposable as possible. This maximizes opportunities to adjust any part of the system, as objectives, technology, or information about system performance change, and minimizes the extent of disruption to other parts of the system. In the case of emission rights for the disposal of trade waste, for example, it may prove beneficial to eventually allow substitution of chromium for nickel into an estuary or other marine ecosystem. This is facilitated easily if the initial specification gives each person a share of all heavy metal disposal rights, but is more difficult if separate rights are allocated to nickel and chromium.

Conclusions and Policy Implications: Ecology, Markets, and Corporate Structures

Earlier in this chapter, we listed the ways that the value of market-based allocations may be enhanced. Providing that the right is divisible and transferable, it is our judgment that the system also is likely to have greatest value if rights are specified in ways that most closely track the ecosystem being exploited and are as close as possible to the action that causes the problem. One example of the importance of being close to the action concerns systems for reducing the emission of chlorofluorocarbons (CFCs) under the Vienna Convention and Montreal Protocol for protecting the ozone layer. Where tradable rights are involved, they would appear to be more cost effectively administered if allocated to CFC manufacturers rather than to people who buy spray cans, air conditioners, and other products that contain CFCs.

A key and difficult consideration is how to specify and condition the bundle of rights in any system. A relatively new innovation now implemented in the New South Wales fishing industry (Young 1995) is the notion of nesting rights within a corporate structure. As Townsend and Pooley (1995) have argued, this is arguably a superior alternative to reliance on either command-and-control or communal systems of governance, in the context of commercial and globalized economies.

As far as possible, the rights system should begin by specifying the ecosystem that is to be managed. In the first instance, the resource, which might be a fishery or a waste stream, is defined as a legal entity and then each rights holder is issued a proportional interest in that entity. In effect, the structure mimics the shares that a person might hold in a limited liability company (Townsend and Pooley 1995). For global commons problems, such as ozone depletion or climate warming, this might mean that, at the national level, policy should specify rights to the ecological functions performed by the stratosphere. Emission rights, or tradable obligations to reduce emissions, would be nested within that framework.

The value of a right can be maximized by first granting each rights holder a perpetual share in the resource, and then using a nested framework within this structure to define and make operational the rights, obligations, and conditions that attach to the right. Security and, hence, value are maximized by devising these proportional shares so that each share holder has a claim to all windfall gains (as well as risks of loss or cutback) that may emerge. This framework preserves many of the options necessary to build resilience, stewardship, and equity into the rights system.

Great care must be taken in specifying the nature of the rights to be given, especially where there is a high degree of risk and uncertainty. The ITQs used in fisheries are part of management regimes based on the notion that the total allowable catch, from which the separate ITQs are proportionally derived, is at a level known as "maximum sustainable yield" (or "optimum yield"; see Larkin 1977). Recent experience, however, suggests that the approach is wrong for many fisheries, because they take place within ecological systems better described as chaotic, with complex interdependencies (Wilson and others 1990). Switching between ecological states is both likely and unpredictable.

Within such fisheries, a rights system based on shares in gear and boats, rather than an allowable catch based on estimates of levels of fishing mortality required to maintain a sustainable yield, may be more effective. Whether any market-based system involving individual property rights is appropriate to this ecological reality is very contentious, but it is arguable that well-designed market-based rights systems can provide the flexibility and adaptability that often is lacking in top-down systems.

The problem of uncertainty and the risk of chaotic behavior characteristic of many ecosystems lends further support to the need for nested and decentralized governance regimes. One of the most difficult decisions in designing any system is to decide where the loci of control should be located and how they should be nested. Some regimes, such as the ITQ systems of Iceland, New Zealand, and elsewhere, are highly centralized within government agencies, but others, such as traditional grazing systems used by Masaii pastoralists, are very decentralized. A resources management system wholly based on market regulation would be another example of extreme decentralization; that is hypothetical, however, because government agencies exercise their roles as representatives of the public trust.

A key issue with any resource is the state of scientific knowledge about the ecosystem being exploited. Where ecosystem performance is predictable, centralized control is possible. Where system performance is unpredictable, fully centralized control is likely to be inefficient and inequitable and likely to encourage resource depletion. In such situations, the most efficient and equitable system is usually one that empowers those who depend upon the system to set and periodically revise the conditions that attach to a resource right. In the case of a fishery, for example, it may be more effective to empower fishers to determine catch rules and for central government to (a) define the fishery and ensure that its potential is not eroded by inequitable processes, (b) record which rights to the fishery are shared and define how those rights may be changed and exchanged, and (c) protect the interests of those not involved directly in catching fish. This is the way most corporations operate. The rights of a corporation are protected by a range of mechanisms and societal institutions; subject to rules that protect wider community interests, a corporation's directors, shareholders, and workers ideally collectively determine how its rights are exercised.

Although cursory and selective in the points addressed and evidence presented, we have covered a broad field concerning market-based property rights for the management of renewable, but vulnerable, natural systems. Recognizing the importance of efficiency as a criterion for such management regimes, we have focused on the criteria of equity, resiliency, and stewardship, offering suggestions about ways these, too, can be built into the design of adaptive and flexible management regimes.

Bibliography

Apostle, R., B. McCay, and K. Mikalsen. 1994. "Deregulation Through Privatization? The Politics of Rights-Based Fishing in Atlantic Canada and Norway." Paper presented at the annual meeting of the American Fisheries Society, Halifax, Nova Scotia, Canada, August 21–25.

Berman, M., and L. Leask. 1994. "On the Eve of IFQs: Fishing for Alaska's Halibut and Sablefish." *Alaska Review of Social and Economic Conditions,* Institute of Social and Economic Research, University of Alaska, Anchorage 29(2):1–20.

Clark, C. 1973. "The Economics of Over-Exploitation." *Science* 181:630–34.

Creed, C., R. Apostle, and B. McCay. 1994. "ITQs from a Community Perspective." Paper presented at annual meetings of the American Fisheries Society, Halifax, Nova Scotia, Canada, August 21–25.

Crowley, R. W., and H. Palsson. 1992. "Rights-Based Fisheries Management in Canada." *Marine Resource Economics* 7:1–21.

Gatewood, John. Personal communication at Beijer Workshop, Rutgers University, New Brunswick, New Jersey, March 1944.

Ginter, J. 1995. "The Alaska Community Development Quota Program." Paper presented at the Fifth Common Property Conference, The International Association for the Study of Common Property, Bodo, Norway, May 24–28.

Godby, R., S. Mestelman, R. A. Muller, and D. Welland. 1995. "Emissions Trading with Shares and Coupons when Control over Discharges is Uncertain." Paper presented at the Fifth Common Property Conference, The International Association for the Study of Common Property, Bodo, Norway, May 24–28.

Jentoft, S., and B. McCay. 1995. "User Participation in Fisheries Management: Lessons Drawn from International Experiences." *Marine Policy* 19(3):227–46.

Larkin, P. 1977. "An Epitaph for the Concept of Maximum Sustained Yield." *Transactions of the American Fisheries Society* 106(1):1–11.

Liew, D. 1995. "Selected Statistics of the Scotia Fundy Groundfish ITQ Fleet." Presented to the *IQ* Committee, Program Coordination & Economics Branch, Canada Department of Fisheries and Oceans, Scotia Fundy Region, February 10.

Major, P. 1994. "Individual Transferable Quotas and Quota Management Systems: A Perspective from the New Zealand Experience." In Karyn Gimbel, ed., *Limiting Access to Marine Fisheries: Keeping the Focus on Conservation* (pp. 98–106). Washington, D.C.: Center for Marine Conservation and World Wildlife Fund—US.

McCay, B. 1994a. "ITQ Case Study: Atlantic Surf Clam and Ocean Quahog Fishery." In Karyn Gimbel, ed., *Limiting Access to Marine Fisheries: Keeping the Focus on Conservation* (pp.75–97). Washington, D.C.: Center for Marine Conservation and World Wildlife Fund—US.

———. 1994b. "Privatization in Fisheries Management: Experiences in the U.S. and Canada." Paper presented at the Third Annual Ocean Governance Study Group Symposium, Lewes, Delaware, April 9–13.

———, and C. Creed. 1994a. "Social Impacts of ITQs in the Sea Clam Fishery." Final Report to the New Jersey Sea Grant College Program, New Jersey Marine Sciences Consortium, February.

———. 1994b. "Individual Transferable Quotas in Clams and Fish: A Comparative Analysis." Paper M.1994/T:15, 82nd Statutory Meeting, International Council for the Exploration of the Seas, St. John's, Newfoundland, Canada, September 22–30.

Monk, G., and G. Hewison. 1994. "A Brief Criticism of the New Zealand Quota Management System." In Karyn Gimbel, ed., *Limiting Access to Marine Fisheries: Keeping the Focus on Conservation* (pp. 107–19). Washington, D.C.: Center for Marine Conservation and World Wildlife Fund—US.

O'Boyle, R., C. Annand, and L. Brander. 1994. "Individual Quotas in the Scotian Shelf Groundfishery Off Nova Scotia, Canada." In Karyn Gimbel, ed., *Limiting Access to Marine Fisheries: Keeping the Focus on Conserva-* *tion*(pp. 152–68). Washington, D.C.: Center for Marine Conservation and World Wildlife Fund.

Pálsson, G., and A. Helgason. 1995. "Figuring Fish and Measuring Men: The Quota System in the Icelandic Cod Fishery." *Ocean and Coastal Management,* forthcoming.

Pinkerton, E. 1994. "Local Fisheries Co-management: A Review of International Experiences and their Implications for Salmon Management in British Columbia." *Canadian Journal of Fisheries and Aquatic Sciences* 51:1–17.

Rawls, J. 1987. "The Idea of Overlapping Consensus." *Oxford Journal of Legal Studies* 7(1):1–25.

Robinson, K. 1993. "The Regional Economic Impacts of Marketable Permit Programs: The Case of Los Angeles." In Kosobud, A. Testa, and A. Hanson, eds., *Cost Effective Control of Urban Smog* (pp. 166–88). Chicago: Federal Reserve Bank of Chicago.

Scott, A. 1993. "Obstacles to Fishery Self-Government." *Marine Resource Economics* 8:187–99.

———. 1955. "The Fishery: The Objectives of Sole Ownership." *Journal of Political Economy* 63:116–24.

Townsend, R., and S. Pooley. 1995. "A Proposal for Corporate Management of the Northwestern Hawaiian Islands Lobster Fishery." *Ocean and Coastal Management Journal,* forthcoming.

Wilson, J., R. Townsend, P. Kleban, S. McKay, and J. French. 1990. "Managing Unpredictable Resources: Traditional Policies Applied to Chaotic Populations." *Ocean & Shoreline Management* 13(3&4):179–97.

———. 1992. *Sustainable Investment and Resource Use; Equity, Environmental Integrity and Economic Efficiency.* Man and the Biosphere Series, Vol.9. Carnforth, United Kingdom: The Parthenon Publishing Group.

———. 1993a. "Opportunities for the Improvement of Wood Rights." CSIRO Division of Wildlife and Ecology Decision Support Systems Program Working Document, 92/2.

———. 1995. "The Design of Fishing-Right Systems—The NSW [New South Wales] Experience." *Ocean and Coastal Management,* forthcoming.

Figure 7–1: An Adaptive Property-Right System with Periodic Reviews

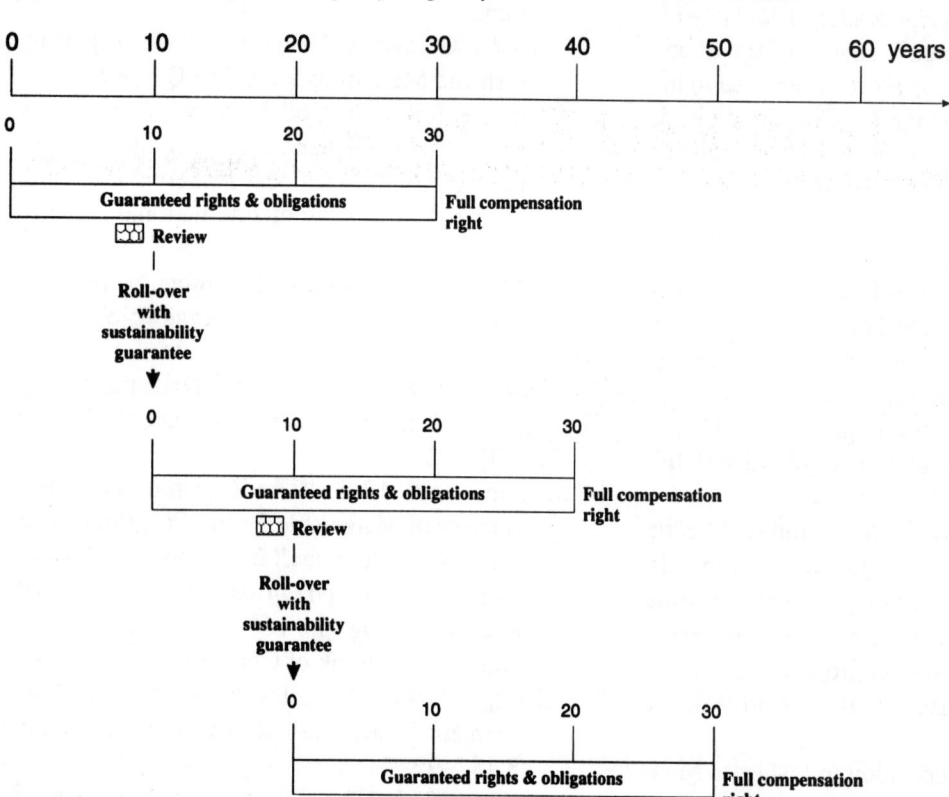

Traditional Knowledge

8

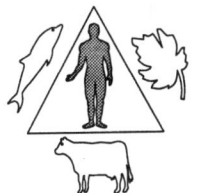

Analysis of Earth Summit Prescriptions on Incorporating Traditional Knowledge in Natural Resource Management

Biliana Cicin-Sain and Robert W. Knecht

Abstract

THE CHAPTER REVIEWS AND ASSESSES major developments at the international level which, in recent years, have emphasized the importance of incorporating systems of traditional knowledge into contemporary approaches to natural resources management.

The authors participated in a number of the pre-UNCED negotiations in 1991 and 1992, in the Earth Summit in 1992, and in several post-UNCED negotiations—most prominently the 1993, 1994, and 1995 substantive sessions of the Commission for Sustainable Development, the Global Conference on Sustainable Development of Small Island Developing States, and the Conference on Straddling Stocks and Highly Migratory Fish Stocks—as NGO representatives accredited to the United Nations Economic and Social Council (UN ECOSOC) on behalf of the International Ocean and Coastal Organization. Thanks are due to the Delaware Sea Grant College Program for its financial support of travel costs to participate in these meetings. Professor Cicin-Sain thanks the Beijer International Institute for Ecological Economics for its invitation to participate in two symposia of the property rights group (in 1993 and 1994) in which indigenous knowledge questions were prominently featured, and for its support of her research on indigenous issues. Special thanks are due to Gregory Fisk, research assistant at the Center for the Study of Marine Policy, for his assistance in preparing the tables using the UNCED CD-ROM.

In particular, the chapter examines prescriptions on the use of traditional knowledge and on participation in decisionmaking by indigenous peoples found in the major international agreements emanating from the 1992 Earth Summit—the Rio Declaration of Principles, Agenda 21, the Convention on Biological Diversity, the Framework Convention on Climate Change, and the Statement of Forest Principles—as well as in the national reports to the Earth Summit prepared by individual nations. The varying conceptions of the role of traditional knowledge and indigenous peoples in these international agreements and in the national reports are analyzed and contrasted. The chapter concludes by discussing implementation challenges that national-level entities will face as they endeavor to implement international prescriptions on indigenous knowledge and participation.

✧

The Legitimization of Indigenous Concerns by the Earth Summit

For some years now, a rich and varied scholarly literature has documented the importance of traditional knowledge and practices in the management of various types of environments and natural resources, such as ocean and coastal resources (see, for example, Ruddle (1994); Ruddle and Akimichi (1984); Ruddle and Johannes (1985, 1990);

Cordell (1989); Hviding (1993)). With the Earth Summit in 1992 (the United Nations Conference on Environment and Development (UNCED)), these ideas moved from the realm of relatively obscure academic circles to the limelight of global negotiations. This extraordinary conference brought together nearly 120 heads of state and government from most countries of the world together with a substantial number of representatives from nongovernmental organizations (NGOs) and the media to consider a set of agreements and international instruments fashioned over a two and one-half year preparatory period.

Indigenous issues figured prominently in Earth Summit discussions and in the agreements that came out of the Earth Summit: the Rio Declaration of Principles, Agenda 21 (the Action Plan emanating from UNCED), the Convention on Biological Diversity, the Framework Convention on Climate Change, and the Statement on Forest Principles. An estimate of this newly gained prominence may be gleaned from Table 8–1, which provides a summary of the number of times the term *indigenous* appears in the various UNCED agreements (prepared using the UNCED CD-ROM):[1]

Although we have not studied this question empirically, we can hypothesize that the large-scale legitimization of the importance of indigenous knowledge and participation took place at the Earth Summit for the following reasons. First, all the Earth Summit outputs, as well as the Bruntland report that preceded them (WCED 1987), put great emphasis on local-level participation in decisionmaking and in local capacity building. Indigenous peoples, of course, figure prominently among local constituents in many parts of the world. Second, one of the main emphases of the Earth Summit negotiations was the notion of interdependence—between environment and development, among various realms (land, sea, air), and among different sectors or activities, such as agriculture and fishing. To address interdependence, Earth Summit discussions highlighted the need for integrated management approaches—management that cuts across geographical areas, jurisdictions, sectors, and subjects. This emphasis mirrors typical indigenous management practices in many areas of the world. In many areas of the South Pacific, for example, traditional marine management practices have focused on management of the entire catchment area from the top of a watershed to the outer limit of a lagoon—a practice which many modern nations are now trying to emulate. A third

---

1. The Earth Summit CD-ROM contains the documentation related to UNCED and its preparatory stages. Major documents included are the final agreements reached at the Earth Summit, documents associated with the UNCED preparatory process, the detailed national and regional reports prepared for UNCED, and NGO statements. Note that the reference *indigenous* in these documents may, on occasion, refer to indigenous plants and animals, in addition to indigenous peoples and their practices. A content analysis of each document is necessary to fully understand the various ways in which the term *indigenous* is utilized.

reason for the strong emphasis on indigenous concerns evident at the Earth Summit was the work done by the many indigenous groups that participated in these international negotiations from all regions of the world. As is well known, the Earth Summit negotiations attracted a larger number of NGOs than any previous international gathering. Out of the approximately 1,400 NGOs participating in the Earth Summit negotiations, 102 were indigenous groups or dealt with indigenous concerns. The regional breakdown of indigenous-related NGOs may be found in Table 8–2. Finally, a fourth reason for the prominent role given to indigenous concerns at the Earth Summit, it seems to us, was the personal leadership lent to this issue by Maurice Strong, UNCED Secretary General. Mr. Strong seemed to utilize every tool at his disposal (for example, the work of the Secretariat, his media contacts) to continuously highlight the special needs, circumstances, knowledge, and rights of indigenous peoples around the globe.

Recognition of the special status of indigenous concerns was not confined to the international agreements reached at the Earth Summit, but was evident in many of the national reports prepared by nations participating in the Earth Summit. In 1992 and in each year subsequent to 1992, nations have been asked to submit annual reports detailing their current efforts and future plans on environment and development issues and on achieving sustainable societies. Table 8–3 provides a summary of the number of references to the term *indigenous* found in the national reports submitted by nations to UNCED in 1992. Leading the list is New Zealand with 60 mentions of the term. Readers will recognize the long-standing concern and experience of this nation with the special and legally recognized rights of the Maori population in the exploitation of New Zealand's natural resources.

These data make it clear that, at least in rhetoric, indigenous issues figured prominently in the Earth Summit negotiations. In the next section, we explore the various ways in which indigenous knowledge and indigenous participation are conceptualized in the UNCED agreements.

Comparing the Content of UNCED Agreements on Indigenous Issues

The Rio Declaration on Environment and Development

The Rio Declaration is a set of 27 principles adopted at Rio which expressed the goals, aspirations, and principles that the nations meeting at Rio believe should guide future actions of national governments, international organizations, and individuals in the years ahead with respect to the environment and sustainable development issues. One of the principles (Principle 22) is devoted to the indigenous issue:

Indigenous people and their communities and other local communities have a vital role in environmental management and development because of their knowledge and traditional practices. States should recognize and duly support their identity, culture and interests and enable their effective participation in the achievement of sustainable development.

This principle emphasizes three different dimensions which are echoed in other parts of the Earth Summit agreements: (a) recognition of the *special knowledge* of indigenous peoples, which makes their role vital in environmental management and development; (b) prescriptions to states to *support this special knowledge (identity, culture, and interests)*; and (c) prescriptions to states *to ensure the effective participation of indigenous peoples and their communities* in the achievement of sustainable development. We should note that Principle 22 is worded in a more explicit way than two companion principles which, respectively, emphasize the importance of the role of women (Principle 20) and the role of youth (Principle 21) in sustainable development.[2] Also, the principle includes "other local communities" and provides

---

2. Principle 20 reads: "Women have a vital role in environmental management and development. Their full participation is therefore essential to achieve sustainable development." Principle 21 reads: "The creativity, ideals, and courage of the youth of the world should be mobilized to forge a global partnership in order to achieve sustainable development and ensure a better future for all."

a general statement of support for the inclusion of any forms of local knowledge and participation of local communities in the pursuit of sustainable development.

Agenda 21

Agenda 21 is the comprehensive forty-chapter Action Plan, which emerged from the Rio Conference after considerable preparatory work. References to indigenous issues in Agenda 21 occur in 166 places throughout the text and, specifically, in 24 of the 40 chapters. By far, the most references occur in Chapter 26, which is in the section of the Agenda 21 document dealing with "Strengthening the Role of Major Groups;" this section deals explicitly with the role of indigenous people and their communities. The title of the chapter is "Recognizing and Strengthening the Role of Indigenous People and Their Communities" (forty-three references). More than ten references to *indigenous* are contained in five other chapters: Chapter 6, "Protecting and Promoting Human Health" (eleven references); Chapter 7, "Promoting Human Settlement Development" (ten references); Chapter 14, "Promoting Sustainable Agriculture in Rural Development" (thirteen references); Chapter 15 "Conservation of Biological Diversity" (eleven references); Chapter 17, "Protection of the Oceans, All Kinds of Seas, including Enclosed and Semi-Enclosed Seas and Coastal Areas and the Protection, Rational Use and Development of their Living Resources" (fourteen references). Between five and nine references to indigenous issues occur in Chapter 11, "Combatting Deforestation" (nine references); Chapter 12, "Managing Fragile Ecosystems: Combatting Desertification and Drought" (seven references); Chapter 16, "Environmentally Sound Management of Biotechnology" (five references); Chapter 18, "Protection of the Quality and Supply of Fresh Water Resources: Application of Integrated Approaches to Development, Management, and Use of Water Resources" (nine references); and Chapter 35, "Science for Sustainable Development" (six references).

Chapters in which there is no reference to the participation of indigenous people and/of their knowledge are also worthy of mention. The Agenda 21 chapters on toxic chemicals, hazardous waste, radioactive wastes, and the protection of the atmosphere are all devoid of any reference

to the indigenous issue. Similarly, with regard to cross-cutting issues, the chapter on transfer of technology includes only one reference to the issue, and the controversial and important chapter on financial arrangements has no specific reference to indigenous questions.

Considering first Chapter 26, which is focused exclusively on indigenous questions, the chapter begins by noting that indigenous peoples and their communities, which represent a significant percentage of the global population,[3] have a historical relationship with their lands and are generally descendants of the original inhabitants of such lands.[4] Over many generations they have developed a "holistic traditional scientific knowledge of their lands, natural resources, and environment" (Section 26.1). The chapter continues by postulating that "indigenous peoples and their communities shall enjoy the full measure of human rights and fundamental freedoms without hindrance or discrimination," and that, therefore, national and international efforts to implement environmentally sound and sustainable development should "recognize, accommodate, promote, and strengthen the role of indigenous people and their communities" (Section 26.1).

Governments and intergovernmental organizations are thus called upon to "empower indigenous peoples and their communities" through measures such as the following:

- Adoption of national policies and/or legal instruments;

- Recognition that indigenous lands should be protected from activities that are environmentally unsound or socially and culturally inappropriate;

- Recognition of the values, traditional knowledge, and resource management practices of indigenous peoples;

- Recognition that traditional and direct dependence on renewable resources and

---

3. The specific percentage is not specified in the Earth Summit documents.

4. *Lands* is broadly construed to include the environment.

ecosystems continues to be essential to the cultural, economic, and physical well-being of indigenous peoples;

- Development and strengthening of national dispute-resolution arrangements in relation to settling land and resource-management concerns;

- Support of alternative environmentally sound means of production to ensure a range of choices on how to improve their quality of life;

- Capacity-building for indigenous communities;

- Establishment of arrangements to strengthen the active participation of indigenous people and their communities in the national formulation of resource management policies, laws, and programs that may affect them; and

- Involvement of indigenous peoples at national and local levels in resource management and sustainable development decisions connected with other program areas of Agenda 21.

The final part of the Chapter sets forth several activities that governments and international entities could take to fulfill the objectives discussed above. Governments, for example, are urged to consider means whereby indigenous peoples may attain greater control over their lands and self-management over their resources, such as through ratification of existing international conventions relevant to indigenous peoples (where not yet done) and adoption of policies and/or legal instruments that will protect indigenous intellectual and cultural property and the right to preserve customary and administrative systems and practices. Governments are also called upon to develop or strengthen national arrangements for consultation with indigenous peoples and to cooperate at the regional level, where appropriate, to recognize and strengthen their participation in sustainable development.

International entities, such as United Nations organizations and international finance organizations, and governments are called upon to under-

take such measures as the following: (a) to appoint a focal point on indigenous issues within each international organization and to organize annual coordination meetings; (b) to provide technical and financial assistance for capacity-building; (c) to strengthen research and education programs aimed at gaining a better understanding of indigenous peoples' knowledge and their management experience, and application of this experience to contemporary development challenges; and (d) to increase the efficiency of indigenous peoples' resource management systems through the adaptation of suitable technological innovations.

Each of the Agenda 21 chapters provides, at the end of the chapter, an estimated total annual cost of implementation for the activities called for in the chapter, prepared by the UNCED Secretariat and not reviewed by governments. The implementation cost estimated for the activities called for in Chapter 26 is about "$3 million on grant or concessional terms." This is a small amount of funding in comparison to projected-needed expenditures found in other Agenda 21 chapters.

In addition to the prescriptions on indigenous knowledge and participation found in Chapter 26, twenty-three other Agenda 21 chapters contain references to indigenous concerns. Considering in some detail the Agenda 21 chapters with ten or more mentions on indigenous issues—chapters on health, human settlements, agriculture and rural development, biodiversity, and oceans and coasts—we can organize references to indigenous issues into six major categories:

1. Recognition of the special values, culture, practices, and knowledge of indigenous peoples.

2. The need to integrate traditional knowledge and practices of indigenous peoples into contemporary management systems.

3. The need to involve indigenous peoples in decisions about the environment and development.

4. The need to target specific initiatives at indigenous peoples, such as initiatives that deal with questions of land tenure.

5. The need to build the capacity of indigenous peoples.

6. The need to build the capacity of governments for dealing with indigenous issues, such as through the training of government staff.

As can be seen in Table 8–4, the five chapters on health, human settlements, agriculture and rural development, biodiversity, and oceans and coasts present a wide range of specific prescriptions in each of these categories.

Convention on Biological Diversity

The major objectives of the Convention on Biological Diversity (which was opened for signature at the Earth Summit and which entered into force in December 1993) has three major objectives: (a) the conservation of biological diversity, (b) the sustainable use of its components, and (c) the fair and equitable sharing of the benefits arising out of the utilization of genetic resources. In ratifying the convention, countries committed themselves to, inter alia, (a) developing national strategies and plans for the conservation and sustainable use of biological diversity; (b) integrating biological diversity issues into relevant sectoral or cross-sectoral plans; (c) identifying and monitoring the components of biological diversity; (d) establishing a variety of measures to conserve biodiversity in situ (in the natural environment), such as through the creation of protected areas; and (e) establishing a variety of measures to achieve ex situ conservation (conservation of the components of biological diversity outside their natural habitats).

Indigenous concerns are addressed in several sections of the Convention. In the Preamble, the Convention recognizes "the close and traditional dependence of many indigenous and local communities embodying traditional lifestyles on biological resources...". The most explicit statement on indigenous issues comes in the section on in situ conservation measures, where the Convention states the following:

Subject to its national legislation, [each Contracting Party shall] respect, preserve and maintain knowledge, innovations, and prac-

tices of indigenous and local communities embodying traditional lifestyles relevant for the conservation and sustainable use of biological diversity and promote their wider application with the approval and involvement of the holders of such knowledge, innovations and practices and encourage the equitable sharing of the benefits arising from the utilization of such knowledge, innovations, and practices. (Article 8 (j))

Other sections of the Convention call for the protection and encouragement of "customary use of biological resources in accordance with traditional cultural practices..." (Article 10 (c)); international exchange of information among nations on "indigenous and traditional knowledge" (Article 17 (2)); and international cooperation on the development and use of technologies, including indigenous and traditional technologies, in pursuance of the objectives of the Convention (Article 18 (4)).

Statement on Forest Principles

Management of forests was one of the most intractable issues at UNCED. Many industrial nations of the North see the expansive rain forest of the South as a necessary and valuable "sink" for greenhouse emissions. The nations from the South—Brazil and Malaysia are good examples—in contrast, see the rain forest as theirs to develop or conserve entirely as they see fit. No consensus could be reached at UNCED on an overall international forest agreement; however, as a first step, an agreement on a set of forest principles was concluded. The Statement of Forest Principles ("Non-Legally Binding Authoritative Statement of Principles for a Global Consensus on the Management, Conservation, and Sustainable Development of all Types of Forests") represents "a first global consensus on forests" (Statement Preamble (d)), and holds that "Forests issues and opportunities should be examined in a holistic and balanced manner, taking into consideration the multiple functions and uses of forests, including traditional uses..." (Preamble (c)).

Much as in the Agenda 21 chapters discussed earlier, there is a strong emphasis in the Statement of Forest Principles on indigenous knowledge and participation in decisionmaking, and in the sharing of benefits. Section 5 (a) prescribes that "National forest policies should recognize and duly support the identity, culture and the rights of indigenous peoples, their communities and other communities and forest dwellers. Appropriate conditions should be promoted for these groups to enable them to have an economic stake in forest use, perform economic activities, and achieve and maintain cultural identity and social organization, as well as adequate levels of livelihood and well-being, though, inter alia, those land tenure arrangements which serve as incentives for the sustainable management of forests." Section 12 (d) holds that "Appropriate indigenous capacity and local knowledge regarding the conservation and sustainable development of forests, should, through institutional and financial support and in collaboration with the people in the local communities concerned, be recognized, respected, recorded, developed and, as appropriate, introduced in the implementation of programs. Benefits arising from the utilization of indigenous knowledge should therefore be equitably shared with such people." Finally, Section 2 (d) of the Statement prescribes that "Governments should promote and provide opportunities for the participation of interested parties, including local communities and indigenous peoples...forest dwellers...in the development, implementation, and planning of national forest policies."

Framework Convention on Climate Change

The Climate Change Convention, consistent with the climate change chapter in Agenda 21, contains no reference to the indigenous issue. Clearly, discussions of issues that seem to be largely technically and scientifically oriented and that have been largely developed by the global scientific community (with the exception of the biological diversity issue) appear not to be sensitive to the role of indigenous peoples.

Conclusions and Policy Implications

The recognition of the importance of traditional knowledge in the quest for sustainable development is of relatively recent origin. Little if any real discussion of the role of indigenous people and the traditional knowledge that they bring to the management of natural resources appears to have taken place at the Stockholm Conference on the Human Environment in 1972.

Indeed, it seems that the matter did not arise in a serious way until the deliberations of the World Commission on Environment and Development (WCED) during the 1984–87 period. The report of WCED contains reference to indigenous peoples and the value of traditional knowledge in the sustainable development process. The WCED report also observes that indigenous people are largely marginalized in today's society (WCED 1989).

As we have seen, the Earth Summit carried the topic considerably further, and developed a number of aspects in much greater detail. Our review of the UNCED prescriptions suggest that there are three key ideas contained within them:

1. The recognition that the traditional knowledge of indigenous peoples is often relevant and helpful in the management of natural resources and in the quest for sustainable development in general.

2. That this knowledge should be integrated into contemporary natural resources decision-making as appropriate.

3. That indigenous people should participate fully in such decisionmaking, especially as it affects lands, waters, and resources in which they have had a traditional interest.

Like other UNCED recommendations, those involving indigenous peoples and the use of traditional knowledge are, unfortunately, not self-implementing. Governments must act to put such ideas into action. However, the UNCED recommendations do provide a comprehensive justification for action that has been endorsed by virtually all the nations of the world. Indeed, NGO groups and individuals sympathetic to these issues and wishing to promote these prescriptions have been provided with a well-articulated rationale for action by national governments and international organizations on a number of fronts. In this connection, three questions suggest themselves:

1. How best can the momentum generated by the UNCED process be maintained?

2. What kinds of actions should be sought in the next step?

3. Is there a natural sequence of steps for national governments to consider as they attempt to follow through on the UNCED prescriptions on indigenous peoples and traditional knowledge?

Maintaining the Momentum

In our view, this is a task that falls to all NGOs and others who actively support the UNCED prescriptions. In addition, certain governments that have been actively involved in these issues, most notably New Zealand, Brazil, and the United States, can be expected to seek discussion of the topic and additional action by other states. The Commission for Sustainable Development, as the body created especially to monitor the implementation of UNCED recommendations, can also play a critically important role in monitoring national action (or inaction) and in giving wide notice to the results.

Action by Nation States

Nation states vary widely in their populations of indigenous peoples. Some, like New Zealand, the United States, Australia, and Canada, have significant numbers of such peoples still living within their borders and, in many cases, still actively involved in the use of natural resources. Other nations that have not had a history of colonial domination may still be largely populated by the original inhabitants although they may have gone through periods of foreign influence. Hence, nation states fall into rather diverse groupings on the indigenous peoples issue. In the Pacific region, for example, a number of traditional resource management systems continue in existence, especially in Melanesia and Micronesia (Ruddle 1994).

In a significant group of developed nations—the United States perhaps foremost among them—the problem is one of a reorientation in attitudes and goals. In these countries in the recent past, emphasis has been on "righting past wrongs" and on questions of equity and fairness. Programs have focused on providing secure access to land and water and the resources that they contain. Typically, however, the dialogue has been conflictive in nature and the outcome determined not by intellectual considerations, but rather by a court order or a political settlement in a legislative context.

National governments must now see the issue in a different light. Indigenous peoples and their traditional knowledge must be seen as important resources in the movement toward a sustainable future. The lessons that these peoples have learned over long expanses of time living in harmony with nature must be rediscovered and adapted to modern needs and approaches. To lose this learning would be inexcusable. Nation states must seek to stimulate, encourage, and facilitate work that assists in this process. Innovative ways must be found to uncover traditional knowledge and to evaluate its relevance to today's problems and needs. Obviously, communities of indigenous people can assist greatly in this activity. Funding can be made available to stimulate studies of traditional methods of planting, harvesting, fishing, and herding, and oral histories can be commissioned to supplement archeological information related to natural resource use.

National governments can be urged to create positions in resource management agencies for individuals experienced in traditional methods of resource use and management. Governments can be encouraged to require consideration of traditional knowledge in new resource management plans. Governments can also encourage their university extension activities to consider integrating traditional knowledge and techniques into their programs. Funding and technical assistance can be made available to indigenous peoples groups to increase their capacity for effective participation in contemporary resource management programs.

Ultimately, nations must ensure that indigenous peoples once again become fully functional members of the societies of which they are rightfully a part, and that benefits flowing from the use of natural resources are equitably shared with them.

References

Berkes, Fikret. 1993. "Traditional Ecological Knowledge in Perspective." In: J. T. Inglis (ed.) *Traditional Ecological Knowledge: Concepts and Cases*. Canadian Museum of Nature/International Development Research Centre, Ottawa.

Berkes, Fikret, Carl Folke, and Madhav Gadgil. 1993. "Traditional Ecological Knowledge,

Biodiversity, Resilience, and Sustainability," Beijer International Institute of Ecological Economics, Beijer Discussion Paper Series No. 31.

Hviding, E. 1993. "Isophormism or Disparity? On "Scientific" and "Folk" Models of Coastal Resources and Their Management," Paper presented at the workshop on Integrative Quantitative Analysis and Tropical Coastal Zone Management, San Jose, Costa Rica, November 22–28, 1993.

Ruddle, K. 1994. *A Guide to the Literature on Traditional Community-Based Fishery Management in the Asia-Pacific Tropics.* FAO Fisheries Circular. No. 869. Rome: Food and Agriculture Organization (FAO).

Ruddle, K., and T. Akimichi, eds. 1984. *Maritime Institutions in the Western Pacific. Senri Ethnological Studies* 17. Osaka: National Museum of Ethnology.

Ruddle, K., and Robert E. Johannes, eds. 1985. *The Traditional Knowledge and Management of Coastal systems in Asia and the Pacific.* Jakarta: United Nations Educational, Scientific, and Cultural Organization (UNESCO), Regional Office for Science and Technology for Southeast Asia (ROSTSEA).

Ruddle, K., and R. E. Johannes, eds. 1990. *Traditional Marine Resource Management in the Pacific Basin: An Anthology.* Jakarta: UNESCO-ROSTSEA.

United Nations Department of Public Information. 1992. *Agenda 21, Rio Declaration, Forest Principles. The Final Text of Agreements Negotiated by Governments at the United Nations Conference on Environment and Development (UNCED), 3–14 June 1992, Rio de Janeiro, Brazil.*

World Commission on Environment and Development (WCED). 1987. *Our Common Future.* Oxford, U.K.: Oxford University Press.

Table 8–1: Number of References to Indigenous *in the Main* UNCED *Documents*

UNCED document	No. of references
Agenda 21	166*
Forest Principles	5
Biodiversity Convention	4
Rio Declaration of Principles	1
Climate Change Convention	0

*Forty-three from Chapter 26 on Indigenous People and Management; fourteen from Chapter 17 on Oceans and Coasts; thirteen from Chapter 14 on Sustainable Development; and other mentions contained in other chapters.

Source: UNCED.

Table 8–2. Number of Groups with Reference to Indigenous *from the List of Accredited* NGOs

Region	No. of NGOs with references to Indigenous
Africa	5
Asia, Australia, Oceania, Middle East	17
Europe and Confederation of Independent States (CIS)	19
Latin America and the Caribbean	32
North America	29
Total	102

Note: References can appear in the organization's title, membership list, or "Activities Relevant to UNCED" description.

Source: UNCED.

Table 8–3. Number of Citations of Indigenous *in the 1992 National Reports to the United Nations Conference on Environment and Development*

Country	Cit.	Country	Cit.	Country	Cit.
New Zealand	60	Norway	6	Oman	2
Brazil	41	Niue	6	Netherlands Antilles	2
United States	39	India	6	Mongolia	2
Samoa (Western)	32	Switzerland	5	Marshall Islands	2
Zimbabwe	28	Bangladesh	5	Korea, DPR	2
Malawi	27	Afghanistan	5	Israel	2
Philippines	25	Tonga	4	Honduras	2
Colombia	25	Tokelau	4	Ethiopia	2
Australia	25	Suriname	4	Denmark	2
South Africa	24	Lesotho	4	Belize	2
Swaziland	23	Ghana	4	Barbados	2
Fiji	23	Germany	4	Antigua and Barbuda	2
Mauritius	20	Zambia	3	Yugoslavia	1
Mozambique	17	Yemen	3	Vietnam	1
Sri Lanka	15	Turks and Caicos Islands	3	Tunisia	1
Tanzania	13	Singapore	3	Seychelles	1
Vanuatu	10	Papua New Guinea	3	Netherlands	1
Namibia	10	Nigeria	3	Nepal	1
Uruguay	9	Myanmar	3	Lithuania	1
Pakistan	9	Malta	3	Korea, Republic of	1
Kenya	9	Maldives	3	Japan	1
Greece	9	Ireland	3	Italy	1
Solomon Islands	8	Cyprus	3	Indonesia	1
Panama	8	Canada	3	Egypt	1
Gambia	8	Botswana	3	Burundi	1
Malaysia	7	Bahamas	3	British Virgin Islands	1
Guyana	7	Austria	3	Bahrain	1
Iceland	7	Uganda	2		
Finland	7	Turkey	2		
Sierra Leone	6	Portugal	2		

Source: UNCED.

Table 8–4. Prescribed Actions Regarding Indigenous Peoples in Selected Agenda 21 Chapters

Chapter	Recognition of their special knowledge	Need to integrate knowledge in decisionmaking	Participation in decisions	Target initiatives to them	Build indigenous capacity	Build government capacity on indigenous issues
6: Health		Integrate traditional knowledge and experience into health systems (6.27 D(i))		Health initiative (6.22)	Strengthen through preventive and curative health services (6.27 D (ii))	Governments to organize symposia on health issues affecting indigenous peoples (6.31)
7: Human Settlements		Development in accordance with indigenous practices (7.41(c)) Take account of traditional cultural practices of indigenous peoples and their relationship to the environment (7.76)	Participation in urban decisions (7.20(a))	Provide security of land tenure (7.30(f))	Establish indigenous community-based organizations (7.16 b(iii)) Raise awareness (7.45(a)) Establish indigenous materials industry based on locally available material resources (7.70 (a))	
14: Agriculture and Rural Development	Initiate and maintain on-farm and off-farm programs to collect and record indigenous knowledge (14.28(b))	Promote indigenous technology in farming (14.26(b)) Collect and record information on indigenous conservation and rehabilitation practices and farming systems as a basis for research and extension programs (14.47(c))	Ensure equitable access of indigenous peoples to land, water, and forest resources, and to technologies (14.17(b)) Achieve wider access to resource above (14.18(b))			Promote greater public awareness of role of indigenous peoples (14.17(a)) Train field staff and land users in indigenous and modern techniques of consideration and rehabilitation (14.51)

Table 8–4. Prescribed Actions Regarding Indigenous Peoples in Selected Agenda 21 Chapters (continued)

Chapter	Recognition of their special knowledge	Need to integrate knowledge in decisionmaking	Participation in decisions	Target initiatives to them	Build indigenous capacity	Build government capacity on indigenous issues
15: Biodiversity	Recognize and foster traditional methods and knowledge of indigenous people in the conservation of biological resources and in their sustainable use (15.4(g))		Ensure opportunity for participation of indigenous peoples in economic and commercial benefits derived from use of traditional methods and knowledge (15.4(g)) Participate in long-term studies on the importance of biodiversity for the functioning of ecosystems (15.5(f)) and in inventory taking (15.6(c))			Take action to respect, record, and promote the wider application of traditional knowledge (15.5(e))
17: Oceans and Coasts	Marine living resources are of major importance to indigenous peoples (17.71)	Take into account trad. knowledge and interests of indigenous peoples in development and management programs (17.75(b)) (17.80(b))	Involve indigenous peoples in marine education planning (17.136)	Coastal states should support the sustainability of small-scale artisanal fisheries, including indigenous peoples' rights to subsistence (17.82, 17.83)	Training in integrated coastal management for indigenous peoples (17.15) Support indigenous peoples with technical and financial assistance to organize, maintain, exchange, and improve traditional knowledge of marine living resources and fishing techniques (17.95)	Coordinating mechanisms for integrated management of oceans and coasts should consult with indigenous peoples, among others (17.6) Adapt Geographic Information System (GIS) for needs of small island states, taking into account traditional and cultural values of island indigenous peoples (17.129(d))

Source: UNCED Agenda 21.

Linking Mechanisms

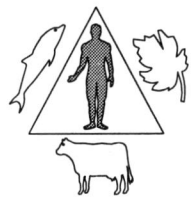

9

Mechanisms that Link Property Rights to Ecological Systems

Carl Folke and Fikret Berkes

Abstract

THIS CHAPTER ADDRESSES LOCAL COMMONS and their interrelationships with environmental resources and ecosystems. We discuss the commons and property rights, and provide some major lessons from the common property literature with regard to the interface between ecological and social systems. Next, a systems view of social and ecological interactions is presented, stressing the need for active social adaptations to environmental feedback. Such adaptations are discussed in relation to traditional ecological knowledge. Through a number of case studies, we search for the mechanisms guiding ecological adaptation of human groups to their diverse environments.

This chapter is based on Berkes 1993a; Berkes and Folke 1994b; and Berkes, Folke, and Gadgil 1993.

121

Each case study is designed to contribute to a social-ecological framework presented here, which tries to synthesize the following: What lessons can be learned to assist in the design of more sustainable resource management systems? How can adaptiveness and resilience be built into institutions so that they are capable of responding to the processes that contribute to the resilience of ecosystems? Are there similarities, general patterns, principles, and policy recommendations that can be drawn from the case studies? Understanding the mechanisms guiding sustainability of the combined social-ecological systems could help design more effective and adaptive management for ecological systems in general.

❖

The property rights issue of concern in this chapter is mainly in the domain of a class of resources which are neither pure private goods or pure public goods. Thus, the scope does not include industries, services, most agricultural land, mineral resources, and state-owned reserves and parks, but includes common property (or common-pool) resources. Further, in the realm of commons, the focus of this chapter is local commons, which is the focus of most literature on the interface of ecological and social systems.

The chapter presents some perspectives on the linkages between social and ecological systems, and cover some aspects of the state of knowledge and search for social mechanisms behind sustainable uses of ecosystems. Four points are presented in the chapter. First, we know enough to improve on Hardin's conceptual model of the commons that so dominated the thinking of some scholars and resource managers that it was widely assumed that individuals using resources jointly were helpless to change the incentives they faced. Second, it is argued that the focus on property rights necessarily expands the scope of ecological and economic analysis to include the social-institutional-cultural dimension. Elsewhere, we have characterized this linkage as natural capital–cultural capital–human-made capital interaction (Berkes and Folke 1994a). Third, traditional ecological knowledge represents a summation of millennia of ecological adaptation of the social-institutional-cultural

dimension to its diverse environments. This knowledge is important for its potential to help design more effective and adaptive management for ecological systems in general. Fourth, we search for the mechanisms that improve the use of environmental resources and ecosystems, and increase the well-being and sustainability of the integrated social-ecological system.

The Commons and Property Rights

By far the best known of the various formulations of the commons dilemma is the "tragedy of the commons," as used by Hardin as a parable to explain overgrazing in a hypothetical medieval English commons. Each herdsman seeking individual gain wants to increase the size of his herd. However, the commons is finite, and sooner or later the total number of cattle will exceed the carrying capacity of the land. Yet it is in the rational self-interest of each herdsman to keep adding animals: his personal gain from adding one more animal (+1) outweighs his personal loss (a fraction of -1), from the damage done to the commons. However, since all herdsmen use the same logic, eventually they all lose. Hence, the overexploitation of the commons is an inevitable result, and a tragedy in the sense of ancient Greek tragedies, according to Hardin, in which the characters know that disaster is coming but are unable to do anything about it.

Hardin's (1968, p. 1244) notion that "freedom in the commons brings ruin to all" was taken quite literally, and accorded by some the status of scientific law. Many scholars, however, knew that the case study would not hold up to historical scrutiny and that the generalization about commons was inappropriate (Feeny and others 1990). Improving upon Hardin's analysis of commons required, among others, an organizing framework of property rights regimes applicable to common property resources.

Hardin's seminal "tragedy of the commons," with its group of medieval English herders locked in a downward spiral of resource degradation is a powerful metaphor for the consequences of the lack of property rights on the commons, although it is not a very good characterization of what really happens in many commons cases. Much of the commons literature suggests instead a "bucket brigade" metaphor. Given a resource management problem, a group of people will often organize themselves in a way that is similar to the formation of a bucket brigade to put out the fire in a rural community.

Figure 9–1 attempts to summarize the two metaphors as simple feedback models of an integrated natural-social system. The major differences between the two models are in the stabilizing feedback loops that connect the social system and the natural system. For common property resource use to be sustainable, there should be feedback informing the management institution about the state of the resource; there should also be feedback between the regime and the resource user. When these stabilizing feedbacks are absent (or assumed away, as Hardin assumed), one is left with a runaway positive feedback loop, and this integrated social-natural system cannot be sustainable in the long term.

Such an interpretation is consistent with the literature. Much of the common property literature is notable in its attempt to study the interface between natural and social systems, and to establish a dialogue between natural resource specialists and social science specialists. Some of this literature is captured and interpreted in a series of fairly recent volumes, for example, McCay and Acheson (1987), Berkes (1989), Ostrom (1990), and Bromley (1992).

Some of the major lessons from the common property literature with regard to the interface between ecological and social systems, may be summarized as follows:

- Resource users are often not a collection of independent individuals; rather they tend to be connected through formal or informal institutions, and they are capable of communication and altering incentive structures.

- From a historical perspective, the use of common property resources has rarely been a free-for-all (open access), except for short periods of rapid change.

- There often is a resource management regime, which may be a government regime, but more often a local, informal regime that regulates the way in which resources are used.

- In the case of local, informal regimes, the resource use behavior of individuals is often mediated by a variety of social controls or social sanctions.

- The presence of a "community" is an important (e.g., Taylor 1982) but insufficient condition to solve the commons problem (Ostrom 1992).

- Many of the principles that may be derived from local commons cases are applicable to, or have their parallels with, international commons cases (Keohane, McGinnis, and Ostrom 1992).

- There are design principles (Ostrom [1990 and 1992] identifies eight) which may be used as predictors of success for common property institutions.

- There often are numerous feedback loops in most natural-social systems involved in the use of common property.

Here, we are interested in such social-ecological feedbacks.

A Systems View of Social and Ecological Interactions

In general terms, property rights institutions are part of the "cultural capital" by which societies convert "natural capital," that is, resources and ecological services, into "human-made capital" or the produced means of production. We have used the term cultural capital (Berkes and Folke 1992, 1994a) to refer to factors that provide human societies with the means and adaptations to deal with the natural environment and to actively modify it. As we see it, cultural capital includes what others have called social capital and institutional capital. It also includes how people view the natural world, values, and ethics, including religion, along with culturally transmitted knowledge of the environment—indigenous knowledge (IK).

Figure 9–2 presents a view of how the three kinds of capital may be interrelated. Natural capital is the basis for cultural capital. For example, property rights institutions are closely related to the characteristics of the resources used by that society (Geertz 1963). In turn, the attitudes and practices of a society regulate the exploitation of its natural capital (Freeman, Matsuda, and Ruddle 1991; Posey and Balee 1989). Thus, human-made capital is generated jointly by natural and cultural capital; the use of natural capital under a particular set of institutions, attitudes, and technology produces human-made capital. Human-made capital may, in turn, alter cultural capital. For example, technologies may mask a society's dependence on natural capital and provide a false sense of control over nature. Thus, cultural capital is closely linked to how natural capital will be used, while technologies reflect cultural values, world view, and institutions (Gadgil, Berkes, and Folke 1993; Warren, Slikkerveer, and Brokensha 1994).

How would the three capitals interact under different property rights regimes? The short answer is that we do not know. There is as of yet no well-developed literature in this area. However, some tentative observations and speculations may be offered:

- Ways of enhancing the turnover of information within the larger social-ecological system will enhance the performance of natural resource systems.

- New adaptations or a constant elaboration of cultural capital will be necessary to keep up with changes in human-made capital.

- The sustainable use of natural capital will be facilitated by those property rights regimes capable of responding to feedbacks from natural capital.

- Property rights regimes must be flexible, adaptive, diverse, and capable of self-renewal.

The introduction of the notion of cultural capital, with all the informal and intangible dimensions that it embodies, no doubt complicates the more manageable ecology-economics dichotomy. But it also serves to highlight systems, many of which are informal and thus largely "invisible" to conventional analyses. These informal systems (such as local common property institutions and traditional knowledge systems) tend to be found more in the developing world than the industrial West, more in rural than in urban areas, and in many cases, more in female-dominated than in male-dominated

activities. These are not areas in which conventional analyses are known to be strong.

In contrast to the detailed studies of institutions and economic performance, there seem to be no detailed studies or syntheses that focus on the performance of the ecological system itself under different property rights regimes. What is available, however, is a rich literature on local and traditional management systems.

Traditional Ecological Knowledge and Resource Management

This section discusses the role of traditional ecological knowledge for sustainable use of resources and ecosystems. Traditional knowledge represents a summation of millennia of ecological adaptation of human groups to their diverse environments, and is important not just for its own sake but for its potential to help design more effective and adaptive management for ecological systems in general.

The term indigenous knowledge (IK) is broadly defined as the local knowledge held by indigenous peoples or local knowledge unique to a given culture or society (several definitions are offered in various issues of the *Indigenous Knowledge and Development Monitor*), and is used here interchangeably with traditional knowledge. More specifically, we use the term traditional ecological knowledge (TEK) as a subset of IK, defined here as a cumulative body of knowledge and beliefs, handed down through generations by cultural transmission, about the relationship of living beings, including humans, with one another and with their environment (Berkes 1993b). IK or TEK is an attribute of societies with historical continuity in resource use practices; by and large, these are nonindustrial societies—many of them indigenous or tribal (Warren, Slikkerveer, and Brokensha 1994).

Traditional knowledge is important for its own sake and for its social-cultural value. It is also significant for a number of practical reasons. The following list is adapted from the World Conservation Union (IUCN) Programme on Traditional Knowledge for Conservation (World Conservation Union 1986) by Berkes (1993b):

- TEK offers new biological knowledge and ecological insights.

- Some TEK systems provide models for sustainable resource management.

- TEK is relevant for protected areas and conservation education.

- The use of TEK is often crucial for development planning.

- TEK may be used in environmental impact assessment.

There are many similarities between TEK and scientific knowledge. Both are attempts to make sense of the world, to render it comprehensible to the human mind. Both are based on observations and on generalizations deriving from those observations. Many parallels can be drawn between these two kinds of knowledge. For example, Gadgil and Berkes (1991) suggested that a number of "rules of thumb" developed by ancient resource managers and enforced by social means parallel rules that may be derived from the science of ecology, and may function in much the same ways.

There are, however, also some notable differences between the two kinds of knowledge. In particular, IK differs from scientific knowledge in its:

- restricted geographical scale of observations,

- reliance on mainly qualitative (rather than quantitative) information,

- lack of a built-in drive to accumulate more and more facts,

- slower speed in the accumulation of facts,

- more reliance on trial and error, rather than on systematic experimentation,

- limited scope for the verification of predictions, and

- lack of interest in general principles or theory-building.

As well, a number of additional characteristics of IK systems are suggested by detailed studies of traditional ecological knowledge in indigenous cultures and tribal peoples (see references in Berkes, Folke, and Gadgil 1994). A number of generalizations can be offered on the basis of these studies. It appears that IK differs from scientific knowledge in being moral, ethically-based, spiritual, intuitive, and holistic; it has a large social context. Social relations are not separated from relations between humans and nonhuman entities. The individual self-identity is not distinct from the surrounding world. There often is no separation of mind and matter. Traditional knowledge is an integrated system of knowledge, practice, *and* beliefs.

A major strength of IK lies in the long time series of observations on particular local and regional ecosystems. That is, IK is based on diachronic data (long-term series), as opposed to synchronic data (short time series over a large area) characteristically produced by Western science. Thus, the two kinds of data may be compatible and complementary. There is great potential value in historical series of observations about particular areas, based on cultural transmission of knowledge from generation to generation, provided that the particular environment has not in the meantime been drastically perturbed.

Western science of resource management has until recently emphasized efficiency of exploitation, in terms of physical and monetary yields, rather than sustainability in resource use. Resource harvesting proceeds most effectively with simplified systems, as in agriculture and forestry, and on the basis of understanding of only part of the larger system. Gadgil and Berkes (1991) and McNeely (1991), among others, have pointed out that scientific management has its roots in the utilitarian and exploitive world view that assumes that humans have dominion over nature, and that scientific management is best geared for the efficient utilization of resources as if they were limitless. The replacement of a diversity of local systems by a monolithic scientific management vision has not, in most cases, led to sustainable outcomes. There are many examples of natural resource depletion or degradation due to the replacement of locally adapted, subtle, and complex common property systems by government management or private property, especially in the developing world (McCay and Acheson 1987; Berkes 1989).

By contrast, managing for sustainability requires an understanding of the system in all its complexity. The relevance of IK for the sustainable management of tropical forest, dryland, mountain, and arctic-subarctic ecosystems is recognized not only by a few specialists, but also by international agencies (WCED 1987, p.12; IUCN, UNEP, and WWF 1991). IK, with its long-term view and the contextual understanding of the local environment, can also be of value in developing a new science of sustainability. However, there has been little discussion that directly addresses this area; exceptions include Oldfield and Alcorn (1991) who discussed the role of TEK mainly in biodiversity conservation in tropical forests, and Warren (1992) who emphasized IK mainly in the conservation of crop genetic resources.

Many traditional societies view the biophysical environment and human societies as being linked together in a web of relationships. This view—common among many traditional Amerindian (Tanner 1979; Berkes 1988), Asian (Callicott and Ames 1989), and African (Engel and Engel 1990) peoples—was probably common among pre-Christian European peoples as well (White 1967). The contemporary Western assumptions that the basic human relationship with nature is one of separation and dominance (Callicott and Ames 1989; Engel and Engel 1990), is not shared by a great many traditional cultures. For example, from North America to Oceania, many traditional cultures cannot accept the idea that land can be bought and sold. Instead, they maintain that humans can have only use rights over the land resource, which is something permanent and which can belong only to a supreme power, not to mortals (Berkes 1989).

If traditional peoples had a prescientific conceptualization of ecosystems, we might expect to find traces of it today in the way ecosystems are locally conceived and used. One evidence of an ecosystem-like view comes from Indonesia where traditional systems combined rice and fish culture (*subak*); wastes from this system often flowed downstream into brackish water aquaculture systems (*tambak*). The *tambaks* themselves were polyculture ponds, often combining fish, vegetables, and tree crops (Costa-Pierce 1988). The *subak* itself was often

part of a water temple system, and the entire regional rice terrace irrigation system was often managed as a system, as in Bali. Thus, the integration of *subak-tambak* systems for combined production of rice, fish, and downstream crops is an ecologically sophisticated application.

Ancient conceptualizations of ecosystems, especially as watershed-based units, exist in several Amerindian, European, and Asian cultures (Gadgil and Berkes 1991). It appears, however, that it is Southeast Asia and Oceania which had, and to some extent still have, a wealth of such prescientific ecosystem concepts and applications. Examples include ancient Hawaiian *ahupua'a* (Costa-Pierce 1987), the Yap *tabinau*, the Fijian *vanua*, and the Solomon Islands *puava* (Ruddle, Hviding, and Johannes 1992). The *puava* refers to an intimate association of a group with land, reef, lagoon, and all that grows on or in them. It is an integrated corporate estate (Ruddle, Hviding, and Johannes 1992), but effectively the "personal ecosystem" of the group in question: "*puava* is a defined, named area of land and in most cases sea. A *puava* in the widest sense includes all areas and resources associated with a *butubutu* (descent group) through ancestral rights, from the top of the mainland mountains to the open sea outside the barrier reef" (Hviding 1990). Similarly, in the Hawaiian *ahupua'a*, river drainage basins were managed as integrated systems, fishponds and agriculture were combined, and headwater forests were protected by taboo (Costa-Pierce 1987).

For analytical purposes, traditional knowledge may be considered at several levels. First, there is the local TEK of animals, plants, soils, and landscape; all such knowledge has obvious survival value, but may not be sufficient by itself for the sustainable use of resources. Second, there is the traditional resource management system, as in the Bora agro-forestry example, which uses local environmental knowledge *and* also includes an appropriate set of tools, techniques, and practices. Third, such traditional systems of management require appropriate social institutions; examples would include the Indonesian *subak* and the Solomon Islands *puava*. For a group of interdependent hunters, fishers, or agriculturalists to function effectively, there must be a social organization for coordination, cooperation, rule-making (as in social restraints), and rule enforcement. Finally, the world view, which shapes the environmental perception and gives meaning to social relations, may be considered a fourth level of traditional knowledge. Not all TEK may be adaptive, and a given practice, such as a particular taboo against killing or consuming an animal, may be of obscure adaptive value. But different levels of TEK may be adaptive at different scales, analogous to the proximate and ultimate levels of significance in evolutionary ecology.

These different levels of TEK need to be considered together. Our impression is that there has probably been a disproportionate amount of interest in local environmental knowledge held in TEK systems (consider the photos of befeathered New Guineans peering at obscure medicinal plants on the cover of popular weekly magazines). But there has not been a great deal of interest in traditional management systems, institutions, or world views. Or worse, there is "emphasis on the *extraction* of knowledge with little, if any, identification of the place of this knowledge in indigenous societies, as in the special status which it confers to some individuals" (Baines 1993). And yet, the protection of local environmental knowledge held by TEK systems depends in the long run on the conservation of the integrity of TEK systems at all levels, including social and institutional levels.

What insights do TEK systems offer for management of resources and ecosystems? Consider for a moment that the Northeast Indian *jhum* system described by Ramakrishnan (1992) employed a monoculture crop on the hill slopes year after year regardless of the ecological feedback. Such an approach may produce a reasonably good crop one year or perhaps even several years in a row, although it is not likely to produce food that would sustain a group of people in the long run. A different strategy would be much more likely to work better for long-term survival: plant a diversity of species and varieties, make a note of which species grow best where, apply this information to adjacent areas, and pass the knowledge on to your offspring. As Ramakrishnan (1992) has shown, the multispecies strategy using a mix of plant species does in fact make a great deal of ecological sense. It also minimizes the risk of total crop

failure by making sure that at least some of the crops will grow well in any given year.

Contrast this with the results of the more intensive applications of science and technology, such as the current practices of agriculture or intensive aquaculture. Resource management based on Western scientific knowledge often generates simplified ecosystems, either directly through excessive resource extraction and monoculture-based production, or through pollution and degradation that cause ecosystem stress. Subsidies to these production systems, such as energy inputs, technological innovations, or the use of a series of substitutions (often with the sequential depletion of resources from elsewhere) tend to mask the degradation of the resource base (Berkes and Folke 1994a).

Resource management practices are also designed to lock out the feedbacks from the environment; resource management agencies work hard to avoid natural perturbations, as in fire management in forestry. Blocking out perturbations and feedbacks may be "efficient" in a limited sense in the short term, but may make the ecosystem "brittle" by inviting even larger and less predictable feedbacks from the environment. These feedbacks, termed surprises by Holling (1986), may be even harder to cope with and can have devastating effects on the ecosystem and on societies that depend on these resources (Gunderson, Holling, and Light 1995).

Traditional systems of knowledge are not just curiosities; they are important for rediscovering new principles for the more sustainable uses of the natural environment. Traditional knowledge and management systems, developed by trial and error through millennia, enable many societies to use their resources in a way that maintains the integrity of their local ecosystems.

The process that gives rise to TEK is the natural process of adaptation. Thus, the evolution of TEK can be seen as part of the general self-organizing process of all natural systems. Related to increasing the potential for survival, TEK evolves from the necessity for the society to deal with feedbacks from the environment. It is a capital of knowledge that contains not only the simpler "Is this good to eat?" type of information, but also the codified information essential for societal survival on how to respond to changes in the environment, such as game depletion, soil exhaustion, and forest succession.

In short, it contains the recipes for responding to and managing ecological feedbacks.

Searching for Mechanisms that Link Social and Ecological Systems for Resilience and Sustainability

The general objective of our subproject of the Beijer Institute's research program on *Property Rights and the Performance of Natural Resource Systems* is to study social mechanisms that have evolved for dealing with ecological feedbacks to secure sustainability of the combined social-ecological system. We investigate how the resilience (capacity to buffer disturbances, to absorb them) of certain selected ecosystems can be improved by learning from traditional and newly-emergent, social-ecological systems. Social and ecological linkages in the management of selected resources and ecosystem are investigated systematically, using a common analytical framework, which is summarized in the following.

The Analytical Framework

The research questions posed by the subproject explicitly link ecology, economics, and social science. They require an interdisciplinary, international, case study approach. To ensure focus, creative synthesis, and direction, the subproject uses a common framework for the case studies. This includes the identification of the relevant characteristics of the ecosystem in question, and the identification of property rights arrangements, institutions, and knowledge systems that characterize the case study.

The framework shown in Figure 9–3 distinguishes seven sets of variables which can be used to describe social and ecological system linkages in any resource case study: (1) ecosystem, (2) resource users and technology, (3) local knowledge, (4) property rights, (5) institutions, (6) pattern of interactions, and (7) outcomes. The framework borrows from the Oakerson (1992) framework for the analysis of common property resources and from the framework for institutional analysis used by Ostrom and colleagues (Ostrom 1990). The following sections describe each of the attributes, followed by sections dealing with interactions and outcomes.

The Ecosystem

Particular attention is directed to factors affecting the resilience of particular ecosystems. The concept of resilience has been defined in two very different ways in the ecological literature (Holling and others 1995). The first definition concentrates on stability at a presumed steady state, and stresses resistance to a disturbance and speed of return to the equilibrium point. This is the conventional, equilibrium-centered, linear, cause-and-effect view of a predictive science as generally used in ecology, economics, and some other sciences. In resource management science, this view leads to the assumption that resources are in fact manageable and yields predictable. Discrete yield levels, such as maximum sustained yields of fish or timber, can be calculated and perturbations (such as fire and pest outbreaks) excluded from the system.

The experience is that the very success of such management, efficient in the short term, freezes the ecosystem at a certain stage by actively blocking out environmental perturbations and feedbacks. Instead of allowing smaller perturbations to act on the system, management causes the accumulation of larger perturbations, inviting larger and less predictable feedbacks at a level and scale which may threaten the functional performance of the ecosystem, and thereby the social and economic activities dependent on this performance. Holling and Bocking's (1990) favorite examples are budworm control in Canadian forests (more and more control seems to lead to larger and larger infestations when they do finally occur) and forest fire suppression (following a century of fire suppression, nearly half of Yellowstone National Park burned down in one major fire in 1988).

In contrast to the first definition of resilience, the second definition, and the one we use here, emphasizes conditions in which disturbances (or perturbations) can flip a system from one equilibrium to another. In this case, the important measure of resilience is the magnitude or scale of disturbance that can be absorbed before the system changes in structure by changing the variables and processes that control behavior. This is the emerging, multi-equilibrium, nonlinear view of science, Holling's (1986) "science of surprise," in which causal effects and predictions are not simple matters. Rather, systems are complex and self-organizing, permeated by uncertainty and discontinuities, as in irreversible thermodynamic systems (Prigogine and Stengers 1984). Resilience in this context is a measure of robustness and buffering capacity of the ecosystem and associated social systems to changing conditions.

The science in which the second definition of resilience is embedded represents a move away from the positivist emphasis on objectivity and towards a recognition that fundamental uncertainty is large, yields are unpredictable, certain processes are irreversible, and qualitative judgments do matter.

Resource Users and Technology

The description of the social system starts with the user communities and the technology employed by them. In many case study areas, investigators will limit their case to certain resources and user communities, for example, the fishers of the Baltic, the hunter-trappers of James Bay, and the herders of semiarid East Africa. Even within the bounded case studies, there will be considerable complexity in the user communities, the resources they pursue, and the technology they use, for example, the smaller-scale inshore and the larger-scale offshore fisheries of the Baltic (Hammer, Jansson, and Jansson 1993). The type of technology available to potential users for exploiting a resource will be important; for example, gill nets used by the small-scale fishers in the Baltic limit their areas of use, whereas the trawlers of the offshore fleet will, almost by necessity, be more mobile and exploit a larger area.

The use or choice of technology may also provide clues to distinguish user communities and perhaps also the sustainability of their practices. To illustrate, in South Kalimantan, Indonesia, there are two kinds of shifting cultivators: the local indigenous forest people and urban-based, opportunistic, shifting cultivators. The latter group consists of nonlocal, market-oriented farmers, often outfitted with chain saws and trucks, who follow logging roads into the hills, burn the remaining timber and plant cash crops. After two to three years, when the land is no longer productive, they move up the logging road and begin again. This kind of shifting cultivation is considered destructive, in contrast to that practiced by local indigenous forest people who have the capability of maintaining their environment in a productive state (Dove 1993).

Local Knowledge

Having established who the resource users are, it is then necessary to know something about their knowledge and understanding of the local environment. A farmer, fisher, logger, or hunter will have a certain amount of local environmental knowledge that will allow him or her to carry out a particular activity. In many cases, this local knowledge may be very substantial, especially if it includes culturally transmitted knowledge accumulated over generations. Many indigenous groups, as well as other historically continuous communities, such as certain groups of North Atlantic fishers, possess traditional knowledge (Palsson 1991). In some cases, local knowledge may be organized and used in a form that in effect amounts to a traditional management system. Such is the case with certain shifting cultivators, Amerindian hunter-trappers, Asian-Pacific aquaculturists and others (Alcorn 1984; Costa-Pierce 1987; Gadgil, Berkes, and Folke 1993; Berkes, Folke, and Gadgil 1994).

Of particular interest to the project are groups that may have systems of knowledge different from Western knowledge (Banuri and Apffel Marglin 1993). We refer especially to knowledge related to the maintenance of ecosystem resilience, as in the case of traditional agricultural and aquacultural systems that use a variety of species as opposed to monocultures (Warren, Slikkerveer, and Brokensha 1994), and the case of integrated human-nature concepts of the environment (Ruddle, Hviding, and Johannes 1992). There is more than one possible way to organize environmental knowledge, and the diversity of systems of knowledge and environmental world views deserve reexamination. Cultural diversity may be related to biodiversity (Gadgil and Berkes 1991), and both may be important for improving the sustainability of the world's ecological systems, as well as for their own sake.

Property Rights

Western resource management science often assumes a very limited set of property rights:

there is state property, and there is private property, or else a "tragedy of the commons." This limited view has been criticized by many scholars and practitioners who find that the real world also contains many working examples of common property (or communal property) systems in which an identifiable group of users holds the rights and responsibilities for a resource (McCay and Acheson 1987; Berkes 1989; Ostrom 1990; Bromley 1992). There are also many systems that show intermediate characteristics of property rights, including power and responsibility-sharing arrangements (comanagement) between users and government agencies (Pinkerton 1989; Hanna 1990).

Property rights arrangements in a given area may be complex because resource tenure often involves "bundles of rights" ranging from use rights to the right of sale (Schlager and Ostrom 1992). Determining actual rights is often a challenge, as in many marine resources (Palsson 1991). Even within an administrative area with common legal and fiscal interventions, the actual status of local property rights to resources may vary from village to village (Jodha 1986). Also, different resources within a given area may be held under different property right regimes. For example, in the case of forest resource management in mountainous areas in Asia, patches of privately-owned cropland may alternate with state-controlled and managed forest land, common grazing land, common grass, and bush land from which users may be obtaining diverse products (Messerschmidt 1993).

Generally speaking, local social systems of rights and responsibilities develop for any resource deemed important for a community; few resources, if any, are truly open access. Claims of lack of local property rights and self-governance often indicate a lack of research more than anything else. Even under rapidly changing conditions, there are usually incipient property rights. A historical and evolutionary perspective has often provided new management insights (Hanna 1990; Ostrom 1990). In many cases, rules arise and evolve according to local needs (Berkes 1989).

Institutions

Local knowledge and traditional knowledge do not exist in a vacuum; rather they are embedded in local institutions. Similarly, property rights, which are embedded in institutions, are the set of rules actually used, as Ostrom (1992) defines them. Rule-making, enforcement, dispute management, and decisionmaking in general are all matters pertaining to property rights; they are also part of the question of institutions. Ostrom (1990; 1992) has elaborated on a set of eight design principles for long-enduring institutions for management of commons.

In addition to community-based management, institutions also include questions of jurisdictions and government management agencies. Often the user community is dependent on the enforcement and protection of local rights by higher levels of government. Even those indigenous groups with well-functioning local management systems are dependent on the central government for the legal recognition of their rights and their protection against outsiders. The literature contains many examples of the necessity of local dependence on the government for the protection of communal resource management systems (Berkes 1989; Ostrom 1990; Bromley 1992). Conversely, government intervention may often be the cause of disruption of the local institution.

Patterns of Interaction

Rules, by themselves, are no guarantee for successful outcomes. In Oakerson's (1992) analysis, patterns or strategies of interaction are the means by which rules are translated into outcomes through the choices made by individuals and groups. In the case of common property resource management, such strategies include cooperation, reciprocity, free-riding, or destructive competition leading to a "tragedy of the commons." Users are interdependent, and the behavior of individual users may be modeled as a Prisoner's Dilemma game in which cooperative outcomes become likely if the "game" is repeated, if the number of players is relatively small, and if the probability of repeat encounters is relatively large. The availability of information and the openness of communication also improve the chances of success (Ostrom, Walker, and Gardner 1992).

Just as participants in the social system are interdependent, elements of the ecological system are also interdependent. Consider the case of a mountain watershed ecosystem. The vegetation cover, soil, and surface and ground water are all interdependent. But further, the social system and the ecological system are also mutually dependent. If the ecological system on the mountain watershed deteriorates, fewer and fewer environmental benefits flow from it, and the people depending on the natural capital of the ecosystem for their crops, fuel, fiber, fertilizer, and other goods will become impoverished. Damage to the functional performance of the ecosystem will likely result in damage to the social system and management institutions based on it.

Outcomes

Patterns of interaction produce certain outcomes. The biophysical environment may or may not be used sustainably; the functional performance of the ecosystem may or may not be damaged; total benefits from the natural system may or may not be optimized; and benefits may or may not be shared equitably or fairly. The question of performance of natural resource systems begs the question of evaluative criteria. Oakerson (1992) suggested two criteria: efficiency (defined as Pareto Optimality) and equity. Other criteria include empowerment and livelihood security, as suggested, for example, by some development professionals (ICLARM 1993).

In seeking a criterion that is both human-centric and resource-centric, and not exclusively one or the other, Feeny and others (1990) suggested sustainability (see WCED 1987). However, there are operational problems with this concept. Whereas the criteria for ecological sustainability are relatively well known, there are no agreed-upon criteria for economic and social-cultural sustainability. In this study, our working assumption is that social-ecological systems that have survived for extended periods are sustainable. This assumption is consistent with Ostrom (1990) and will facilitate the search for *mechanisms* for the resilience of the integrated social-ecological system.

Hypotheses for the Framework

We attempt to develop case studies that deal with both ecological and social systems and their interactions. Identifying and understanding a few of the key feedbacks would be of great value. Linkages of social and ecological systems need to deal with the relevant attributes of the ecosystem, resource users and their technology, and the users' local knowledge, property rights, and institutions, as indicated in Figure 9–3. Perhaps more important, however, the ecological-social system, the linkages, and the outcomes need to be analyzed from a systems point of view. The three boxes in Figure 9–3 may be considered components of a system, and are in dynamic interrelationship with one another. Feedback loops among the three components are indicated with arrows.

The ecological and social system, treated together with emphasis on resilience, results in certain linkages. These linkages result in certain outcomes. Depending on the outcome, the linkages may be modified. For example, the herders in a hypothetical grazing commons may see that the range is deteriorating, and decide on collective action to limit the number of cattle, and on enforcement and sanctions, thus replacing the impending "tragedy of the commons" with a cooperative strategy. The scenario is highly plausible on both theoretical and practical grounds (Feeny and others 1990; Hanna 1990).

The other possibility, as sketched in Figure 9–3, is that, depending on the outcome, the interaction of ecological and social systems may be modified. One mechanism by which such a modification may come about is co-evolution. In a detailed study of Indonesian irrigation and farming systems, Geertz (1963) showed that society and the natural environment mutually modified one another over a period of hundreds of years, and that property rights institutions were closely attuned to the resources used. Another way in which the interaction of social and ecological systems may be modified is through adaptations for resilience.

Some non-Western resource management systems are of special interest because they seem to allow less intensive use and greater biological diversity, and thus help maintain resilience. These are systems in which ecosystem processes (as well as populations of target species) may be maintained and ecological feedbacks managed for sustainability. *We hypothesize that maintaining resilience may be important for both resources and social institutions—that the well-being of social and ecological systems is thus closely linked.*

It is possible that traditional and neo-traditional knowledge and resource management systems may in some ways be an improvement over conventional scientific resource management with its assumptions of controllable nature, predictable yields, and exclusion of environmental perturbations. If so, *we hypothesize that such successful traditional knowledge systems will allow perturbations to enter on a scale that does not threaten the structure and functional performance of the ecosystem and the services it provides*. Resource management under such a traditional knowledge system continuously adapts to, is modified by, and even evolves with these fluctuations. *We hypothesize that there will be evidence of co-evolution, making the local community and their institutions "in tune" with the natural processes of the particular ecosystem.*

Many Western resource management systems focus on high-yield resources that provide a high monetary value. The production of these resources is extensively supported by the socioeconomic infrastructure, which masks the impairment of the functional performance of the ecosystem, as in modern intensive agriculture. Ecosystem simplification leads to reduced flexibility and reduced capacity to absorb stress. In contrast, many traditional knowledge systems consciously or unconsciously consider the insurance value of diversity and the information value of ecological feedbacks.

A major objective for our subproject is to analyze, through various case studies, how damages to the functional performance of an ecosystem have been avoided. That is, we aim to study local social systems that have adapted to and developed a knowledge system for coping with their resource base in a sustainable fashion. In particular, we are interested in what the feedbacks—the mechanisms serving sustainability—within and between the social and ecological systems look like, and how they are managed.

Conclusions and Policy Implications

The conventional resource management science, best geared for exploitive development ("business in liquidation"), but not for sustainable use, is in need of fundamental rethinking. The range of changes includes those regarding world views and, more pertinent to the present subject, property rights and institutional arrange-

ments. The issue has been raised that changes in property rights through Western-oriented management, from communal ownership to private or state ownership, have disrupted behavioral patterns and social-self-regulatory mechanisms that once ensured sustainable uses of environmental resources and ecosystems (Berkes 1989; Gadgil and Berkes 1991; Gadgil and Guha 1992).

We have argued that resource management characterized by traditional ecological knowledge systems allows unpredictable perturbations to enter the system, instead of locking them out. In indigenous cultures, a knowledge base has evolved to provide guidance on how to adapt to such perturbations, and how to respond to change. Such cultural practices are not only adapted to, but they actively modify their natural environment by managing the feedbacks for the sustainable use of the resource base. These adaptations to the resource base have ensured that traditional societies have prevailed for extensive periods within dynamic ecological thresholds; those that did not disappeared long ago. Through a number of case studies, we are presently searching for the mechanisms guiding such behavior. Each case study is designed to contribute to the overall project, which will try to synthesize the following: Are there similarities, general patterns and principles, and policy recommendations that can be drawn from the case studies? What lessons can be learned to assist in the design of more sustainable resource management systems? How can adaptiveness and resilience be built into institutions so that they are capable of responding to the processes that contribute to the resilience of ecosystems? The task is to make institutional arrangements more diverse, not less so; to make natural system-social system interactions more responsive to feedbacks; and to make management systems more flexible and accommodating of environmental perturbations.

As local communities and traditional peoples are integrated into the global economy, they lose their attachment to their own restricted resource catchments. This could lead to a loss of motivation to observe social restraints toward the sustainable use of a diversity of local resources, along with the pertinent traditional knowledge that goes with it. Self-interest in sustainable uses of environmental resources and ecosystems may be maintained, however, as long as the local population continues to have at least some expectation of benefits, economic or otherwise.

Common property theory provides some general guidelines and policy prescriptions for community-based management of environmental resources and ecosystems: (a) eliminate open-access conditions in areas to be conserved, (b) balance resource use rights of the local population with responsibilities, and (c) legally protect land tenure and marine tenure of local communities (Berkes 1989). Sharing responsibility and benefits requires cooperative management (comanagement) arrangements between the local organization and the government, and the rights and benefits may be spelled out in a management plan (Pomeroy 1993).

In this chapter, we have focused on sustainable resource management systems, and on ecological insights from local communities and traditional knowledge for the design of more diverse and more resilient systems of production. Understanding the mechanisms guiding sustainability of the combined social-ecological systems could provide insights for redirecting the behavior of the industrial world towards a more sustainable path. The irony is that, just as globalization has liberated local communities and traditional peoples from their local ecosystems on which they used to depend, they are receiving attention as a source of inspiration so that the industrial world does not destroy the larger global ecosystem on which all people depend.

Bibliography

Alcorn, J. B. 1984. "Development Policy, Forest and Peasant Farms: Reflections on Huastec-Managed Forests' Contributions to Commercial Production and Resource Conservation." *Economic Botany* 38:389–406.

Baines, Graham. 1993. Chair, World Conservation Union (IUCN) Working Group on TEK, personal communication. Brisbane, Australia.

Banuri, T., and F. Apffel Marglin, eds. 1993. *Who Will Save the Forests?* London: the United Nations University/Zed Books.

Berkes, Fikret. 1988. "Environmental Philosophy of the Chisasibi Cree people of James Bay." In M. M. R. Freeman and L. N. Carbyn, eds., *Traditional Knowledge and Renewable Resource Management in Northern Regions*. Edmonton: University of Alberta.

Berkes, Fikret, ed. 1989. *Common Property Resources. Ecology and Community-Based Sustainable Development*. London: Belhaven.

Berkes, Fikret. 1993a. "The Interface Between Natural and Social Systems." Beijer Discussion Paper No. 37.

Berkes, Fikret. 1993b. "Traditional Ecological Knowledge in Perspective." In J. T. Inglis, ed., *Traditional Ecological Knowledge. Concepts and Cases*. Ottawa: Canadian Museum of Nature/International Development Research Centre.

Berkes, Fikret, and C. Folke. 1992. "A Systems Perspective on the Interrelations Between Natural, Human-Made, and Cultural Capital." *Ecological Economics* 5:1–8.

Berkes, Fikret, and C. Folke. 1994a. "Investing in Cultural Capital for the Sustainable Use of Natural Capital. In: Investing in Natural Capital: The Ecological Economics Approach to Sustainability." In A. M. Jansson, M. Hammer, C. Folke, and R. Costanza, eds., *Investing in Natural Capital: The Ecological Economics Approach to Sustainability*. Washington, D.C.: Island Press.*

Berkes, Fikret, and C. Folke. 1994b. "Linking Social and Ecological Systems for Resilience and Sustainability." Beijer Discussion Paper No. 52.

Berkes, Fikret, C. Folke, and Madhav Gadgil. 1993. "Traditional Ecological Knowledge, Biodiversity, Resilience and Sustainability." Beijer Discussion Paper No 31.

Berkes, Fikret, C. Folke, and Madhav Gadgil. 1994. "Traditional Ecological Knowledge, Biodiversity, Resilience and Sustainability." In C. Perrings, K.-G. Mäler, C. Folke, C. S. Holling, and B.-O. Jansson, eds., *Biodiversity Conservation: Policy Issues and Options*. Dordrecht: Kluwer Academic Publishers.

Bromley, D. W., ed. 1992. *Making the Commons Work. Theory, Practice and Policy*. San Francisco: Institute for Contemporary Studies Press.

Callicott, J. B., and R. T. Ames, eds. 1989. *Nature in Asian Traditions and Thought*. Albany: State University of New York Press.

Costa-Pierce, B. A. 1987. "Aquaculture in Ancient Hawaii." *BioScience* 37:320–30.

Costa-Pierce, B. A. 1988. "Traditional Fisheries and Dualism in Indonesia." *Naga* 11 (2):3–4.

Dove, M. R. 1993. "A Revisionist View of Tropical Deforestation and Development." *Environmental Conservation* 20:17–24.

Engel, J. R., and J. G. Engel, eds. 1990. *Ethics of Environment and Development.* London: Belhaven Press.

Feeny, D., Fikret Berkes, B. J. McCay, and J. M. Acheson. 1990. "The Tragedy of the Commons: Twenty-Two Years Later." *Human Ecology* 18:1–19.

Freeman, M. M. R., Y. Matsuda, and K. Ruddle, eds. 1991. "Adaptive Marine Resource Management Systems in the Pacific." Special issue of *Resource Management and Optimization* 8(3/4).

Gadgil, Madhav, and Fikret Berkes. 1991. "Traditional Resource Management Systems." *Resource Management and Optimization* 18:127–41.

Gadgil, Madhav, Fikret Berkes, and C. Folke. 1993. "Indigenous Knowledge for Biodiversity Conservation." *Ambio* 22:151–56.

Gadgil, Madhav, and R. Guha. 1992. *This Fissured Land: An Ecological History of India.* New Delhi: Oxford University Press.

Geertz, C. 1963. *Agricultural Involution.* Berkeley: University of California Press.

Gundersson, L. H., C. S. Holling, and S. S. Light, eds. 1995. *Barriers and Bridges to the Renewal of Ecosystems and Institutions.* New York: Columbia University Press.

Hammer, M., A. M. Jansson, and B.-O. Jansson. 1993. "Diversity Change and Sustainability: Implications for Fisheries." *Ambio* 22:97–105.

Hanna, S. 1990. "The 18th Century English Commons: A Model for Ocean Management." *Ocean and Shoreline Management* 12:155–72.

Hardin, G. 1968. "The Tragedy of the Commons." *Science* 162:1243–48.

Holling, C. S. 1986. "The Resilience of Terrestrial Ecosystems: Local Surprise and Global Change." In W.C. Clarke and R.E. Munn, eds., *Sustainable Development of the Biosphere.* Cambridge: Cambridge University Press, pp. 292–317.

Holling, C. S., and S. Bocking. 1990. "Surprise and Opportunity: In Evolution, in Ecosystems, in Society." In C. Mungall and D. J. McLaren, eds., *Planet under Stress.* Oxford: Oxford University Press.

Holling, C. S., D. W. Schindler, B. W. Walker, and J. Roughgarden. 1995. "Biodiversity in the Functioning of Ecosystems: An Ecological Primer and Synthesis." In C. Perrings, K.-G. Mäler, C., Folke, C. S. Holling, and B.-O. Jansson, eds., *Biodiversity Loss: Ecological and Economic Issues.* Cambridge: Cambridge University Press.

Hviding, E. 1990. "Keeping the Sea: Aspects of Marine Tenure in Marovo Lagoon, Solomon Islands." In K. Ruddle and R. E. Johannes, eds., *Traditional Marine Resource Management in the Pacific Basin: An Anthology.* Jakarta: United Nations Educational, Scientific, and Cultural Organization (UNESCO)–ROSTSEA.

Indigenous Knowledge and Development Monitor. Available from CIRAN/Nuffic, P.O. Box 29777, 2502 LT The Hague, Netherlands.

International Center for Living Aquatic Resources Management/International Institute of Rural Reconstruction (ICLARM). 1993. "Workshop on Community Management and Common Property of Coastal Fisheries in Asia and the Pacific." ICLARM/International Institute of Rural Reconstruction, Silang, Philippines.

Jodha, N. S. 1986. "Common Property Resources and Rural Poor in Dry Regions of India." *Economic and Political Weekly* 21(27):1169–81.

Keohane, R., M. McGinnis, and E. Ostrom. 1992. *Proceedings of a Conference on Linking Local and Global Commons*, held at Harvard University, April, Cambridge, Mass.

McCay, B. J., and J. M. Acheson, eds. 1987. *The Question of the Commons. The Culture and Ecology of Communal Resources.* Tucson: University of Arizona Press.

McNeely, Jeffrey A. 1991. "Common Property Resource Management or Government Ownership: Improving the Conservation of Biological Resources." *International Relations* 1991:211–25.

Messerschmidt, D. A., ed. 1993. "Common Resource Management. Annotated Bibliography of Asia, Africa and Latin America." Community Forestry Note 11: 265 pp. Rome: FAO.

Oakerson, R. J. 1992. "Analyzing the Commons: A Framework." In D. W. Bromley, ed., *Making the Commons Work: Theory, Practice, and Policy.* San Francisco: Institute for Contemporary Studies.

Oldfield, M. L., and J. B. Alcorn, eds. 1991. *Biodiversity: Culture, Conservation and Ecodevelopment.* Boulder: Westview Press.

Ostrom, E. 1990. *Governing the Commons. The Evolution of Institutions for Collective Action.* Cambridge: Cambridge University Press.

Ostrom, E. 1992. *Crafting Institutions for Self-Governing Irrigation Systems.* San Francisco: Institute for Contemporary Studies Press.

Ostrom, E., J. Walker, and R. Gardner. 1992. "Covenants with and without a Sword: Self-Governance Is Possible." *American Political Science Review* 86:404–17.

Palsson, G. 1991. *Coastal Economies, Cultural Accounts. Human Ecology and Icelandic Discourse.* Manchester and New York: Manchester University Press.

Pinkerton, E., ed. 1989. *Co-operative Management of Local Fisheries: New Directions for improved Management and Community Development.* Vancouver: University of British Columbia Press.

Pomeroy, R. S. 1993. "A Research Framework for Coastal Fisheries Co-management Institutions." *Naa* 16(1):14–16.

Posey, D. A., and W. Balee, eds. 1989. "Resource Management in Amazonia: Indigenous and Folk Strategies." Special issue of *Advances in Economic Botany*, vol. 7.

Prigogine, I., and I. Stengers. 1984. *Order out of Chaos: Man's New Dialogue with Nature.* New York: Bantam.

Ramakrishnan, P. S. 1992. *Shifting Agriculture and Sustainable Development. An Interdisciplinary Study from North-Eastern India.* Paris: UNESCO/Parthenon.

Ruddle, K., E. Hviding, and R.E. Johannes. 1992. "Marine Resources Management in the Context of Customary Tenure." *Marine Resource Economics* 7:249–73.

Schlager, E., and E. Ostrom. 1992. "Property-Rights Regimes and Natural Resources: A Conceptual Analysis." *Land Economics* 68:249–62.

Tanner, A. 1979. *Bringing Home Animals.* London: Hurst.

Taylor, M. 1982. *Community, Anarchy, and Liberty.* New York: Cambridge University Press.

Warren, D. M. 1992. "Indigenous Knowledge, Biodiversity Conservation and Development." Keynote paper presented at the International Conference on Conservation of Biodiversity in Africa, Nairobi.

Warren, D. M., L. J. Slikkerveer, D. Brokensha, eds. 1994. *Indigenous Knowledge Systems: The Cultural Dimension of Development.* London: Zed Books.

World Conservation Union (IUCN). 1986. IUCN Programme on Traditional Knowledge for Conservation. Occasional Newsletter TEK No. 4. Gland, Switzerland: IUCN.

World Conservation Union (IUCN), United Nations Environment Programme (UNEP), and World Wide Fund for Nature–International (WWF). 1991. *Caring for the Earth. A Strategy for Sustainable Living.* Gland, Switzerland.

World Commission for Environment and Development (WCED). 1987. *Our Common Future. The World Commission on Environment and Development.* Oxford and New York: Oxford University Press.

White, L., Jr. 1967. "The Historical Roots of Our Ecological Crisis." *Science* 155:1205–07.

Figure 9–1. A View of the Differences Between Common Property and Open-Access Systems

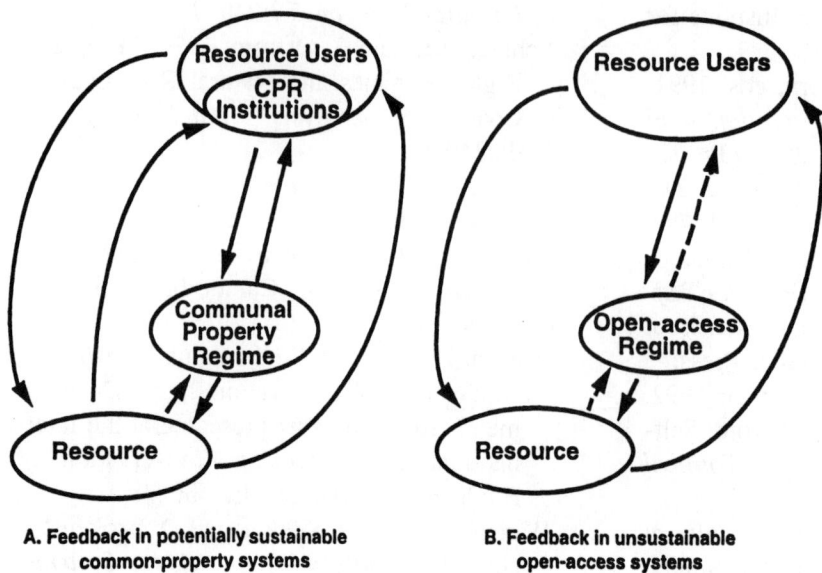

A. Feedback in potentially sustainable common-property systems

B. Feedback in unsustainable open-access systems

Source: Berkes 1993a.

Figure 9–2. First-Order Interrelationships among Natural Capital (NC), Human-Made Capital (H-MC), and Cultural Capital (CC)

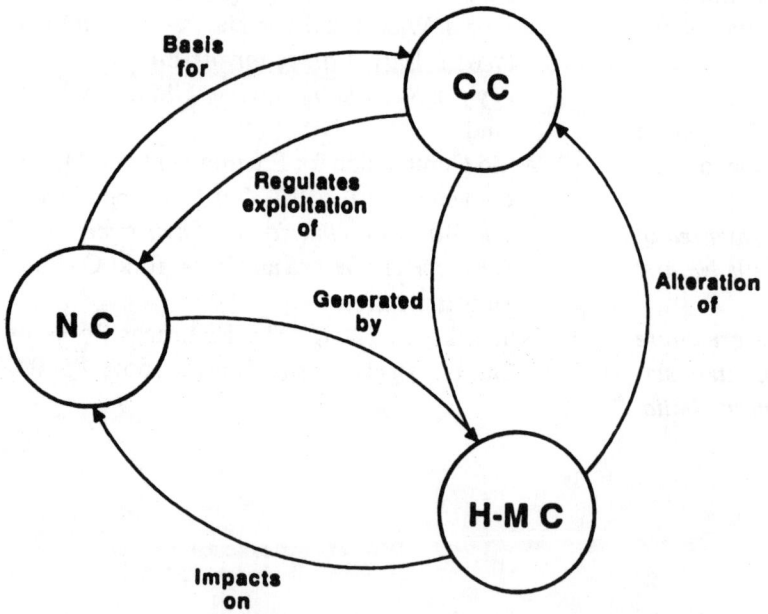

Note: Natural capital is a prerequisite, a necessary but insufficient condition for culture and welfare. Tools and techniques are created by an interplay between nature and culture. Technical development affects nature's life support systems, for good and for bad, as well as the cultural view of humanity's relationship with nature in a sustainable or unsustainable direction.

Source: Berkes and Folke 1994a.

Figure 9–3. A Framework for Analyzing the Links Between Social and Ecological Systems for Resilience and Sustainability

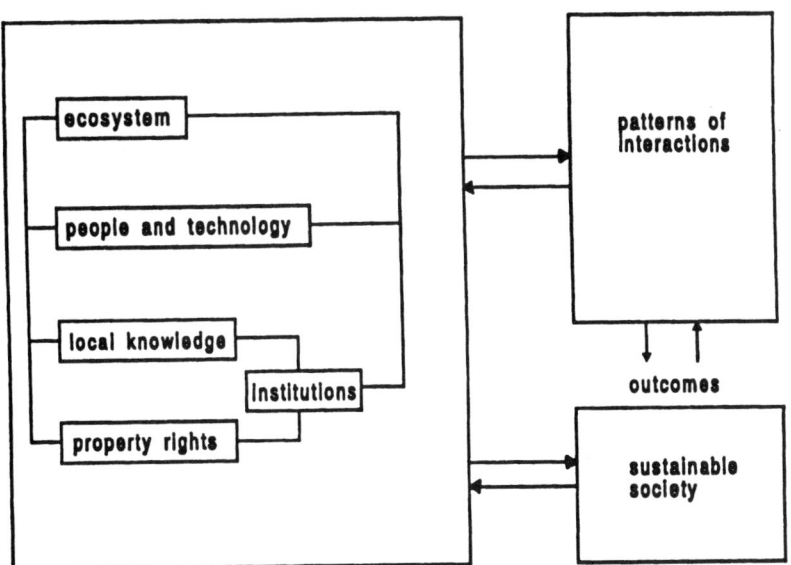

Source: Berkes and Folke 1994b.

Poverty and Population

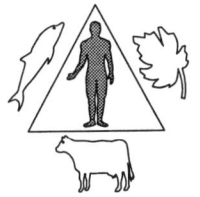

10

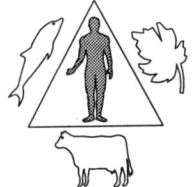

Poverty, Population, and the Environment

Partha Dasgupta

Abstract

This chapter applies economic analysis to rural households in poor countries to see what one may mean by a "population problem." It is argued that there is a serious population problem in certain regions of the world, and that it is in varying degrees linked to poverty, to gender inequalites in the exercise of power, to communal sharing of child-rearing, and to an erosion of the local environmental-resource base.

It is argued that some of the links may, to an extent, be synergistic. One manifestation of the problem is that very high fertility rates are experienced by women bearing risks of death that should now be unacceptable. An argument is sketched to show how the cycle of poverty, low birth-weight and stature, and high fertility rates can perpetuate within a dynasty. The one general policy conclusion that emerges is that a population policy in these parts should not only contain such measures as family-planning programs, improved female education, and employment opportunities, but also those measures that are directed at the alleviation of poverty, such as improved credit, insurance, and savings opportunities, and a ready availability of basic household needs, such as potable water and fuel. It is argued that these latter measures lower the net private benefits of procreation.

Introduction: Motivation and Scope

As with politics, we all have widely differing opinions about population. Some point to population growth as the cause of poverty and environmental degradation. Others permute the elements of this causal chain, arguing, for example, that poverty is the cause rather than the consequence of increasing numbers. Yet even when studying the semiarid regions of sub-Saharan Africa and the Indian subcontinent, economists have usually not regarded population growth, poverty, and the state of the local environmental resource-base as interconnected. Inquiry into each factor has in large measure gone along its own narrow route, with discussions of their interactions dominated by popular writings (see, for example, Paul and Anne Ehrlich 1990), which, while often informative, are in the main descriptive, not analytical.[1]

Over the past several years, though, a few investigators have studied the interactions between the three ingredients more closely. Our approach has been to fuse theoretical modeling with empirical findings drawn from a number of disciplines. The resulting construction regards none of the three factors to be the prior cause of the other two; rather, it sees each as influencing the others and in turn being influenced by them. Focusing on people in small, rural communities in the poorest regions of the world, the work has even identified circumstances in which population growth, poverty, and degradation of the local environmental resource base can fuel one another over extended periods of time. In this article I will present an outline of this work, laying stress on the arguments that have shaped it and on the policy recommendations that have emerged from it. As we will see, this body of work offers something like a new perspective on what may be called *the Population problem*.

A decade ago an inquiry was made into the economic consequences of population growth in poor countries (National Research Council 1986). Drawing on time series and cross-regional data, the investigators observed, among other things, that population size and its growth can have both positive and negative effects. The investigators recognized that population growth should not be regarded as exogenously given. Nevertheless, for tractability, they treated it as a causal factor in their inquiry, and concluded that, while economic development in most poor countries would be faster with slower rates of population growth, there is no cause for alarm over the high rates being experienced there.[2]

That population growth is best regarded as endogenous is the hallmark of a strand in demographic theory—often called the "new economic demography" (Schultz 1988)—that had been developed earlier.[3] It contains an elaborate account of the determinants of fertility behavior. One weakness of this literature is that, with but relatively few exceptions, it has focused on decisions made by a single household; it has not studied in detail social mechanisms in which a myriad of individual household decisions lead to outcomes that are a collective failure. In short, the literature has often equated private and social benefits (and costs) of having children. Schultz

---

1. Nancy Birdsall (1988), Allen Kelley (1988), and T. Paul Schultz (1988) are three authoritative surveys on the subject of population growth in poor countries. None of them focuses on the interactions I am concerned with in this article. Nor does a large literature on poverty (see, for example, Jean Dreze and Amartya Sen 1990) address our theme.

---

2. Kelley (1988) is an excellent review of the findings.

3. Gary Becker (1981) is often regarded as the canonical formulation.

(1988:418) points out that "The next step is to apply…micro economic models [of household behavior] to understand aggregate developments in a general equilibrium framework. But progress in this field has been slow." The new perspective, in contrast, focuses on various types of externalities that could be associated with fertility decisions. It notes that a number of such externalities can, over time, lead to wide divergences between individual intentions and social realizations (see from *Birth Control* to *Positive Feedbacks and Poverty Traps* below). The theory also peers more closely into the character of decisionmaking within rural households and relates fertility behavior to gender issues (see *The Household, Power, and Gender* below).

To anyone who is not a demographer, economic demography can be a most frustrating subject. It would seem that for any theoretical inference (say, on fertility matters), no matter how innocuous, there is some set of data from some part of the world over some period that is not consonant with it. Over forty years of demographic research have uncovered that the factors underlying fertility behavior include not only the techniques that are available to households for controlling their size (see *Birth Control* below), but also the household demand for children (see *Children as Ends* and *Children as Productive Assets* below). The latter in particular is influenced by a number of factors, whose relative strengths would be expected to differ across cultures, and over time within a given culture, responsive as they are to changes in income and wealth and the structure of relative prices. Thus, the factors that would influence the drop in the total fertility rate in a society from, say, seven to five should be expected to be different from those that would influence the drop from five to three in that same society.[4] Across societies the matter is still more difficult. The springs of human behavior in an activity at once so personal and social as procreation are complex and interconnected, and empirical confirmation of ideas is always shot through with difficulty.

These observations are merely a reminder that a general theory of fertility behavior is not currently available. The findings I will be reporting here enable us to weave a narrative (see *Positive Feedbacks and Poverty Traps* below) of the circumstances in which *some* people are born, what they aspire to, and the manner in which they live and die. The findings cannot be applied universally. But there are reasons for thinking that it may have a bearing in parts of the Indian subcontinent and sub-Saharan Africa. The account offers us an interpretation of the population problem in some of the poorest regions of the world. It sees the problem as consisting of unacceptable risks of maternal death for poor, illiterate women, and of new lives doomed to extreme poverty amidst deterioration of the local environmental resource base. In this sense, the new perspective regards current rates of population growth in these regions to be overly high and thus a matter for concern. This is in marked contrast to the views expressed in both the strands of the demographic literature I have just alluded to.

Population, GNP, Food Production, and the Environment

Why did demographic writings a decade ago not regard high rates of population growth in poor countries a troubling matter? In particular, why did investigators arrive at what Kelley (1988:1686) calls a "revisionist interpretation" of the evidence?[5]

It seems to me there were at least two reasons. One is the preoccupation of those who developed the new household economics. Attention was paid in great part to choices made by a single, optimizing household; and the study of a single household is not a propitious one in which to explore the possibilities of collective failure.

A second reason stems from empirical findings. As Figure 10–1 shows, richer countries on average have been associated with lower fertility

---

4. *Total fertility rate* is the number of live births a woman would expect to give if she were to live through her childbearing years and to bear children at each age in accordance with the prevailing age-specific fertility rates. The measure pertains to the number of live births, not pregnancies.

5. The "revision" pertains to a decided shift from an earlier view, expressed, for example, in the 1971 National Academy of Sciences report entitled *Rapid Population Growth: Consequences and Policy Implications*, which found little good in population growth.

rates. A regional breakdown of even the Chinese experience displays a general pattern: fertility is lower in higher-income regions (Birdsall and Dean Jamison 1983). Furthermore, except for sub-Saharan Africa over the past twenty-five years or so, gross income per head has grown in nearly all poor regions since the end of the Second World War. In addition, growth in world food production since 1960 has exceeded the world's population growth by an annual rate of approximately 0.6 percent. This has been accompanied by improvements in a number of indicators of human well-being, such as the infant survival rate, life expectancy at birth, and literacy. In poor regions all this has occurred in a regime of population growth rates substantially higher than in the past: except for East Asia and parts of Southeast Asia, modern-day declines in mortality rates have not been matched by reductions in fertility. A number of places that did experience a decline in fertility rates for a while (for example, Costa Rica and India), appear to have stabilized at levels well above the population replacement rate (the fertility rate at which population size would be expected to stabilize in the long run, a figure just over 2.1).[6]

Table 10–1 presents (total) fertility rates in several countries and groups of countries. Toward the end of the 1980s, the fertility rate in the World Bank's list of low-income countries (excluding China and India) was 5.6. The figures for China and India were 2.3 and 4.2, respectively. (In contrast, fertility rates in western industrial countries today lie between 1.5 and 1.9.) The oft-expressed fear that rapid population growth will accompany deteriorations in living standards has not been borne out by experience so far, at least not when judged from the vantage point of the world as a whole. Taken together, these observations suggest not only that population growth is not a serious hindrance to economic growth, but that the process of economic growth itself can be relied upon to reduce the rate of population growth. This elucidates the reasoning behind the revisionist interpretation.

But there is a problem with it. Conventional indicators of the standard of living pertain to commodity production, not to the environmental resource base upon which all production ultimately depends. This base includes soil and its cover, freshwater, breathable air, fisheries, and forests. Statistics on past movements of gross income and agricultural production say nothing about this base. They do not say if, for example, increases in gross national product (GNP) per head are not being realized by means of a depletion of natural capital; in particular, if increases in agricultural production are not being achieved by a "mining" of the soil. By concentrating on GNP (and other current welfare measures, such as life expectancy at birth), economists have wrongly bypassed the concerns that ecologists have repeatedly expressed about the links that exist between continual population growth, increased output, and the state of the environment. Dasgupta and Geoffrey Heal (1979), Henry Peskin (1981), and Dasgupta and Karl-Goran Maler (1991) have shown precisely how gross national product, if it is to function effectively as an index of social well-being, should include the value of changes in the environmental resource base. They have also shown that, when it is properly defined, this index, which measures *net* national product (NNP), takes into account the effect of changes in stocks of natural capital on future consumption possibilities. Thus it is possible for GNP per head to increase for an extended period even while NNP per head is declining. We should be in a position to say if this has been happening in poor countries. But the practice of national income accounting has lagged so far behind theory that we have little idea of what the facts have been.[7]

Conventional statistics can also lull us into thinking that human ingenuity can be relied

---

6. It will be noticed that the curve in Figure 10–1 does not fit the data well. It will also be noticed that, among the poor countries in the sample, total fertility rates in Asia are below what the curve would predict, while those in Africa are above. Part of my intention in this article is to discuss possible reasons for these systematic differences.

7. Attempts at estimating NNP, thus defined, are now being made at the World Bank. However, the principles underlying the construction of NNP that I have sketched in the text assume that production possibility sets are convex. This is a bad assumption: there would appear to be significant nonlinearities in ecological processes (for example, threshold effects; see Edward Wilson 1992; Kenneth Arrow and others 1995). This means that NNP on its own is not an adequate index of social well-being. We need to supplement NNP with estimates of the stocks of appropriate environmental resources. On this see Dasgupta (1993, ch. 10).

upon to overcome the stresses that growing populations would otherwise impose on the natural environment, that for every vanishing resource there would always be substitutes available for our use. But analyzes of biodiversity tell us why this would be an error. Ecologists stress that biodiversity plays a central role in the evolution of ecosystems (Wilson 1992). Not only does biodiversity provide the units through which both energy and materials flow (thus giving the system its functional properties, such as those of preserving and regenerating soil, recycling nutrients, pollinating crops, and filtering pollutants), it also provides an ecosystem with *resilience*.

Resilience is the capacity of an ecosystem to recover from perturbations, shocks, and surprises. If a system loses its resilience, it can flip to a wholly new state when subjected to even a small perturbation. (This is where threshold effects assume importance.) Thus, field studies suggest that an ecosystem that is diverse in its biota withstands stress (for example, occasioned by violent events), in that it manages to sustain many of its functions even when the composition of species changes. (Resilience should, therefore, be thought of as a functional, as opposed to structural, stability of complex systems.) This is because there are species that are "waiting in the wings" to take over the functions of those that are denuded or destroyed.

Now this is reminiscent of the assumption of substitutability among inputs in commodity production, an assumption that is often made in economic models of technological processes. But resilience presupposes that there *are* species waiting in the wings. So, to invoke the idea of substitutability among natural resources in commodity production in order to play down the utilitarian value of biodiversity, as is frequently done (see, for example, Julian Simon 1981, 1994), is to make a mistake. The accounting price of natural capital could well be a good deal in excess of what it is implicitly taken to be. For example, Peter Vitousek and others (1986) have estimated that 40 percent of the net energy created by terrestrial photosynthesis (that is, the net primary production of the biosphere) is currently being appropriated for human use. To be sure, this is a very rough estimate; moreover, net terrestrial primary production is not exogenously given and fixed. But the figure does put the scale of the human presence on the planet in perspective.

In stressing the importance of biodiversity, popular writings on the environment and population growth have taken a global, future-oriented view: they have emphasized the deleterious effects that a large population would have on our planet in the future. This slant has its uses, but it has drawn attention away from the economic misery endemic in large parts of the world today. Disaster is not something the poorest have to wait for; it is occuring even now. Moreover, in poor countries, decisions on fertility and on allocations concerning education, food, work, health care, and on the use of local environmental resources are in large measure reached and implemented within households that are unencumbered by compulsory schooling, visits from social workers, and so forth. The new perspective—the subject of this article—studies the interface of population growth, poverty, and environmental degradation from a myriad of household, and ultimately individual, viewpoints. It adopts a microcosmic, contemporary outlook, rather than a macroscopic, futuristic one.

The Household, Power, and Gender

The *household* as a concept is not without its difficulties. It is often taken to mean a housekeeping or consumption unit. The household in this sense is the eating of meals together by members, or the sharing of meals derived from a common stock of food (John Hajnal 1982). This definition has the merit that it is in accordance with most modern censuses, but there is a problem with it: in rural communities it does not yield exclusive units.[8] A household shares a "table" and may, for example, include live-in servants who do not cook for themselves. In many cases some meals are eaten together, while others are not; and often raw and cooked food is passed to parents in adjacent cottages, apartments, and even rooms. The boundaries vary with context, especially where food is not consumed together around a table (as in Europe) but in bowls in distinct groups (as in sub-Saharan Africa). In none of these cases is the housekeep-

---

8.   Here I am borrowing from Jack Goody (1990, 1991).

ing unit the same as the consumption unit, nor is the consumption unit necessarily well-defined.

In his famous analysis of fertility differences between seventeenth- and eighteenth-century Northwest Europe on the one hand and modern preindustrial societies on the other, Hajnal (1982) drew upon the distinction between "nuclear" and "joint" household systems. He observed that in Northwest Europe marriage normally meant establishing a new household, which implied that the couple had to have, by savings or transfer, sufficient resources to establish and equip the new household. This requirement in turn led to late marriages. It also meant that parents bore the cost of rearing their children. Indeed, fertility rates in France dropped before mortality rates registered a decline, before modern family-planning techniques became available, and before women became literate (Ansley Coale 1969). Hajnal contrasted this with the Asiatic pattern of household formation, which he saw as joint units consisting of more than one couple and their children.

Whether this two-way classification is ultimately fruitful for interpreting differences in fertility behavior between the two regions in question is open to doubt: it does not easily help to explain modern fertility declines in East and Southeast Asia.[9] Across several continents the matter is even more doubtful. For example, it can be argued that the rules of inheritance are a critical factor governing interpersonal relations, and that differences in inheritance rules explain in large measure why households in sub-Saharan Africa are strikingly dissimilar to the "joint" household system that has for so long been taken to be the hallmark of the Asiatic form. But inheritance rules themselves require explanation, and it is tempting to search for this in the mode and technology of agricultural production (such as the hoe versus the plough), and thereby in ecological factors, for example, soil quality, population density, rainfall, and availability of domestic animals. These are delicate matters of historical analysis, and the causal links are not

well understood.[10] Fortunately for our purposes here, we can bypass such analytical problems by studying instead the underlying motivations of those agencies whose decisions most affect fertility. Rather than regard the household as the unit of analysis, it proves more fruitful to start with *individuals*, view them as agencies of action, and study their choices in the context of the social ties to which they are, or they become, attached. Seen from this perspective, the relative costs and benefits of procreation to the various agencies differ much across societies, in ways that we will study in this chapter.

Traditionally, economists have taken households to mean *decision-units* concerned with the allocation of consumption, work, leisure, health care, education, and fertility. In so doing, they have developed an idealized version of the concept in order to explore how choices made by these units would respond to changes in the outside world, such as employment opportunities, credit, insurance, health care, and education facilities (Becker 1981; Inderjit Singh, Lyn Squire, and John Strauss 1986). The view is idealized, in that the process by which decisions are reached in the household model is taken to be a benign one. Thus it has been customary to interpret household behavior by assuming that its choices reflect a *unitary* view among its members of what constitutes their well-being: the model is that of a utility-maximizing household. This is as true of general competitive analyzes (for example, Gerard Debreu 1959) as it is of the new economic demographies (for example, Marc Nerlove, Assaf Razin and Efraim Zadka 1987). However, if this, now traditional, interpretation were correct, household choices would be independent of which member actually does the choosing. Unfortunately, the assumption is at variance with recent findings, which have revealed, for example, that income in the hands of the mother has a bigger effect on her family's health (for example, nutritional status of children) than income under the control of the

9. On the Asian experience in recent years, see Richard Leete and Iqbal Alam (1993).

10. See, in particular, Goody (1976, 1990) for a thorough investigation. Prabhu Pingali and Hans Binswanger (1987) have also offered an economic rationale for hoe agriculture in sub-Saharan Africa in terms of population density and soil quality. See Mark Rosenzweig, Binswanger, and John McIntire (1988) for further analyses of the effect of population density on agrarian relations more generally.

father (Eileen Kennedy and Ruth Oniang'o 1990). Moreover, in some parts of the world, like the northern parts of the Indian subcontinent, household choices have been found to reflect allocations that favor some members, for example, men and boys over women and girls, and the young over the elderly.[11] These inequalities cannot be explained by differences in needs. Household decisions would assume strong normative significance only if the underlying basis upon which they are made took each member's interests into reasonable account. But this may not be common, at least not when the family is impoverished and the stresses and strains of hunger, illness, and physical weakness make themselves felt. Thus, there is a case for moving from unitary to *collective* models of the household (see also Harold Alderman and others 1994).

Since we know that gender inequities often prevail in education, food, and health care allocations, it should not be surprising that they prevail over fertility choices as well. Here also men typically wield greater influence, even though women bear the greater cost. To grasp how great the burden can be, consider that in sub-Saharan Africa the total fertility rate is between six and eight (Table 10–1). Now each successful birth involves at least a year and a half of pregnancy and breastfeeding. On making the obvious corrections, we can then conclude that in a society where female life expectancy at birth is fifty years, and where the total fertility rate is, say, seven, about half of a woman's adult life is spent either carrying a child in her womb or breastfeeding it. And we have not allowed for unsuccessful pregnancies.

Another indicator of the price that women pay is maternal mortality. In most poor countries, complications related to pregnancy constitute the largest single cause of death among women in their reproductive years. In sub-Saharan Africa (for example, in Ethiopia), maternal mortality

rates as high as one in fifty have been recorded.[12] We may conclude that, at a total fertility rate of seven and over, the chance that a woman who enters her reproductive years will die because of complications related to pregnancies is about one in six. Producing children therefore involves playing a kind of Russian roulette. This is one manifestation of the population problem.

As the cost they incur for procreation is so high, one expects that, given a choice, women would opt for fewer children. Thus birth rates should be expected to be lower in societies where women are more empowered. Data on the status of women from seventy-nine developing countries (Table 10–2) confirms this and displays an unmistakable pattern: high fertility, high rates of female illiteracy, low share of paid employment, and a high percentage working at home for no pay—all hang together. From the data alone, it is of course difficult to discern which of these measures are causing, and which are merely correlated with, high fertility. But the findings are consistent with the possibility that lack of paid employment and education limits a woman's ability to make decisions and therefore promotes population growth.

The beneficial effects of parents' education, particularly mothers' education, on the well-being of their children have been much documented.[13] Studies suggest also that education helps mothers to process information more effectively, and enables them to use more intensively the various social and community services that may be offered. Among other things, education appears to impart a degree of self-confidence that enables a woman to avail herself of whatever new facilities may be offered. This is

---

11. Lincoln C. Chen, Emdadul Huq, and Stan D'Souza (1981) is a pioneering quantitative study. Dasgupta (1993) contains references to what is now an extensive literature on these matters.

12. By way of contrast, we should note that the maternal mortality rate in Scandinavia today is 1 per 20,000 (World Bank 1988).

13. They have investigated household consumption of nutrients, the use of contraceptives, child health in general, infant and child survival rates, and children's height (see Dasgupta 1993, ch. 12, for references). However, not all the studies are methodologically immune to criticism. Indeed, in a few studies endogenous variables are treated as though they are exogenous. Strauss (1990) has a good discussion of such failings.

invaluable for rural populations living through changing circumstances.[14]

The links between female education, especially secondary education, and reproductive behavior are, however, varied (Susan Cochrane 1983). The acquisition of education delays the age of marriage, which would be expected to reduce fertility. Moreover, at low levels of education and contraceptive prevalence, literacy and receptiveness to new ideas would be expected to complement the efforts of family planning programs.[15] Furthermore, family planning programs have been known to result in longer birthspacing. This in turn results in a reduction in infant mortality rates. Turning to a different set of links, education increases women's opportunities for work, and thus their opportunity cost of time: the cost of child-rearing is higher for educated mothers. And finally, educated mothers would be expected to value education for their children more highly, and so would be more likely to make a conscious tradeoff between the quality and number of their children. Each of these forces would be expected to reduce fertility rates.

Set against these is an effect on fertility that runs the other way. Taboos against post-partum female sexual activity, where they exist, may well be weakened through education. In sub-Saharan Africa, where polygyny is widely practiced, post-partum female sexual abstinence can last up to three years after birth. It is also not uncommon for women to practice total abstinence once they have become grandmothers. The evidence is curious: in Latin America and Asia, increased female enrollment in secondary education has had the effect of lowering fertility rates, while in parts of sub-Saharan Africa there is evidence that the effect has been the opposite. Table 10–2 displays this curiosity.

Since 1960 total fertility rates in a number of poor countries have declined by 50 percent or more. Schultz (1993) has shown that family-planning outreach activities help little to explain either cross-country variations in fertility or changes over time in fertility within a country. He has found that the level and gender composition of education (affecting, for example, child mortality), the extent of agricultural employment (affecting the cost of raising children), and the level of nutrition (affecting, once again, child mortality), taken together, explain most of both types of variation.

As noted earlier, there are reasons for thinking that the extent of economic dependency of women on men also plays a role in fertility decisions. This dependency is enormous in the Indian subcontinent, especially in the north (David Sopher 1980; Tim Dyson and Mick Moore 1983). In patrilineal societies women rightly perceive sons as having especially high value as insurance against personal calamities, such as widowhood and abandonment. But sons cannot be guaranteed. So one has to keep trying. In East and South Asia, South India, and Sri Lanka, women's economic dependency would appear to be less severe. Among those that were the world's poorest countries in the early 1970s, fertility rates have fallen most dramatically in this part of the world. In a wide-ranging essay on the old-age security hypothesis, Mead Cain (1984) used the median age difference between spouses as an index of female economic dependence in patrilineal societies to demonstrate a remarkably high correlation between this and the total fertility rate in a cross-sectional study of nations. Thus, in poor societies marked by gender differences in employment opportunities and power, women's professed reproductive goals need not necessarily differ noticeably from those of men despite the differences in reproductive costs incurred by men and women (Karen Mason and Anju Taj 1987).

Opportunities for paid employment among women would appear to empower them more than educational opportunities (Mayra Buvinic 1994). This has implications for policy. It is all well and good, for example, to urge governments in poor countries to invest in literacy programs. But the results could be disappointing. Many factors militate against poor households taking advantage of subsidized education. If children are needed for work inside and outside the home, for example, then keeping them in school (even a subsidized one) is costly for

---

14. Here is an indication of orders of magnitude. The infant mortality rate in households in Thailand where the mother has had no primary or secondary education was found to be 122 per 1000. See World Bank (1991).

15. Above low levels, however, female education and family-planning outreach activities appear to be substitutes.

poor households. In places that are experiencing high unemployment rates among school graduates, the benefits are also uncertain. In patriarchal societies, educated girls can be perceived as less pliable and harder to marry off. We should expect a gender-bias in educational attainment. Today it is a commonplace that there is such a bias (see, for example, the World Tables in World Bank 1991). Indeed, the benefits of subsidies even to primary education are captured disproportionately by families that are better off.

In contrast, policies aimed at increasing women's productivity at home and improving their earnings in the marketplace would directly empower women, especially within the household. Greater earning power would also raise for men the implicit costs of procreation (which keeps women from bringing in cash income). One would then expect families to have fewer children. This is not to deny the value of public investment in primary and secondary education in poor countries. It is only to say that we should be wary of claims that such investment is a panacea for the population problem.

The nature of income-earning opportunities influences the extent to which women are able to exercise choice, because neither the habit of making decisions nor the confidence with which one is able to make decisions comes easily: they are both acquired. Employment as a manual worker does not involve decisionmaking in quite the extent as does self-employment as an entrepreneur. Seen from this perspective, employment programs involving loans for commercial ventures (as, say, those developed by the Grameen Bank in Bangladesh) are more useful than public works.[16]

The importance of gender inequality to overpopulation in poor nations is fortunately gaining international recognition. Indeed, the focal point of the United Nations Conference on Population and Development in Cairo in September 1994, namely, women's reproductive rights and the means by which they could be protected and promoted, is consonant with the new perspective. But the Cairo Conference came very near to treating the problems as identical. This was a mistake. There is more to the population problem than gender inequalities, a fact that has been uncovered by inquiring into the various instruments that are available to people for controlling fertility and into the motives they have for procreation. These matters are discussed next.

Birth Control

Except under conditions of extreme nutritional stress, nutritional status does not appear to affect fecundity (John Bongaarts 1980). During the 1974 famine in Bangladesh, the rural population lost over 1.5 million additional children. The stock was replenished within a year (Bongaarts and Cain 1981). Of course, undernourishment can still have an effect on sexual reproduction, through its implications on the frequency of stillbirths, maternal and infant mortality, and a possible reduction in the frequency of sexual intercourse.

A most obvious determinant of fertility is the available technology for birth control. Cross-country regressions (see, for example, Lant Pritchett 1994) confirm that the fraction of women of reproductive age who use modern contraceptives is strongly and negatively correlated with total fertility rates.[17] So it should not be surprising that family planning programs are often seen as a prerequisite for any population policy. But these regression results mean only that contraception is a proximate determinant of fertility, not a causal determinant. They could mean, for example, that differences in fertility rates across nations reflect differences in fertility goals, and thereby differences in contraceptive use. Nevertheless, it is frequently held that high fertility is a consequence of an unmet need for modern birth control devices, as in the claim "…contraceptives are the best contraceptive," (Bryant Robey, Shea Rutstein and Leo Morris 1993:35).

---

16. The case of sub-Saharan Africa (especially West Africa) is, as in many other matters, different. Women do most of the (subsistence) agricultural work there, but have little control over their reproduction (see *Children As Ends* below).

17. For example, in East Asia over 65 percent of married women age 15–49 use contraceptives, as opposed to somewhat under 10 percent in sub-Saharan Africa. In South Asia as a whole the figure in the early 1980s was about 25 percent, but in Sri Lanka it was a high 55 percent. Sri Lanka has one of the lowest fertility rates in Asia (see World Bank 1984, Table 7.1).

To social scientists, this is altogether too narrow an account for comfort. It is also at variance with recent findings (such as those of Schultz 1993, mentioned earlier) which suggest that, even in poor countries, it is parental demand for children rather than an unmet need for contraceptives that in large measure explains reproductive behavior. We will inquire into the various reasons why parental demand would be expected to be high in those regions where fertility rates are high, and low where the rates are low. But it is useful to bear in mind that people in all societies practice some form of birth control: fertility is below the maximum possible in all societies. Even in poor countries, fertility is not unresponsive to the relative prices of goods and services. As we noted earlier, extended breastfeeding and postpartum female sexual abstinence have been common practices in Africa. In a study on !Kung San foragers in the Kalahari region, Richard Lee (1972) observed that the nomadic, bush-dwelling women among them had an average birthspacing of nearly four years, while those settled at cattleposts gave birth to children at much shorter intervals. From the viewpoint of the individual nomadic !Kung San woman, it is significant that the social custom is for mothers to nurse their children on demand, and to carry them during their day-long trips in search of wild food through the children's fourth year of life. Anything less than a four-year birth interval would, therefore, increase mothers' carrying loads enormously, impose a threat to their own capacity to survive, and reduce their children's prospects of survival. In contrast to bush dwellers, cattlepost women are sedentary, and are able to wean their children earlier.

Traditional methods of birth control have included abortion, abstinence, or rhythm, coitus interruptus, and prolonged breastfeeding.[18] These options are often inhumane and unreliable: modern contraceptives are superior. Nevertheless, successful family planning programs have proved more difficult to institute than could have been thought possible at first. In a wide-ranging commentary on the findings of the World Fertility Survey, Cochrane and Samir Farid (1989) observed that in parts of sub-Saharan Africa, modern contraceptive methods have been used by households for altering the spacing of births, not so much the number of births. The authors remark that the high levels of fertility in sub-Saharan Africa are a consequence of early and universal marriage, allied to little reliance on contraception. As Table 10–3 shows, the average age at marriage for sub-Saharan women is 18.9 years, and the proportion of those 15–19 years of age who are mamed is 40 percent. The corresponding figures for Asia are 21.3 and 26 percent, respectively, and for Latin America, 21.5 years and 19.8 percent, respectively.

But the proximate determinants identified by Cochrane and Farid are themselves in need of explanation, and we will look at those. Sub-Saharan Africa's population growth rate has increased during the two decades from 1960–80 from about 2.5 percent per year to around 2.9 percent per year. We will see below that the absence of a strong conjugal bond there (in particular the practice of polygyny[19]) has something to do with such high rates, as do their concept of the *self* and its ties with kinship, which are different from those in Eurasia (Goody 1976; Meyer Fortes 1978). But it is not clear if any of this has much to do with the fact that, barring a few countries, fertility rates there have not shown any significant decline in recent years, despite a decline in infant mortality rates. The importance of women in farming has often been adduced to explain, in part, sub-Saharan Africa's marriage patterns. But, as we observed in the previous section, differences between the genders in the net benefits of having children are a key ingredient in the population problem facing both the Indian subcontinent and sub-Saharan Africa, not just the latter.

Households would be expected to adopt new methods of birth control to satisfy unmet needs. However, over time it is the net demand for children that would be expected to dominate household decisions. We should not be surprised, therefore, that, in those regions where family planning programs have had an impact, it has occurred mostly in the initial stages. One

---

18. Anthropologists have, however, argued that in sub-Saharan Africa prolonged breastfeeding is not a birth control measure, but a means of reducing infant mortality: traditionally, animal milk has been scarce in the region.

19. In West Africa between 40 and 50 percent of wives are in polygynous marriages (John and Pat Caldwell 1990).

example is that starting in 1977, seventy "treat-ment" villages were serviced by a program of birth control in the famous experiment in Matlab Thana in Bangladesh, while seventy-nine "con-trol" villages were offered no such special service. The contraceptive prevalence in the treatment villages increased from 7 to 33 percent within eighteen months, and then more gradually to a level of 45 percent by 1985. The prevalence also increased in the control villages, but only to 16 percent in 1985. By 1980 the difference in total fertility rates between the two groups reached a figure of 1.5 (Kenneth Hill 1992). The question is whether the Matlab experiment should be viewed as an exception, or whether it could be replicated easily in other places.

In a notable paper, Pritchett (1994) has argued that it would be unrealistic to use the Matlab program as an indicator of the effectiveness of birth control programs, for the reason that it was both massive and expensive. The fertility re-sponse was certainly large, but he estimates that the cost of each prevented birth was about 120 percent of Bangladesh's GDP *per capita*, a very high figure.

Pritchett (1994) also analyzed data from household surveys conducted by the World Fertility Survey and the Demographic and Health Surveys programs, which included women's responses to questions regarding both their preferences and their behavior on fertility matters. Demographers had earlier derived several indicators of the demand for children from these data. One such indicator, the "wanted total fertility rate" (Bongaarts 1990), can be compared to the actual total fertility rate for the purpose of classifying births or current pregnan-cies in a country or region as wanted or un-wanted. Regressing actual fertility on fertility desires on a sample of forty-three countries in Asia, Africa, and Latin America, Pritchett found that about 90 percent of cross-country differ-ences in total fertility rates are associated with differences in desired fertility. Moreover, excess fertility was found not to be systematically related to the actual total fertility rate, nor to be an important determinant of the rate. The figure *90 percent* may prove to be an overestimate, but

it is unlikely to prove to be off by much.[20] Even in poor households, the use of modern contra-ceptives would involve only a small fraction (1 percent or thereabouts) of income.

It is reasonable to conclude, then, that even in poor countries fertility rates today are dependent mostly (perhaps by 70 to 80 percent) on the net demand for children and not on the extent of family planning outreach activities. The impor-tance international agencies continue to place on family planning programs as a way of eliciting lower fertility rates is at odds with these find-ings. We should instead be seeking to under-stand the determinants of the demand for chil-dren. This issue is taken up next.

Children as Ends

One motive for procreation, common to humankind, relates to children as ends in them-selves. We are genetically programmed to want and to value them. It has also been said that children are the clearest avenue open to "self-transcendence" (David Heyd 1992).[21] Viewing children as ends ranges from the desire to have children because they are playful and enjoyable to a desire to obey the dictates of tradition and religion. One such injunction emanates from the cult of the ancestor, which, taking religion to be the act of reproducing the lineage, requires women to bear many children.[22] This latter

---

20. I am grateful to John Bongaarts for helpful conversations on this matter.

21. Note that in evolutionary biology, phenotypic costs and benefits of reproduction are important only to the extent that they are correlated with reproductive measures. Offspring in this theory are valued in terms of the end of increasing fitness. This is not the point of view in economic demography.

22. Writing about West Africa, Fortes (1978:125–6) says "…a person does not feel he has fulfilled his destiny until he or she not only becomes a parent but has grandchildren…. [Parenthood] is also a fulfillment of fundamental kinship, religious and political obligations, and represents a commitment by parents to transmit the cultural heritage of the community…. Ancestry, as juridically rather than biologically defined, is the primary criterion…for the allocation of economic, political, and religious status." See also Goody (1976). Cochrane and Farid (1989) remark that both the urban and rural, the educated and uneducated in sub-Saharan Africa have more,

motivation has been emphasized by Caldwell and Caldwell (1990) to explain why sub-Saharan Africa has for the most part proved so resistent to fertility reduction.

The problem with this argument is that, although it explains why fertility rates in sub-Saharan Africa are high, it does not explain why the rates have not responded to declines in mortality. The cult of the ancestor may prescribe reproduction of the lineage, but it does not stipulate an invariant fertility rate. Even in sub-Saharan Africa, total fertility rates have been below the maximum possible rate; so they should be expected to respond to declines in mortality, a matter I shall come back to in *Children as Productive Assets* below.[23]

The view that children are an end in themselves provides several pathways by which reasoned fertility decisions at the level of every household could lead to an unsatisfactory outcome from the perspectives of all households.[24] One such pathway arises from the fact that traditional practice is often perpetuated by imitative behavior. Procreation in closely-knit communities is not only a private matter; it is also a social activity, influenced by both family experiences and the cultural milieu (Goody 1976, 1990; Fortes 1978; Richard Easterlin, Robert Pollak, and Michael Wachter 1980;

---

and want more, children than their counterparts in other regions. Thus, even the younger women there expressed a desire for an average of 2.6 more children than women in the Middle East, 2.8 more than women in North Africa, and 3.6 to 3.7 more than women in Latin America and Asia.

23. Between 1965 and 1987 the infant mortality rate in a number of the poorest countries in sub-Saharan Africa declined from about 200 per 1,000 live births to something like 150 per 1,000 live births (World Bank 1989). Caldwell, Orubuloye, and Caldwell (1992) suggest that the declines in fertility rates that have been observed in recent years in Botswana, Kenya, Zimbabwe, and parts of Nigeria are due to the further declines in mortality rates that these places have recently enjoyed.

24. Reproductive externalities have not been much studied in the "new economic demography" so far. Surveying the field, Schultz (1988:417) writes, "Consequences of individual fertility decisions that bear on persons outside of the family have proved difficult to quantify, as in many cases where social external diseconomies are thought to be important."

Susan Cotts Watkins 1990). Formally speaking, imitative behavior would occur if every household's most desired family size were an increasing function of the average family size in the community.[25] This is, of course, a "reduced form" of the concept (Dasgupta 1993, Ch. 12), and the source of a desire to imitate could lie in reasons other than an intrinsic desire to be like others. It could be that similar choices made by households generate mutual positive externalities, say, because people care about their status, and a household's choice of actions signals its predispositions, and thereby affects its status (B. Douglas Bernheim 1994).

Whatever the basis of imitative behavior, there would be practices encouraging high fertility rates that no household would unilaterally desire to break. Such practice could well have had a rationale in the past, when mortality rates were high, rural population densities were low, the threat of extermination from outside attack was large, and mobility was restricted. But practices can survive even when their original purpose has disappeared. It can then be that, so long as all others follow the practice and aim at large family sizes, no household on its own wishes to deviate from the practice; however, if all other households were to restrict their fertility rates, each would desire to restrict its fertility rate as well. In other words, imitative behavior can be a reason for the existence of multiple equilibria.

That said, it must also be acknowledged that testing for multiple equilibria is a most difficult matter. For the moment it is analytical reasoning that tells us that a society could in principle get stuck in a self-sustaining mode of behavior, characterized by high fertility and low educational attainment, even when there is another, potentially self-sustaining, mode of behavior that is characterized by low fertility and high educational attainment (Dasgupta 1993, Ch. 12).

This does not mean that society would be stuck with high fertility rates forever. As always, people differ in the extent of their absorption of traditional practice. There would inevitably be those who, for one reason or another, experiment, take risks, and refrain from joining the

---

25. This is an instance of "strategic complementarities." See Russell Cooper and Andrew John (1988).

crowd. They are the tradition breakers, and they often lead the way. Educated women are among the first to make the move toward smaller families (see, for example, Ghazi Farooq, Ita Ekanem, and Sina Ojelade 1987 for a commentary on West Africa). Female education is thus a potent force for creating tradition breakers, as are wage-earning opportunities for women. A concerted social effort toward furthering these ends could help dislodge such a society from the rapacious hold of high fertility rates and low educational attainment to a mode of behavior where fertility is low and educational attainment high. A more direct route would be social coordination through education and public exhortation, aimed particularly at men if the society is strongly patriarchal. In this context, the role of television and radio in transmitting information about other life styles can be especially important (Ronald Freedman 1995).

Children as Productive Assets

Still other motives for procreation involve viewing children as productive assets. In a rural economy where the avenues for saving are highly restricted, or where public support for the elderly is weak, parents value children as a source of security in their old age. Cain (1981, 1983) has studied this aspect extensively on the basis of data from Bangladesh, and Jeffrev Nugent and Thomas Gillaspy (1983) have used Mexican evidence to argue that old-age pension and social security do act as a substitute for children. One way of formalizing this is to assume that parents are interested in household welfare, subject to the requirement that the chance of there being an offspring to care for them in old age—providing sustenance, time, and attention—is no less than a certain amount. In many regions (for example, the Indian subcontinent) this translates into a requirement that the chance of there being a *son* alive when the parents are old is no less than a certain amount. As a numerical example, we may consider the simulation study by David May and David Heer (1968), who estimated that an average Indian couple in the 1960s needed to have 6.3 children in order to be 95 percent sure of having a surviving son when the father reaches the age of 65. This is a high figure, about the same as the total

fertility rate in India during the decade of the 1950s.[26]

Old-age security provides a potentially strong motive. In 1980 people aged 65 and over in South Asia formed about 4 percent of the total population. The sex composition among the aged is far from even, being of the order of 80–85 men for every 100 women among the elderly. In South and Southeast Asia, female life expectancy at birth is 59 years, while that of males is about 54 years; at age 60, however, they are approximately 15 and 14 years, not much less than the life expectancy at age 60 in advanced industrial countries. In the Indian subcontinent the proportions of the elderly who live with their children (for the most part, sons) is of the order of 80 percent or more. (In the United States, the corresponding figure is about 15 percent.) Sons are a necessity in these circumstances. A poor widow with no sons in northern parts of the Indian subcontinent is faced with the prospect of destitution.[27]

Related to this is a phenomenon that has been observed by Jane Guyer (1994) in a Yaruba area of Nigeria. In the face of deteriorating economic circumstances, some women are bearing children by different men so as to create immediate lateral links with them. Polyandrous motherhood enables women to have access to more than one resource network.

Children differ in their potential. One would expect parents in a poor household to develop the most promising of their children, even if this were to mean that the remaining ones are somewhat marginalized. This is confirmed by both economic theory and evidence (Becker and Nigel Tomes 1976; Caroline Bledsoe 1994). Daughters are a net drain on parental resources in the Indian subcontinent (dowries can be bankrupting). This goes some way toward

---

26. Sam Preston (1978) is a useful collection of essays on the effects that have been observed on fertility rates of reductions in rates of infant mortality.

27. Urbanization tends to break households down into "nuclear" units, thereby raising the parental costs of procreation (Coale and Edgar Hoover 1958; Schultz 1993). Urbanization in a growing economy also offers children better employment prospects, which improve their bargaining strength relative to their parents. This in turn lowers the return on children as investment, since children become less dependable as a source of income to their parents in their old age.

explaining the preference parents show for sons there (Sopher 1980; Cain 1984). It also helps explain why daughters receive less education and are expected to work relatively harder for their parents, a matter we come to next.

In poor countries children are also useful as income-earning assets. This provides households in these parts with another motive for procreation. It has consequences that have only recently been explored in theoretical analyses (Dasgupta and Maler 1991, 1993; Marc Nerlove 1991; Nerlove and Anke Meyer 1993).

Poor countries in great part are biomass-based subsistence economies. Rural folk there eke out a living from products obtained directly from plants and animals. Production throughput is low. Much labor is needed even for simple tasks. Moreover, households there do not have access to the sources of domestic energy available to households in advanced industrial countries. Nor do they have water on tap. In semi-arid and arid regions, water supply is often not even close at hand. Nor is fuelwood near at hand when the forests recede. This means that the relative prices of alternative sources of energy and water faced by rural households in poor countries are quite different from those faced by households elsewhere. In addition to cultivating crops, caring for livestock, cooking food and producing simple marketable products, members of a household may have to spend as much as five to six hours a day fetching water and collecting fodder and wood. These are complementary activities. They have to be undertaken on a daily basis if the household is to survive. Each is time-consuming. Labor productivity is low not only because capital is scarce, but also because environmental resources are scarce. From about the age of six, children in poor households in poor countries mind their siblings and domestic animals, fetch water, and collect fuelwood, dung, and fodder. Children are then needed as workers by their parents, even when the parents are in their prime.

In their study of work allocation among rural households in the foothills of the Himalayas, C.S.E (1990) recorded that children between the ages of ten and fifteen work one-and-a-half times the number of hours adult males do, their tasks consisting of collecting fuelwood, dung, and fodder, grazing domestic animals, perform-

ing household chores, and marketing.[28] Indeed, children can add so much to household income that, in some places, the cost of rearing them is negated by the time they reach adolescence. Cain (1977) studied data from the village Char Gopalpur in Bangladesh. He estimated that male children become net producers at as early an age as twelve years, and work as many hours a day as an adult. Using a zero (calorie) rate of interest, he calculated that male children compensate for their own cumulative consumption by the age of fifteen. This may not be typical in Bangladesh. I cite it, nevertheless, to show the vast difference in the motivation for having children between households in rich countries and poor households in poor countries. Each household would appear to need many hands, and it can be that the overall usefulness of each additional hand increases with declining resource availability, at least over some range.[29]

Positive Feedbacks and Poverty Traps

The need for many hands can lead to a destructive situation, especially when parents do not have to pay the full price of rearing their children but share those costs with their community. In recent years, mores that once regulated local resources have changed. Since time immemorial, rural assets such as village ponds and water holes, threshing grounds, grazing fields, and local forests have been owned communally. This form of ownership and control enabled households in semi-arid regions to pool their risks. James Howe (1986), Robert Wade (1988), Kanchan Chopra, Gopal Kadekodi, and M. N. Murty (1990), Jean-Marie Baland and Jean-Philippe Platteau (1995) and others have shown that, traditionally, communities have protected local commons from overexploitation by relying on norms, imposing fines for deviant behavior, and other means. But the very process of economic development can erode traditional methods of control, say, by way of increased urbanization and mobility (Dasgupta 1993, Ch. 10).

---

28. See Julia Falconer and J. E. A. Arnold (1989) for a similar investigation for sub-Saharan Africa.

29. This can happen if households discount the future at a sufficiently high rate. See Nerlove (1991).

Social norms are also endangered by civil strife and by the usurpation of resources by landowners or the state. As norms degrade, parents pass some of the costs of children on to the community by overexploiting the commons. Indeed, even a marginal decline in compliance in agreements can trigger a process of cumulative causation. Over time the effect could be large. If access to shared resources continues, parents produce too many children, which leads to greater crowding and susceptibility to disease as well as to more pressure on local environmental resources. But no household, on its own, would take into account the harm it would inflict on others when bringing forth another child. This is another instance of a demographic free-rider problem.

Parental costs of procreation are also lower when the cost of rearing the child is shared among the kinship. In sub-Saharan Africa, "foster age" within the kinship is a commonplace: chil-dren are not raised solely by their parents; the responsibility is more diffuse within the kinship group (Goody 1976; Bledsoe 1990). Foster age in the African context is not adoption. It is not intended to, nor does it in fact, break ties between parents and children. The institution affords a form of mutual insurance protection in semi-arid regions. There is some evidence that, as savings opportunities are few in the low-productivity agricultural regions of sub-Saharan Africa, foster age also enables households to spread their consumption across time.[30] In parts of West Africa, up to half the children have been found to be living with their kin at any given time. Nephews and nieces have the same rights of accomodation and support as do biological offspring. There is a sense in which children are seen as a common responsibility. However, the arrangement creates yet another free-rider problem if the parents' share of the benefits from having children exceeds their share of the costs. From the point of view of the parents, taken as a collective, too many children would be produced in these circumstances.[31]

In sub-Saharan Africa, communal land tenure of the lineage social structure offers yet another inducement for men to procreate. In addition, as conjugal bonds are weak, fathers often do not bear the costs of siring a child. Anthropologists have observed that the unit of African society is a woman and her children, rather than parents and their children. Often, there is no common budget for the man and woman. Descent in sub-Saharan Africa is, for the most part, patrilineal, and residence is patrilocal (an exception are the Akan people of Ghana). Patrilineality, weak conjugal bonds, communal land tenure, and a strong kinship support system of children, taken together, are a broad characteristic of the region. In principle they provide a powerful stimulus to fertility. Admittedly, patrilineality and patrilocality are features of the northern parts of the Indian subcontinent also. But conjugal bonds are substantially greater there. Moreover, as agricultural land is not communally held, large family sizes lead to fragmentation of landholdings. In contrast, large families in sub-Saharan Africa are—or, at least *were*, until recently—rewarded by a greater share of land belonging to the lineage or clan.

The perception of both low costs and high benefits of procreation in sub-Saharan Africa induces "couples" to produce too many children. Theoretical considerations suggest that, in cer-

---

30. This latter motivation has been explored by Renata Serra in a graduate thesis at the University of Cambridge.

31. To see that there is no distortion if the shares were the same, suppose c is the cost of rearing a child and N the number of couples within a kinship. For simplicity's sake,

assume that each child makes available y units of output (this is the norm) to the entire kinship, which is then shared equally among all couples, say, in their old age. Suppose also that the cost of rearing each child is shared equally by all couples. Let n^* be the number of children each couple other than the one under study chooses to have. (We will presently endogenize this.) If n were to be the number of children this couple produces, it would incur the resource cost $C=[nc+(N-1)n^*c]/N$, and eventually the couple would receive an income from the next generation equalling $Y=[ny+(N-1)n^*y]/N$. Denote the couple's aggregate utility function by the form $U(Y)-K(C)$, where both $U(.)$ and $K(.)$ are increasing and strictly concave functions. Letting n be a continuous vari-able for simplicity, it is easy to confirm that the couple in question will choose the value of n at which $yU'(Y)=cK'(C)$. The choice sustains a social equilibrium when $n=n^*$. (This is the symmetric noncooperative Nash equilibrium of the social system.) It is easy to check that this is also the condition which is met in a society where there is no reproductive free-riding. It is a simple matter to confirm that there is free-riding if the parents' share of the benefits from having children exceeds their share of the costs.

tain circumstances, a disastrous process can thereby begin. As the community's natural resources are depleted, more hands are needed to gather fuel and water for daily use. More children are then produced, further damaging the local resource base and in turn providing the "household" with an incentive to enlarge. When this happens, poverty, fertility, and environmental degradation reinforce one another in an escalating spiral. By the time some countervailing set of factors stops the spiral—whether because of public policy or because of diminished benefits from having further children due, say, to a scarcity of land—millions of lives may have suffered through worsening poverty.[32]

Kevin Cleaver and Gotz Schreiber (1994) provide some evidence for this thesis in the context of rural sub-Saharan Africa. They report positive correlations between poverty, fertility, and deterioration of the local environmental-resource base. Such data cannot reveal causal connections, but they are not inconsistent with the idea of a positive feedback mechanism such as I have described. Over time, the effects of this spiral would be expected to have large effects, as manifested by battles for resources (William Durham 1979; Thomas Homer-Dixon, Jeffrey Boutwell, and George Rathjens 1993).

And there is evidence that is more indirect. The victims of such a process as we are discussing would be born and raised in poverty. A large proportion would suffer from undernourishment. They would remain illiterate and would often be both stunted and wasted. Undernourishment would retard their cognitive (and often motor) development and compromise their future capacity to work. Labor productivity would be dismally low. Investment credit would for the most part be unavailable to them, and the avenue of savings would consequently be that much more constrained for them. Stunting and wasting would have a tendency of begetting more stunting and wasting down the generations of a dynasty (Dasgupta 1993, Chs. 14–16). Among those who would survive, the victims hit hardest would be society's outcasts—the migrants and dispossessed, some of whom in time would become the emaciated beggars seen on the

streets of large towns and cities in poor countries. Nutritional findings (John Waterlow 1986, 1992), historical studies (Robert Fogel 1994a,b) and theoretical explorations (Dasgupta 1993, Ch. 16; 1995b), when taken together, show that the spiral I have outlined here is one way in which destitutes are created. Emaciated beggars are not lazy; they have to husband their precarious hold on energy. Having suffered from malnutrition, they cease to be marketable.

Families with greater access to resources would, however, be in a position to limit their size and propel themselves into still higher income levels. I have not been able to locate published data on the matter, but my impression is that among the urban middle classes in north India the transition to a low fertility rate has already been achieved. This does not mean there is an inexorable "vicious circle of poverty." People from the poorest of backgrounds have been known to lift themselves out of the mire. Nevertheless, there are forces at work which pull households away from one another in terms of their living standards. India provides a possible example of how the vicious cycle I have described can enable extreme poverty to persist amid a growth in the living standards in the rest of society. The Matthew Effect ("For unto everyone that hath shall be given, and he shall have abundance; but from him that hath not shall be taken away even that which he hath") would appear to work relentlessly in poor countries.

Against this backdrop, it is hard to make sense of the oft-expressed suggestion (see, for example, Simon 1981) that there are cumulative benefits to be enjoyed from increases in population size even in poor countries, that human beings are a valuable resource. To be sure, they are potentially valuable as doers of things and originators of ideas, but for this they require the means for personal development. Moreover, historical evidence on the way pressure of population led to changes in the organization of production, property rights, and ways of doing things, which is what Esther Boserup (1981) studied in her far-reaching work, also does not seem to speak to the population problem as it exists today in sub-Saharan Africa and the northern parts of the Indian subcontinent.

---

32. Nerlove (1991) has provided a formal analysis of such positive feedback processes.

Public Policy

The analysis presented here suggests that the way to reduce fertility would be to break the destructive spiral where such a spiral is in operation. Since parental demand for children, rather than an unmet need for contraceptives, in great measure explains reproductive behavior in poor countries, we should try to identify policies that would so change the options men and women face that their reasoned choice would be to lower their fertility.

In this regard, civil liberties, as opposed to coercion, would appear to play a particular role. In Dasgupta (1990) I showed by the use of statistical analysis of data pertaining to the decade of the 1970s from fifty-one of the then poorest countries that political and civil liberties are positively and significantly correlated with *improvements* in income per head, life expectancy at birth, and the infant survival rate. Correlation is not causation, but there are now reasons for thinking that such liberties are not only desirable in themselves, but also have instrumental virtues in empowering people to flourish in the economic sphere. The causal chain may well be that political and civil liberties provide sustenance to the rule of law, and thereby to security of property and the enforcement of contracts. In fact, Adam Przeworski and Fernando Limongi (1995) have shown that fertility, as well, is lower in countries where citizens enjoy more civil and political liberties. (An exception is China, which represents only one out of some 100 countries in their sample.)

The most potent solution in semi-arid regions of sub-Saharan Africa and the Indian subcontinent is to deploy a number of policies simultaneously. Family planning services, especially when allied with health services and measures that empower women, are certainly desirable. As social norms break down and traditional support systems falter, those women who choose to change their behavior become financially and socially more vulnerable. So a literacy and employment drive for women is essential to smooth the transition to lower fertility. But improving social coordination and directly increasing the economic security of the poor are also essential. Providing infrastructural goods, such as cheap fuel and potable water, will reduce the usefulness of extra hands. When a child becomes perceived as expensive, we may finally have a hope of dislodging the rapacious hold of high fertility rates. Neither evidence nor analysis has yet disproved the notion that the poor in poor countries know, at least in a rough manner, what is in their self interest. But each of the prescriptions offered by our new perspective is desirable by itself, and not just when we have the population problem in mind. It seems to me that this consonance of means and ends is a most agreeable fact in what is otherwise a depressing field of study.

Admittedly, in saying all this we are looking at matters wholly from the perspective of the parents. This is limiting.[33] But developing the welfare economics of population policies has proved to be extremely difficult (Dasgupta 1994): our ethical intuition at best extends to actual and future people; we do not yet possess a good moral vocabulary for including potential people in the calculation. What I have tried to argue in this essay is that there is much that we can establish even if we were to leave aside such conceptual difficulties. Population policy involves a good deal more than making family planning centers available to the rural poor. It also involves more than a recognition that poverty is a root cause of high fertility rates. The problem is deeper, but as I have tried to show, it is possible to subject it to analysis.

Bibliography

Alderman, Harold and others. 1995. "Unitary versus Collective Models of the Household: Time to Shift the Burden of Proof." Mimeo. Washington, D.C.: The World Bank.

Arrow, Kenneth and others. 1995. "Economic Growth, Carrying Capacity, and the Environment." Mimeo. Stockholm: Beijer International Institute of Ecological Economics, Royal Swedish Academy of Sciences.

Baland, Jean-Marie, and Jean-Philippe Platteau. 1995. *Halting Degradation of Natural Re-*

---

33. Stephen Enke (1966) is a notable exploration of the value of prevented births when the worth of additional lives is judged to be based entirely on their effect on the current generation. As a simplification, Enke took the value of a prevented birth to be the discounted sum of the differences between an additional person's consumption and output over the person's lifetime.

sources: Is There a Role for Rural Communities? Oxford: Oxford University Press.

Becker, Gary. 1981. *A Treatise on the Family.* Cambridge, MA: Harvard University Press.

Becker, Gary S., and Nigel Tomes. 1976. "Child Endowments and the Quantity and Quality of Children." *Journal of Political Economy* (Supplement) (August):S143–S162.

Behrman, S. J., Leslie Corsa, and Ronald Freedman. 1969. *Fertility and Family Planning: A World View.* Ann Arbor, Michigan: University of Michigan Press.

Bernheim, B . Douglas. "A Theory of Conformity," *Journal of Political Economy*, October 1994, 02(5), pp. 841-77.

Birdsall, Nancy. 1988. "Economic Approaches to Population Growth." In Hollis Chenery and T. N. Srinivasan, *Handbook of Development Economics, Vol. 1.* Amsterdam: North Holland. 477–542.

Birdsall, Nancy, and Dean Jamison. 1983. "Income and Other Factors Influencing Fertility in China." *Population and Development Review* 9(4):651–75.

Bledsoe, Caroline. 1990. "The Politics of Children: Fosterage and the Social Management of Fertility Among the Mende of Sierra Leone." In W. Penn. Handwerker, *Births and Power: Social Change and the Politics of Reproduction.* London: Westview Press. 81–89.

Bledsoe, Caroline. 1994. "'Chidren are Like Young Bamboo Trees': Potentiality and Reproduction in sub-Saharan Africa." In Kerstin Lindahl-Kiessling and Hans Landberg, *Population, Economic Development, and the Environment: The Making of Our Common Future.* Oxford: Oxford University Press. 105–38.

Bledsoe, Caroline, and Gilles Pison. 1994. *Nupitality in Sub-Saharan Africa: Contemporary Anthropological and Demographic Perspectives.* Oxford: Clarendon Press.

Bongaarts, John. 1980. "Does Malnutrition Affect Fecundity? A Summary of the Evidence." *Science* 208(4444)(9 May 1980):564–9.

Bongaarts, John. 1990. "The Measurement of Wanted Fertility." *Population and Development Review*, September 1990, 16(3), pp. 487-506.

Bongaarts, John, and Mead Cain. 1981. *Demoaraphic Responses to Famine.* New York: Population Council.

Boserup, Esther. 1981. *Population Growth and Technological Change.* Chicago: Chicago University Press.

Bulatao, Rudolfo, and Ronald Lee. 1983. *Determinants of Fertility in Developing Countries,* Vol II. New York: Academic Press.

Buvinic, Mayra. 1994. "Population Policy and Family Planning Programmes: Contribution from a Focus on Women." In Francis Graham-Smith, *Population—The Complex Reality.* London: The Royal Society. 211–28.

Cain, Mead. 1977. "The Economic Activities of Children in a Village in Bangladesh." *Population and Development Review* 3(3) (September):201–27.

Cain, Mead. 1981. "Risk and Insurance: Perspectives on Fertility and Agrarian Change in India and Bangladesh." *Population and Development Review* 7(3) (September):435–74.

Cain, Mead. 1983. "Fertility as an Adjustment to Risk." *Population and Development Review* 9(4) (December):688–702.

Cain, Mead. 1984. "Women's Status and Fertility in Developing Countries: Son Preference and Economic Security." World Bank Staff Working Paper No. 682. Washington, D.C.: The World Bank.

Caldwell, John C., and Pat Caldwell. 1990. "High Fertility in sub-Saharan Africa." *Scientific American* 262(5) (May):82–89.

Caldwell, John C., I. O. Orubuloye, and Pat Caldwell. 1992. "Fertility Decline in Africa: A New Type of Transition?" *Population and Development Review* 18(2) (June):211–42.

Chen, Lincoln C., Emdadul Huq, and Stand D'Souza. 1981. "Sex Bias in the Family Allocation of Food and Health Care in Rural Bangladesh." *Population and Development Review* 7(1) (March):55–70.

Chenery, Hollis, and T. N. Srinivasan, T.N. 1988. *Handbook of Development Economics, Vol. 1.* Amsterdam: North Holland.

Chopra, Kanchan, Gopal Kadekodi, and M. N. Murty. 1990. *Participatory Development: People and Common Property Resources.* New Delhi: Sage Publications.

Cleaver, Kevin M., and Gotz A. Schreiber. 1994. *Reversing the Spiral: The Population,*

Agriculture, and Environment Nexus in Sub-Saharan Africa. Washington, D.C.: World Bank.

Coale, Ansley J. 1969. "The Decline of Fertility in Europe from the French Revolution to World War II." In S. J. Behrman, Leslie Corsa, and Ronald Freedman, *Fertility and Family Planning: A World View.* Ann Arbor, Michigan: University of Michigan Press. 3–24.

Coale, Ansley J., and Edgar M. Hoover. 1958. *Population Growth and Economic Development in Low-Income Countries.* Princeton, NJ: Princeton University Press.

Cochrane, Susan. 1983. "Effects of Education and Urbanization on Fertility." In Rudolfo Bulato and Ronald Lee, *Determinants of Fertility in Developing Countries, Vol II.* New York: Academic Press. 587–626.

Cochrane, Susan, and Samir Farid. 1989. "Fertility in Sub-Saharan Africa: Analysis and Explanation." World Bank Discussion Paper No. 43. Washington D.C.: World Bank.

Cooper, Russell and John, Andrew. "Coordinating Coordination Failure in Keynesian Models," *Quarterlv Journal of Economics,* August 1988, *103*(3), pp. 441–63.

C.S.E. (Centre for Science and Environment). 1990. *Human-nature Interactions in a Central Himalavan Village: A Case Studv of Village Bemru.* New Delhi: Centre for Science and Environment.

Dasgupta, Partha. 1990. "Well-Being and the Extent of its Realization in Poor Countries." *Economic Journal* 100 (March):1–32.

Dasgupta, Partha. 1993. *An Inquirv into Well-Being and Destitution.* Oxford: Clarendon Press.

Dasgupta, Partha. 1994. "Savings and Fertility: Ethical Issues." *Philosophy & Public Affairs* 23(2) (Spring):99–127.

Dasgupta, Partha. 1995(a). "Population, Poverty and the Local Environment." *Scientific American* 272(2) (February):40–45.

Dasgupta, Partha. 1995 (b). "Energy Intake, Work Capacity, and the Allocation of Resources." Forthcoming in *Journal of Econometrics.*

Dasgupta, Partha, and Geoffrey Heal. 1979. *Economic Theory and Exhaustible Resources.* Cambridge: Cambridge University Press.

Dasgupta, Partha, and Karl-Goran Maler. 1991. "The Environment and Emerging Development Issues." Proceedings of the Annual Bank Conference on Development Economics 1990 (Supplement to the *World Bank Economic Review*):101–32.

Dasgupta, Partha and Karl-Goran Maler. 1993. "Poverty, Institutions, and the Environmental-Resource Base." Development Research Programme No. 39, London School of Economics. Forthcoming in Jere Behrman and T. N. Srinivasan, *Handbook of Development Economics, Vol III.* Amsterdam: North Holland.

Dasgupta, Partha, and Karl-Goran Maler, and others. 1993. *The Environment and Emerging Development Issues.* Forthcoming. Oxford: Clarendon Press.

Debreu, Gerard. 1959. *Theory of Value.* New York: John Wiley.

Dreze, Jean, and Amartya Sen. 1990. *Hunger and Public Action.* Oxford: Clarendon Press.

Durham, William. 1979. *Scarcity and Survival in Central America: Ecological Origins of the Soccer War.* Stanford, CA: Stanford University Press.

Dyson, Tim and Mich Moore. 1983. "On Kinship Structure, Female Autonomy, and Demographic Behaviour in India." *Population and Develop-ment Review* 9(1) (March):35–60.

Easterlin, Richard, ed. 1980. *Population and Economic Change in Developing Countries.* Chicago: University of Chicago Press.

Easterlin, Richard, Robert Pollak, and Michael Wachter. 1980. "Toward a More General Model of Fertility Determination: Endogenous Preferences and Natural Fertility." In Richard Easterlin, ed., *Population and Economic Change in Developing Countries.* Chicago: University of Chicago Press. 81–135; 14 1–49.

Ehrlich, Paul, and Anne Ehrlich. 1990. *The Population Explosion.* New York: Simon and Schuster.

Enke, Stephen. 1966. "The Economic Aspects of Slowing Population Growth." *Economic Journal* 76(1) (March):44–56.

Falconer, Julia, and J. E. M. Arnold. 1989. *Household Food Security and Forestry: An Analysis of Socio-Economic Issues.* Rome: Food and Agriculture Organization.

Farooq, Ghazi, Ita Ekanem, and Sina Ojelade. 1987. "Family Size Preferences and Fertility in South-Western Nigeria." In Christine Oppong, ed., *Sex Roles, Population and Development in West Africa*. London: James Currey. 75–85.

Fogel, Robert. 1994. "Economic Growth, Population Theory, and Physiology: The Bearing of Long- Term Processes on the Making of Economic Policy." *American Economic Review* 84(3) (June):369–95.

Fogel, Robert. 1994. "The Relevance of Malthus for the Study of Mortality Today: Long-Run Influences on Health, Mortality, Labor Force Participation, and Population Growth." In Kerstin Lindahl-Kiessling, Hans Landberg, and others, *Population, Economic Development, and the Environment: The Making of Our Common Future*. Oxford: Oxford University Press. 231–84.

Fortes, Meyer. 1978. "Parenthood, Marriage and Fertility in West Africa." *Journal of Development Studies* 14(4) (July):121–49.

Freedman, Ronald. 1995. "Asia's Recent Fertility Decline and Prospects for Future Demographic Change." Asia-Pacific Population Research Report No. 1. Honolulu: East-West Center.

Goody, Jack. 1976. *Production and Reproduction*. Cambridge: Cambridge University Press.

Goody, Jack. 1990. *The Oriental, the Ancient, and the Primitive*. Cambridge: Cambridge University Press.

Goody, Jack. 1991. "Comparison of Family and Demography in Europe and Asia: Thoughts on the Hajnal Hypothesis." Mimeo. Cambridge: St. John's College.

Graham-Smith, Francis. 1994. *Population: The Complex Reality*. London: The Royal Society.

Guyer, Jane L. 1994. "Lineal Identities and Lateral Networks: The Logic of Polyandrous Motherhood." In Caroline Bledsoe and Gilles Pison, *Nupitality in Sub-Saharan Africa: Contemporary Anthropological and Demographic Perspectives*. Oxford: Clarendon Press. 231–54.

Hajnal, John. 1982. "Two Kinds of Preindustrial Household Formation Systems." *Population and Development Review* 8(3) (September):449–94.

Handwerker, W. Penn. 1990. *Births and Power: Social Change and the Politics of Reproduction*. London: Westview Press.

Heyd, David. 1992. *Genethics: The Morality of Procreation*. Los Angeles: University of Calfornia Press.

Hill, Kenneth. 1992. "Fertility and Mortality Trends in the Developing World." *Ambio* 21(1) (February):79–83.

Homer-Dixon, Thomas, Jeffrey Boutwell, and George Rathjens. "Environmental Change and Violent Conflict." *Scientific American* 268(2) (February):16–23.

Howe, James. 1986. *The Kuna Gathering: Contemporary Villaae Politics in Panama*. Austin, Texas: University of Texas Press.

IED/WRI(International Institute for Environment and Development/World Resources Institute). 1987. *World Resources 1987*. New York: Basic Books.

Johnson, D. Gale, Ronald Lee, and others. 1987. *Population Growth and Economic Development: Issues and Evidence*. Madison, WI: University of Wisconson Press.

Kelley, Allen C. 1988. "Econorrlic Consequences of Population Change in the Third World." *Journal of Economic Literature* 26(4) (December):1685–728.

Kennedy, Eileen, and Ruth Oniang'o. 1990. "Health and Nutrition Effects of Sugarcane Production in Southwestern Kenya." *Food and Nutrition Bulletin* 12 (4) (December):261–67.

Lee, Richard. 1972. "Population Growth and the Beginnings of Sedentary Life among the !Kung Bushmen." In Brian Spooner, ed., *Population Growth: Anthropological Implications*. Cambridge, MA: MIT Press. 329–42.

Lee, Ronald, and others. 1988. *Population, Food and Rural Development*. Oxford: Clarendon Press.

Leete, Richard, Iqbal Alam, and others. 1993. *The Revolution in Asian Fertility: Dimensions, Causes and Implications*. Oxford: Clarendon Press.

Lindahl-Kiessling, Kerstin, Hans Landberg, and others. 1994. *Population, Economic Development, and the Environment: The Making of Our Common Future*. Oxford: Oxford University Press.

Mason, Karen and Anju Taj. 1987. "Differences between Women's and Men's Reproductive

Goals in Developing Countries." *Population and Development Review* 13(4) (December):611–38.

May, David A., and David M. Heer. 1968. "Son Survivorship Motivation and Family Size in India: A Computer Simulation." *Population Studies* 22(2) (July):199–210.

Myers, Norman, and Julian L. Simon. 1994. *Scarcity or Abundance? A Debate on the Environment.* New York: W.W. Norton.

National Research Council. 1986. *Population Growth and Economic Development: Policy Questions.* Washington, D.C.: U.S. National Academy of Sciences Press.

Nerlove, Marc. 1991. "Population and the Environment: A Parable of Firewood and Other Tales." *American Journal of Agricultural Economics* 73(4) (December):1334–57.

Nerlove, Marc, and Anke Meyer. 1993. "Endogenous Fertility and the Environment: A Parable of Firewood." In Partha Dasgupta and Karl-Goran Maler, "Poverty, Institutions, and the Environmental-Resource Base." Development Research Programme No. 39, London School of Economics. Forthcoming in Jere Behrman and T. N. Srinivasan, *Handbook of Development Economics, Vol III.* Amsterdam: North Holland.

Nerlove, Marc, Assaf Razin, and Efraim Sadka. 1987. *Household and Economy: Welfare Economics of Endogenous Fertility.* New York: Academic Press.

Nugent, Jeffrey, and Thomas Gillaspy. 1983. "Old Age Pension and Fertility in Rural Areas of Less Developed Countries: Some Evidence from Mexico." *Economic Development and Cultural Change* 31(4) (July):809–29.

Oppong, Christine, ed. 1987. *Sex Roles, Population and Development in West Africa.* London: James Currey.

Peskin, Henry. 1981. "National Income Accounts and the Environment." *Natural Resources Journal* 21(3) (July):511–37.

Pingali, Prabhu, and Hans Binswanger. 1987. "Population Density and Agricultural Intensification: A Study of the Evolution of Technology in Tropical Agriculture." In D. Gale Johnson, Ronald Lee, and others, *Population Growth and Economic Development: Issues and Evidence.* Madison, WI: University of Wisconson Press. 27–56.

Preston, Sam, ed. *The Effects of Infant and Child Mortality on Fertility.* New York: Academic Press.

Przeworski, Adam and Fernando Limongi. 1995. "Democracy and Development." Working Paper No. 7, Chicago Center on Democracy. Chicago: University of Chicago.

Pritchett, Lant H. 1994. "Desired Fertility and the Impact of Population Policies." *Population and Development Review* 20(1) (March):1–56.

Ranis, Gustav, T. Paul Schultz, and others. 1988. *The State of Development Economics.* Oxford: Basil Blackwell.

Robey, Bryant, Shea O. Rutstein, and Leo Morris. 1993. "The Fertility Decline in Developing Countries." *Scientific American,* 269(6) (December):30–37.

Rosenzweig, Mark, Hans Binswanger, and John McIntire. 1988. "From Land Abundance to Land Scarcity: The Effects of Population Growth on Production Relations in Agrarian Economies." In Ronald Lee and others, *Population, Food and Rural Development.* Oxford: Clarendon Press. 77–100.

Schultz, T. Paul. 1988. "Economic Demography and Development." In Gustav T. Ranis, Paul Schultz, and others, *The State of Development Economics.* Oxford: Basil Blackwell. 416–51.

Schultz, T. Paul. 1993. "Sources of Fertility Decline in Modern Economic Growth and Fertility: Is Aggregate Evidence on the Demographic Transition Credible?" Mimeo. New Haven: Department of Economics, Yale University.

Simon, Julian L. 1981. *The Ultimate Resource.* Princeton: Princeton University Press.

Simon, Julian L. 1994. "Debate Statement." In Norman Myers and Julian L. Simon, *Scarcity or Abundance? A Debate on the Environment.* New York: W.W. Norton. 5–68.

Singh, Inderjit, Lyn Squire, John Straus, and others. 1986. *Agricultural Household Models: Extensions, Applications, and Policy.* Baltimore: Johns Hopkins University Press.

Sopher, David E. 1980. "Sex Disparity in Indian Literacy." In David E. Sopher, *An Exploration of India: Geographical Perspectives on Society and Culture.* Ithica, NY: Cornell University Press. 130–90.

Sopher, David, E., ed. 1980. *An Exploration of India: Geographical Perspectives on Society and Culture*. Ithaca, NY: Cornell University Press, 1980.

Spooner, Brian, ed. 1972. *Population Growth: Anthropological Implications*. Cambridge, MA: MIT Press.

Strauss, John. 1990. "Households, Communities, and Preschool Children's Nutrition Outcomes: Evidence from Rural Cote d'Ivoire." *Economic Development and Cultural Change* 38(2) (January):231–61.

Vitousek, Peter, and others. 1986. "Human Appropriation of the Product of Photosynthesis." *BioScience* 36(6) (June):368–73.

Wade, Robert. 1988. *Village Republics: Economic Conditions for Collective Action in South India*. Cambridge: Cambridge University Press.

Waterlow, John. 1986. "Metabolic Adaptation to Low Intakes of Energy and Protein." *Annual Reviews of Nutrition* 6:495–526.

Waterlow, John. 1991. *Protein-Energy Malnutrition*. Sevenoaks, Kent: Edward Arnold.

Watkins, Susan Cotts. 1990. "From Local to National Cornmunities: The Transformation of Demographic Regions in Western Europe 1870–1960." *Population and Development Review* 6(2) (June):241–72.

Wilson, Edward O. 1992. *The Diversity of Life*. Cambridge, MA: Harvard University Press.

World Bank. 1994, 1990, 1991, 1992. *World Development Report*. New York: Oxford University Press.

World Bank. 1989. *Sub-Saharan Africa: From Crisis to Sustainable Development*. Washington, D.C.: World Bank.

Table 10–1: Total Fertility Rates in the Late 1980s

	Total
Sub-Saharan Africa	6–8
India	4.2
China	2.3
Japan and western indus- trial democracies	1.5–1.9

Source: The World Bank (1990).

Table 10–2: Fertility Rates and Women's Status

N	TFR	PE	UE	I
9	>7.0	10.6	46.9	65.7
35	6.1–7.0	16.5	31.7	76.9
10	5.1–6.0	24.5	27.1	46.0
25	<5.0	30.3	18.1	22.6

Key: N = number of countries
TFR = total fertility rate
PE = women's share of paid employment (%)
UE = percentage of women working as unpaid family workers
I = women's illiteracy rate (%)

Source: IIED/WRI (1987, Table 2.3).

Table 10–3: Marriage Statistics for Women in Developing Countries

	A (years)	B (%)
Sub-Saharan Africa	18.9	40
Asia	21.3	26
Latin America	21.5	19.8

Key: A: Average age of marriage for women.
B: Proportion of women aged 15–19 years who are married.

Source: Cochrane and Farid (1989).

Figure 10–1: Fertility in Relation to Income in Developing Countries, 1982

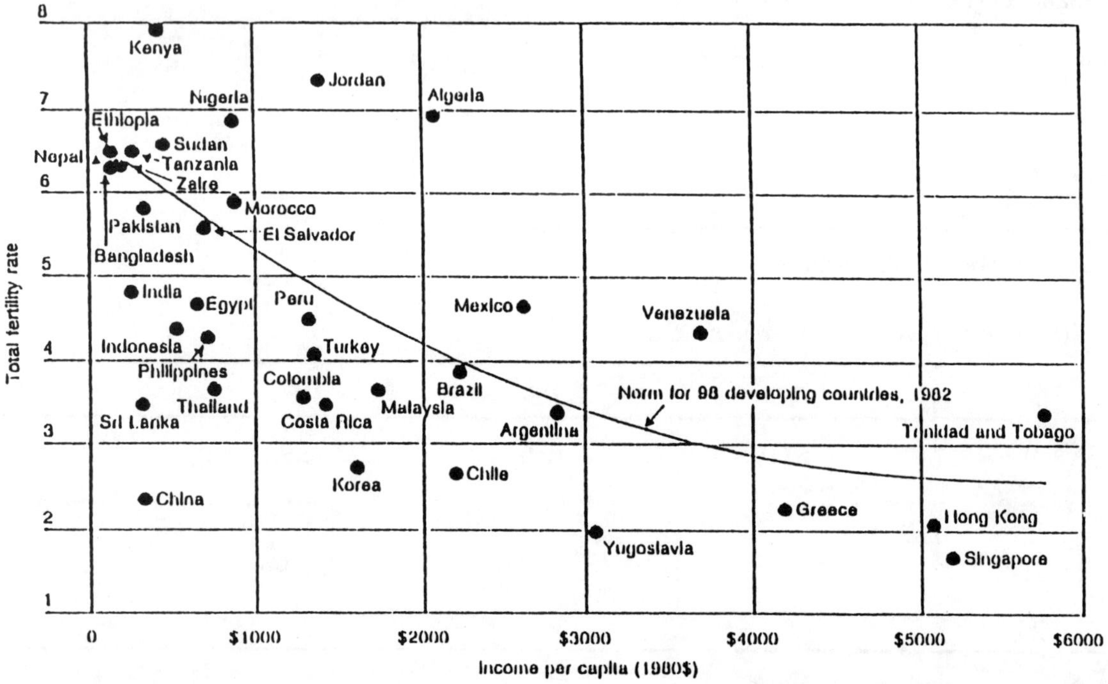

Source: Birdsall (1988).